GLOBAL BUSINESS
Negotiations

A Practical Guide

Claude Cellich
International University

Subhash C. Jain
University of Connecticut

THOMSON

SOUTH-WESTERN

Australia · Canada · Mexico · Singapore · Spain · United Kingdom · United States

Tl

SOL

Global Business N
By Claude Cellich and Subhash C. Jain

VP/Editorial Director: Jack W. Calhoun	**Production Editor:** Carol Spencer	**Design Project Manager:** Stacy Jenkins Shirley
VP/Editor-in-Chief: Dave Shaut	**Production Manager:** Tricia Boies	**Cover Design:** Beckmeyer Design, Inc.
Acquisitions Editor: Steve Momper	**Manufacturing Coordinator:** Charlene Taylor	**Cover Image/Photo:** Courtesy of Getty Images
Channel Manager, Retail: Chris McNamee	**Copyeditor:** Marianne Miller	**Printer:** Phoenix Book Technology
Channel Manager, Professional: Mark Linton	**Compositor:** Lachina Publishing Services	

CONTENTS

PREFACE

Today's globalization requires professionals to deal with their counterparts in countries with different economic, cultural, legal, and political environments. You may need to resolve a dispute with a supplier, finalize a counterproposal for a state owned enterprise, or lead a multicultural team. Thus, in a globalization market, few subjects are as critical as negotiating across cultural boundaries. When negotiators are from diverse cultures, they often rely on quite different assumptions about social interactions, economic interests, and political realities. Consequently, culturally sensitive negotiating skills are necessary for managing in an international setting.

Global Business Negotiations: A Practical Approach has been prepared for all those who negotiate globally: managers, lawyers, government officials, and diplomats. The book provides an insightful, readable, highly organized tour de force of both the conceptual and practical essentials of international business negotiation.

Negotiation is a lifelong activity. In business you can do much better by negotiating successfully. Those not skilled in negotiation will get less than they deserve, perhaps significantly less. Surprisingly, it is often easier to sharpen your negotiating skills by simply trying. To do this, you must acquire proven negotiation strategies and tactics as well as the latest techniques of dealing with the challenges and opportunities of today's complex global alliances and quickly forming partnerships. At the same time, you must know how to navigate across national, organizational, and professional cultures at the negotiating table.

The book provides a clear framework to guide global negotiators around diverse cultural boundaries in order to close deals, create value, resolve disputes, and reach lasting agreements in a constantly changing competitive context. In other words, this book will help managers and professionals acquire knowledge and develop skills that are indispensable in today's global business environment.

The book emphasizes the hardheaded sense of reality at its core. It makes negotiators feel how it will likely to be at the international negotiating table. It tells you how to avoid mistakes and how to optimize your goals. It helps you strengthen the skills that are key to success in conducting business in a multicultural environment. The strength of your agreements and the development of lasting relationships can be the difference between success and failure. Poor agreements with overseas companies results in frequent breakdowns and endless disputes affecting the profitability of the outcome. Mutually beneficial agreements help you reach and exceed your objectives and give the other party greater satisfaction at the same time. This is true whether you are (a) determining the price and terms of the deal, (b) closing with a key customer, (c) persuading others to work with and not against you, (d) setting or meeting budgets, (e) finalizing and managing complex contracts, (f) working on a project with someone important to you, (g) or breaking or avoiding a serious impasse.

While brief, our acknowledgments express our deep gratitude to all who have helped us to design and shape this book over the last several years. Many concepts are grounded upon the work of others and are intended as a tribute to those found in the bibliography—a dedicated group of authors recognized for their research on cross-national negotiations. Some of them may agree or disagree with this book, and that reaction is to be expected.

Closer to home, we wish to acknowledge the support of colleagues: Eric Willumsen and Dora Carbonell at the International University in Geneva; and David Palme and Tome Gutteridge at the University of Connecticut. We are thankful to our students at the International University in Geneva and at the University of Connecticut who read drafts and provided excellent feedback. The staff at the International University in Geneva and the University of Connecticut—particularly Kelly Dunn, Associate Director in the International Programs office, graduate assistants Paula Ehlers and Mami Mishimune, and staff assistants Jennifer Graham and Kelli Francis have been extraordinarily gracious in supporting the project and providing help in numerous ways.

We owe a special word of thanks to the talented staff at South-Western Publishing for their role in shaping the book. Our editor, Steve Momper, furnished excellent advice on the structure of the book and his suggestions in an author friendly manner were very encouraging.

Finally, we are thankful to our wives with love for their graceful support and inspiration in countless ways.

August 2003
Claude Cellich
Geneva, Switzerland
Subhash Jain
Storrs, CT, USA

1

Overview of Global Business Negotiations

In business you don't get what you deserve, you get what you negotiate.—*Chester L. Karras*

Business requires undertaking a variety of transactions. These transactions involve negotiations with one or more parties on their mutual roles and obligations. Thus, negotiation is defined as a process by which two or more parties reach agreement on matters of common interest. All negotiations involve *parties* (i.e., persons with a common interest to deal with one another), *issues* (i.e., one or more matters to be resolved), *alternatives* (i.e., choices available to negotiators for each issue to be resolved), *positions* (i.e., defined response of the negotiator on a particular issue), and *interest* (i.e., underlying needs a negotiator has). These should be identified and stated clearly at the outset.

In the post-World War II period, one of the most important developments has been the internationalization of business. Today companies of all sizes increasingly compete in global markets to seek growth and maintain their competitive edge. This forces managers to negotiate business deals in multicultural environments.

While negotiations are difficult in any business setting, they are especially so in global business because of (a) cultural differences between parties involved and (b) business environments in which parties operate differently. For these reasons, global business negotiations can be problematic and sometimes require an extraordinary effort. Proper training can go a long way in preparing managers for negotiations across national borders. This book provides know-how and expertise for deal making in multicultural environments.

The book is meant for those individuals who must negotiate deals, resolve disputes, or make decision outside their home markets. Often managers take international negotiations for granted. They assume that if correct policies are followed, negotiations can be carried out without any problems. Experience shows, however, that negotiations across national boundaries are difficult and require a painstaking process. Even with favorable policies and institutions, negotiations in a foreign environment may fail because individuals are dealing with people from a different cultural background within the context of a different legal system and different business practices. When negotiators belong to the same nations, their deal making takes place within the same cultural and institutional setup. But where negotiators belong to different cultures, they have different approaches and assumptions relative to social interactions, economic interests, legal requirements, and political realities.

This book provides business executives, lawyers, government officials, and students of international business with practical insights into international business negotiations. For those who have no previous training in negotiations, the book introduces them to the fundamental concepts of global deal making. For those with formal training in negotiation, this book builds on what they already know about negotiation in the global environment.

Negotiation is interdependent, since what one person does affects another party. It is imperative, therefore, that a negotiator, in addition to perfecting his or her own negotiating skills, focus on how to interact, persuade, and communicate with the other party. A successful negotiator works with others to achieve his or her own objectives. Some people negotiate well, while others do not. Successful negotiators are not born; rather, they have taken the pains to develop negotiating skills through training and experience.

NEGOTIATION ARCHITECTURE

The architecture of global negotiations consists of three aspects: negotiation environment, negotiation setting, and negotiation process. The negotiation environment refers to the business climate that surrounds the negotiations and are beyond the control of negotiators. The negotiation setting refers to such aspects as the relative power of the negotiators and the nature of their interdependence. Usually, negotiators have influence and some measure of control over the negotiation setting. The negotiating process is made up of events and interactions that take place between parties to reach an agreement. Included in the process are the verbal and nonverbal communication among parties, the display of bargaining strategies, and the endeavors to strike a deal. Figure 1-1 depicts the three aspects of negotiation architecture.

FIGURE 1-1
Negotiation Architecture

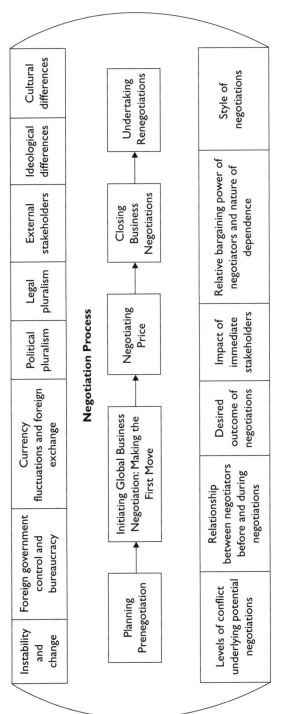

Negotiation Environment

Instability and change	Foreign government control and bureaucracy	Currency fluctuations and foreign exchange	Political pluralism	Legal pluralism	External stakeholders	Ideological differences	Cultural differences

Negotiation Process

Planning Prenegotiation → Initiating Global Business Negotiation: Making the First Move → Negotiating Price → Closing Business Negotiations → Undertaking Renegotiations

Negotiation Setting

Levels of conflict underlying potential negotiations	Relationship between negotiators before and during negotiations	Desired outcome of negotiations	Impact of immediate stakeholders	Relative bargaining power of negotiators and nature of dependence	Style of negotiations

3

Negotiation Environment

The following are the components of the negotiation environment: legal pluralism, political pluralism, currency fluctuations and foreign exchange, foreign government control and bureaucracy, instability and change, ideological differences, cultural differences, and external stakeholders.[1]

Legal Pluralism. Multinational enterprise in its global negotiations must cope with widely different laws. A U.S. corporation not only must consider U.S. laws wherever it negotiates, but also must be responsive to the laws of the negotiating partner's country. For example, without requiring proof that certain market practices have adversely affected competition, U.S. law, nevertheless, makes them violations. These practices include horizontal price fixing among competitors, market division by agreement among competitors, and price discrimination. Even though such practices might be common in a foreign country, U.S. corporations cannot engage in them. Simultaneously, local laws must be adhered to even if they forbid practices that are allowed in the United States. For example, in Europe, a clear-cut distinction is made between agencies and distributorships. Agents are deemed auxiliaries of their principal; distributorships are independent enterprises. Exclusive distributorships are considered restrictive in European Union (EU) countries. The foreign marketer must be careful in making distribution negotiations in, say, France, so as not to violate the regulation concerning distributorships contracts.

Negotiators should be fully briefed about relevant legal aspects of the countries involved before coming to agreement. This will ensure that the final agreement does not contain any provision that cannot be implemented since it is legally prohibited. The best source for such briefing is a law firm that has in-house capability of legal matters of the counterpart's country.

Political Pluralism. A thorough review of the political environment of the party's country with whom negotiation is planned must precede the negotiation process. An agreement may be negotiated that is legal in the countries involved and yet may not be politically prudent to implement. There is no reason to spend effort in negotiating such a deal. Consider the following examples.

A few years ago French president François Mitterand invited Apple Computer executives to lunch at his residence, Élysée Palace. The Apple executives jumped at the invitation; for months, they had been trying to sell their personal computers to the French government. The French government had authorized a $156 million purchase of teaching computers for the French school system, but Apple's foreign citizenship hindered its efforts to get a piece of the order.

During the private two-hour lunch, with a translator present, the Apple executives praised the government's computer program and offered to help in any way they could. But President Mitterand rebuffed them. Later one aide said that the president had invited the Apple executives to discuss technological cooperation with French companies, not the educational computer purchase program.[2]

How Apple tried and failed to get a significant share of the computer order is a revealing tale of international marketing and politics. The total order for 120,000 microcomputers was the biggest single purchase of educational computers in Europe and part of an ambitious campaign to teach French students how to use computers. Although Apple, at that time, was the largest vendor of professional microcomputers in France, when the list of suppliers for the new program was announced, Apple received no order.

The head of Apple's subsidiary near Paris, a French citizen, blamed the company's exclusion on lobbying by competitors and Apple's U.S. nationality. "The color of our passport is wrong," he said.

Upon hearing about Apple's difficulties, the U.S. government complained to France about what it considered the unfair handling of the microcomputer order, raising the possibility of retaliatory moves in U.S. government contracting procedures. Other than registering its annoyance, the U.S. government did not pursue the matter, perhaps for political reasons.

Whether such nationalistic buying resulted in French students getting the best equipment is a matter of debate. Yet this event clearly brings out the political underpinnings of international negotiations.

The federal government officially discourages cigarette smoking in the United States. But if people in other countries are going to smoke, why shouldn't they puff away on American tobacco?

Armed with this logic, the Reagan administration strong-armed Japan, South Korea, and Taiwan to dismantle their government-sanctioned tobacco monopolies. This opened lucrative markets and created such growth for U.S. cigarette makers that skyrocketing Asian sales helped offset the decline at home.

However, Thailand, with a government tobacco monopoly of its own, has been fighting U.S. pressure to open up, and U.S. tobacco companies approached the Bush administration to take up trade sanctions against the Thais. That raises many questions about U.S. trade policy, including these: Should Washington use its muscle to promote a product overseas that it acknowledges is deadly? Are trade disputes to be decided by lawyers and bureaucrats on the basis of commercial regulations, or should health and safety experts get into the act? Should the United States use trade policy to make the world healthier, just as it does to save whales, punish Cuba, or promote human rights?[3] The U.S. should first examine the above questions before deciding to negotiate with the Thais to open their cigarette market.

A thorough review of the political environment of a country must precede the negotiation exercise. A rich foreign market may not warrant entry if the political environment is characterized by instability and uncertainty.

Political perspectives of a country can be analyzed in three ways: (1) by visiting the country and meeting credible people; (2) by hiring a consultant to prepare a report on the country; and (3) by examining political risk analysis worked out by such firms as the Economist Intelligence Unit (EIU), a New York-based subsidiary of the Economist Group, London, or the Bank of America's country Risk Monitor or BERI S.A.'s Business Risk Service.

Currency Fluctuations and Foreign Exchange. A global negotiation may involve financial transfers across national lines in order to close deals. Financial transfers from one country to another are made through the medium of foreign exchange. Foreign exchange is the monetary mechanism by which transactions involving two or more currencies take place. It is the exchange of one country's money for another country's money.

Transacting foreign exchange deals presents two problems. First, each country has its own methods and procedures for effecting foreign exchanges—usually developed by its central bank. The transactions themselves, however, take place through the banking system. Thus, the methods of foreign exchange and the procedures of the central bank and commercial banking constraints must be thoroughly understood and followed to complete a foreign exchange transaction.

A second problem involves the fluctuation of rates of exchange that occurs in response to changes in supply and demand of different currencies. For example, in 1992, a U.S. dollar could be exchanged for about three Swiss francs. In early 2001, this rate of exchange went down to as low as 1.3 Swiss francs for a U.S. dollar. Thus, a U.S. businessperson interested in Swiss currency must pay much more today than in the 1990s. In fact, the rate of exchange between two countries can fluctuate from day to day. This produces a great deal of uncertainty, as a businessperson cannot know the exact value of foreign obligations and claims.

Assume a Mexican representative negotiates to buy a machine from a U.S. manufacturer. The machine price is negotiated at 1.2 million in U.S. dollars, or 7.2 million Mexican pesos. The machine is custom-designed and will be delivered to the Mexican firm in about six months. The U.S. company is willing to accept Mexican pesos for the machine, but currency values fluctuate from day to day. If the Mexican peso goes down by the time the machine is delivered, 7.2 million pesos the U.S. company would receive will amount to much less than $1.2 million it was anticipating. To prevent such a situation, the U.S. firm must negotiate a higher price if the importer wants to pay in pesos. The company must do so because historically the Mexican peso has been unstable and declining in value relative to the U.S. dollar. Before negotiating the price, the U.S. firm should carefully analyze how much the Mexican peso might depreciate in the next six months.

Foreign Government Controls and Bureaucracy. An interesting development of the post–World War II period has been the increased presence of government in a wide spectrum of social and economic affairs it previously ignored. In the United States, concern for the poor, the aged, minorities, consumers' rights, and the environment has spurred government response and the adoption of a variety of legislative measures. In a great many foreign countries, such concerns have led governments to take over businesses to be run as public enterprises. Sympathies for public-sector enterprises, successful or not as businesses, have rendered private corporations suspect and undesirable in many countries. Also, public-sector enterprises are not limited to developing countries. Great Britain and France had many government corporations, from airlines to broadcasting companies to banks and steel mills. Thus, in many nations, negotiations may take place with a government-owned company, where profit motive may not be as relevant as for a private company.

Many nations look upon foreign investment with suspicion. This is true of developed and developing countries. Take, for example, Japan, where it is extremely difficult for a foreign business to establish itself without first generating a trusting relationship that enables it to gain entry through a joint venture. Developing countries are usually afraid of domination and exploitation by foreign businesses. In response to national attitudes, these nations legislate a variety of controls to prescribe the role of foreign investment in their economies. Therefore, a company should review a host country's regulations and identify underlying attitudes and motivations before deciding to negotiate there. For advice on legal matters, the company should contact a law firm, who may know an expert in the host country. Furthermore, the company should examine the political risk analysis of firms such as the Economist Intelligence unit, mentioned previously.

Every country has its own unique administrative scheme. The scheme emerges from such factors as experience, culture, the system of reward and punishment, availability of qualified administrators, and style of leadership. Additionally, the availability of modern means of transportation and communication helps streamline government administration. Businesses often complain about the U.S. federal bureaucracy and its states' agencies. But if they were to compare U.S. administration with other nations, they would be pleasantly surprised to learn that government in the United States is far more efficient than elsewhere. In many African countries, administrators are often unavailable, the telephones do not work, or files are forever lost. Similar difficulties are common in Asia and Latin America too. Such hindrances, in addition to the usual red tape, make business dealings uncomfortable and unpleasant. Although a company would probably not bypass an overseas opportunity solely because of this factor, knowledge about the inefficiency of administrative machinery might warn its managers to lengthen the negotiation schedules—and be mentally prepared to face bureaucratic hassles.

The government of a country sometimes imposes market control to prevent foreign companies from competing in certain markets. For example, until recently, Japan prohibited foreign companies from selling sophisticated communications equipment to the Japanese government. Thus, AT&T, GTE-Sylvania, and ITT could do little business with Japan.

Obviously, in nations with an ongoing bias against home-grown private businesses, a foreign company cannot expect a cordial welcome. In such a situation, the foreign company must contend with the problems that arise because it is a private business as well as a foreign one. Sound business intelligence and familiarity with the industrial policy of the government and related legislative acts and decrees should provide clarification of the role of the private sector in any given economy. This type of information should be fully absorbed before proceeding to negotiate. The same sources of information mentioned previously for seeking insights into political perspectives of a country can be helpful in this regard as well.

Instability and Change. Many countries have frequent changes of government. In such a climate, a foreign business may find that by the time it is ready to implement an agreement, the government with whom the initial agreement was negotiated has changed to one that is not sympathetic to the commitment by its predecessor. Consequently, it is important for international negotiators to examine, before making agreements, whether the current government is likely to continue to be in office for a while. In a democratic situation, the incumbent party's strength or the alternative outcomes of the next election can be weighted to assess the likelihood of change. To learn about the political stability of a country, a company should contact someone who has been doing business in the host country for some time. A company may also gain useful insights on this matter from the International Trade Administration Office (U.S. Department of Commerce) in its area, who may even put the company in touch with a representative in the host country.

More than anything else, foreign companies dislike frequent policy changes by host countries. Policy changes may occur even without a change in government. It is important, therefore, for foreign businesses to analyze the mechanism of government policy changes. Information on the autonomy of legislatures and study of the procedures followed for seeking constitutional changes can be crucial for the global negotiator.

An example of policy change is provided by China. In April 1998, China ordered all direct-sales operations to cease immediately. Alarmed by a rise in pyramid schemes by some direct sellers and uneasy about big sales meetings held by direct sellers, Beijing gave all companies that held direct-selling licensing six months to convert to retail outlets or shut down altogether. The move threatened Avon's China sales, of about $75 million a year, and put Avon, Amway, and Mary Kay Inc.'s combined China investment of roughly $180 million at risk. It also created problems for Sara Lee Corporation and Tupperware Corporation, which had recently launched direct-sales efforts in China.[4] (China withdrew the order after a little arm-twisting from Washington and because over 20 million Chinese were involved in direct sales, with more turning to the businesses as unemployment rose.)

Sovereign nations like to assert their authority over foreign business through various sanctions.[5] Such sanctions are regular and evolutionary and, therefore, predictable. An example is increase in taxes over foreign operations. Many developing countries impose restrictions on foreign business to protect their independence. (Economic domination is often perceived as leading to political subservience.) These countries are protective of their political freedom and want to maintain it at all costs, even when it means proceeding at a slow economic pace and without the help of foreign business. Thus, the political sovereignty problem exists mainly in developing countries.

The industrialized nations, whose political sovereignty has been secure for a long time, require a more open policy for the economic realities of today's world. Today governments are expected simultaneously to curb unemployment, limit inflation, redistribute income, build up backward regions, deliver health services, and avoid abusing the environment. These wide-ranging objectives make developed countries seek foreign technology, use foreign capital and foreign raw materials, and sell their specialties in foreign markets. The net result is that these countries have found themselves exchanging guarantees for mutual access to one another's economies. In brief, among developed countries, multi-nationalism of business is politically acceptable and economically desirable, which is not always true in developing countries.

Any review of a country's political system and its impact on foreign business must remain free of stereotyped notions. Political philosophies change over time. Thus, what a government or party stood for in the 1990s may not hold true in the year 2005. Both current and emerging political perspectives need to be analyzed before negotiations take place in a country.

A basic management reality in today's economic world is that businesses operate in a highly interdependent global economy and that the 100-plus developing countries are significant factors in the international business area. They are the buyers, suppliers, competitors, and capital users. To successfully negotiate in developing countries, a company must recognize the magnitude and significance of these roles.

Cultural Differences. Doing business across national boundaries requires interaction with people nurtured in different cultural environments. Values that are important to one group of people may mean little to another. Some typical attitudes and perceptions of one nation may be strikingly different from those of other countries. These cultural differences deeply affect negotiation behavior. International negotiators, therefore, need to be familiar with the cultural traits of the country with which they want to negotiate. International business literature is full of instances where stereotyped notions of countries' cultures have led to insurmountable problems.

The effect of culture on international business ventures is multifaceted.[6] The factoring of cultural differences into the negotiating process to enhance the likelihood of success has long been a critical issue in overseas operations. With the globalization of worldwide commerce, cultural forces have taken on additional importance. Naiveté and blundering in regard to culture can lead to expensive mistakes. And although some cultural differences are instantly obvious, others are subtle and can surface in surprising ways.

Consider the following example. It was the middle of October, and a marketing executive from the United States was flying to Saudi Arabia to finalize a contract with a local company to supply hospital furnishings. The next day he met the Saudi contacts, wondering if they would sign the deal within two or three days, since he had to report the matter to his board the following Monday. The Saudi executive responded simply, "Insha Allah," which means "if God is willing." The American felt completely lost. He found the carefree response of the Saudi insulting and unbusinesslike. He believed he had made a concerted effort coming all the way to Saudi Arabia so they could question any matter requiring clarification before signing the contract. He thought the Saudi executive was treating a deal worth over $100 million as if it meant nothing.

During the next meeting, the American was determined to put the matter in stronger terms, emphasizing the importance of his board's meeting. But the Saudis again ignored the issue of signing the contract. "They were friendly, appeared happy and calm, but wouldn't sign on the dotted lines," the American later explained. Finally, on orders from the president of his company, he returned home without the contract.

Why did the Saudi executives not sign the sales contract? After all, they had agreed to all the terms and conditions during their meeting in New York. But in Riyadh, they did not even care to review it, let alone sign it.

Unfortunately, the U.S. executive had arrived at the wrong time. It was the time of Ramadan, holy month, when most Muslims fast. During this time, everything slows down, particularly business.[7] In Western societies, religion is, for most people, only one aspect of life, and business goes on as usual most of the time. In Islamic countries, religion is a total way of life for the majority of people. It affects every facet of living. Thus, no matter how important a business deal may be, it will probably not be conducted during the holy month. This U.S. executive was not aware of Muslim culture and its values, and unfortunately, he scheduled a business meeting for the one time of the year when business was not likely to be conducted.

Successful U.S. negotiators advise that in Asian cultures, a low-key, non-adversarial, win/win negotiating style works better than a cut-and-dried businesslike attitude. A negotiator should listen closely, focus on mutual interests rather than petty differences, and nurture long-term relationships.

Four aspects of culture are especially important in negotiating well. They are spoken language, body language, attitude toward time, and attitude toward contracts.[8] For example, fine shades of meaning can get lost in the translation, especially in Japan, where the same spoken word can have three different meanings and where blunt refusals are considered impolite. When the Japanese use a word, it does not mean the same thing to an American or European. When Japanese say something is "difficult" or that "it will take some study," they mean "no." Nor does everyone speak the same body language. Americans may not know that when Japanese audibly suck air through their teeth, they feel pressured. And while a hearty handshake may convey sincerity in New York or London, it makes Asians uncomfortable. Even colors have unexpected significance. For example, a red hat in China signifies joy and prosperity.

Different ideas about punctuality can also confound negotiations. In parts of Sub-Sahara Africa, negotiators might decide to defer action until next year. But Americans get upset if they cannot close a deal in time to catch a four o'clock flight. Differing attitudes toward contracts can cause even more confusion. For instance, the custom of *naniwabushi* allows the Japanese to request a change in a contract if the terms become onerous or unfair, which is not acceptable in Western cultures. A business contract in Japan is like a wedding vow: It means more in spirit than in substance. When a husband disagrees with his wife, he does not go back to the marriage vow to settle the argument. If the relationship is not working, rereading the contract will not help. It is also well-known that the Japanese are insulted when an executive brings a lawyer to negotiations.

Ideological Differences. There are always ideological differences between nations, which influence the behaviors of their citizens.

Ideologies that are attributed to traditional societies imply that they are compulsory in their force, sacred in their tone, and stable in their timeliness. They call for fatalistic acceptance of the world as it is, respect for those in authority, and submergence of the individual in collectivity. In contrast to this, the ideologies of Western societies can be described as stressing acquisitive activities, an aggressive attitude toward economic and social change, and a clear trend toward a higher degree of industrialization. While keeping their ideological differences intact, the traditional societies want to be economically absorbed in Western ways, having a strong emphasis on specificity, universalism, and achievement.

Negotiators should be familiar with and respect each other's values and ideologies. For example, a fatalistic belief may lead an Asian negotiator to choose an auspicious time to meet the other party. The other party should be duly sensitive to accommodate the ideological demands of his or her counterpart.

External Stakeholders. The term *external stakeholders* refers to different people and organizations that have a stake in the outcome of a negotiation. These can be stockholders, employees, customers, labor unions, business groups (e.g., chambers of commerce), industry associations, competitors, and others. Stockholders welcome the negotiation agreement when it increases the financial performance of the company. Employees support the negotiation that results in improved gains (financial and in-kind) for them. Customers favor the negotiation that enables them to have quality products at a lower price. Thus, if a foreign company that is likely to provide good value to consumers is negotiating to enter a country, the consumers will be excited about it. However, the industry groups will oppose such negotiation to discourage competition from the foreign company.

Different stakeholders have different agendas to preserve. They support or oppose negotiation with a foreign enterprise depending on how it will affect them. In conducting negotiation, therefore, a company must examine the likely reaction of different stakeholders.

Negotiation Setting

The negotiation setting refers to factors that surround the negotiation process and over which the negotiators have some control. The following are the dimensions of negotiation setting: the relative bargaining power of the negotiators and the nature of their dependence on each other, the levels of conflict underlying potential negotiation, the relationship between negotiators before and during negotiations, the desired outcome of negotiations, impact of immediate stakeholders, and style of negotiations.

Relative Bargaining Power of Negotiators and Nature of Dependence. An important requisite of successful negotiations is the mutual dependence of the parties on one another. Without such interdependence, negotiations do not take place. The degree of dependence determines the relative bargaining power of each side. The style and strategies adopted by a negotiator depend on his or her bargaining power. A company with greater bargaining power is likely to be more aggressive than one with weaker bargaining power. A company with other equally attractive alternatives may apply a "take it or leave it" posture, while a company with no other choice to fall back upon may adopt a more submissive stance.

Consider a small software firm in a small niche market with tremendous financial problems negotiating with IBM. If the IBM deal fails, the small firm may go out of business. Its survival depends on successfully forming an alliance with IBM. On the other hand, IBM, as a matter of strategy, is acquiring small software companies to strengthen its position in different target markets. The bargaining power of the small firm is limited compared to IBM, but it does have an interest in the alliance since the firm has a unique position in a lucrative market, which motivates IBM to negotiate. Despite its small size, the firm should confidently negotiate based on this strength.

Levels of Conflict Underlying Potential Negotiations. Every negotiation situation has a few key points. When both parties agree to the key points, the negotiation is concluded with supportive attitude. On the other hand, differences over the key points render the potential negotiation to be concluded in a hostile environment.

Where the goals of two parties depend on each other in such a way that the gains of one party have a positive impact on the gains of the other party, the negotiations are concluded in a win-win situation (also called a non-zero-sum game, or integrative bargaining). If, however, the negotiation involves a win-lose situation (i.e., the gains of one side result in losses for the other party), the negotiation will proceed in a hostile setting.

Suppose a U.S. women's fashion company is interested in manufacturing some of its goods in a developing country to take advantage of low wages. The developing country, on the other hand, is interested in increasing employment. This presents a win-win situation, and the negotiation will take place in a friendly setting. Assume another U.S. company is negotiating a joint venture in a developing country. The company desires majority equity control in the joint venture, while the government of the developing country is opposed to it (i.e., the government wants the foreign company to have a minority interest in the joint venture). This case represents a win-lose situation (or a zero-sum game, or distributive bargaining) since the gains of one party come at the cost of the other.

Relationship between Negotiators before and during Negotiations. The history of a positive working relationship between negotiating parties influences future negotiations. When previous negotiations established a win-win situation, both sides undertake current negotiation with a positive attitude, hoping to negotiate another win-win agreement. However, when the previous experience was disappointing, the current negotiation setting may begin with a pessimistic attitude.

Even during the current negotiation, what happens in the first session sets the stage for the next session and so on. Usually, a negotiation involves several sessions over a period of time. When, in the first session, relationships are less than cordial, future sessions may proceed in a negative atmosphere. Therefore, a company should adopt a positive, friendly, and supportive posture in the initial session(s). Every effort should be made to avoid conflicting issues. For example, a German company negotiating with the Japanese need not start with the sad experiences of another German company's dealings with a different Japanese company.

Desired Outcome of Negotiations. The outcomes of global business negotiation can be tangible and intangible. Examples of tangible outcomes are profit sharing, technology transfer, royalty sales, protection of intellectual property, equity ownership, and other outcomes whose values can be measured in concrete terms. Intangible outcomes include the goodwill generated between two sides in a negotiation, the willingness to offer concessions to enhance the relationship between parties (and the outcome through understanding), and give-and-take. The tangible/intangible outcomes can be realized in the short term or long term.

One basic precept of global business negotiation is to compromise for tangible results to happen in the long run. Business deals are long-term phenomena. Even when a company is interested in negotiating with a foreign company only for an ad hoc deal, the importance of a long-term relationship and its positive impact should be remembered. The situation may change in the future such that the company with whom a person negotiated in the past on a minor project may not be a major player for which he or she is currently negotiating. Relationship is an important criterion for conducting successful negotiations. And it takes time to establish a relationship.

Often developing countries want multinational companies to transfer technology to the country. But technology is a very important and unique asset of the company, which it does not want to fall into the wrong hands. Negotiators from developing countries should, in the short term, be willing to live with intangible benefits from the current negotiation, in the interest of realizing the tangible gain of technology transfer in the long run. Similarly, a multinational corporation might initially accept a minority position in a developing country if the latter is willing to reconsider the equity ownership question a few years later. When goodwill is created, the government may approach with an open mind the company's desire to have equity control in the venture.

While relationship building is important for successfully negotiating anywhere in the world, it is more so in Asian nations. Japanese companies, in particular, want to strengthen their relationships with overseas companies before negotiating business deals. Thus, months and years of promoting goodwill and harmony are vital for fruitful negotiations.

Impact of Immediate Stakeholders. The immediate stakeholders in global business negotiation refer to employees, managers, and members of the board of directors. Their experience in global negotiations, their cultural perspectives, and their individual stakes in negotiation outcomes have a bearing on the negotiating process.

Long-term experience in negotiating deals with Japanese, for example, teaches a U.S. manager that the Japanese do not mean yes when they say "okay" to some point. Experience also teaches about the rituals of a culture and the meaning of gestures, jokes, gifts, and so on. Such experience comes in handy in the planning of negotiating tactics and strategies. Likewise, the cultural background of negotiators influences the outcomes. In Russia and Eastern European countries, the emphasis on profits by Western managers is not easy to grasp. In many cultures, people like to deal with their equals. Thus, a lower-ranking manager may have a problem negotiating with the CEO of an Indian company. The ranks of the people involved in negotiation are a consideration in the successful outcome. Other cultural traits such as outside interests, emphasis on time, etc. also impact negotiations.

Different stakeholders have different stakes in the negotiation. Labor in a developed country does not want global negotiation to transfer jobs overseas or to use pressure to institute lower wages. Managers do not like to negotiate an agreement that counters their personal stakes, such as financial gain, career advancement, ego, prestige, personal power, and economic security. Members of a board of directors may be interested in an agreement for prestige sake rather than any financial gain. This means they might compromise on an agreement in terms of profit as long as it ensures the prestige they are seeking.

Style of Negotiations. Every manager has certain traits that characterize his or her way of undertaking negotiation. Some people adopt an aggressive posture and hope to get what they want by making others afraid of them. Some people are low-key and avoid confrontation, hoping their counterparts in negotiations are rational and friendly. Different styles have their merits and demerits.

With regard to negotiations, the best style is the one that satisfies the needs of both parties. In other words, a negotiator should embrace a style that helps in a win-win outcome.

Negotiation Process

Although companies of all sizes run into negotiation problems, managers of small and medium-size firms often lack the business negotiation skills needed to make deals in the international marketplace. These companies may also need negotiation skills for discussions with importers or agents when the firm is exporting its products. Such skills are also necessary when the firm is exploring joint-venture possibilities abroad or purchasing raw materials from foreign suppliers. As mentioned previously, negotiating with business partners located in other countries is more difficult than dealing with local companies when the customs and language of the counterpart are different from those at home. Such cultural factors add to the complexities of the transaction.

Assume the export manager of a small manufacturing company specializing in wooden kitchen cabinets wants to find an agent for the firm's products in a selected target market and has scheduled a visit there for this purpose. The manager has never been to the country and is not familiar with the business practices or the cultural aspects. The manager realizes the need for a better understanding of how to conduct business negotiations in the market before meeting with several potential agents.

The negotiation process introduced in this book (see Figure 1-1) can be of real help to managers who do not have any formal training on the subject. The negotiation begins with prenegotiation planning and ends with renegotiation if necessary. In between are stages of initiating negotiation, negotiating price, and closing the deal.

After completing prenegotiation planning, negotiation begins with contention; i.e., each party starts from a different point concerning what he or she hopes to achieve through negotiation. In the example above, when the export manager meets the potential agents in the target market, he or she has certain interests to pursue in the business dealings that may not necessarily coincide with those of the counterpart. The manager may want the agent to work for only a minimal commission so the extra profits can be reinvested in the company to expand and modernize production. Furthermore, the manager may wish to sign up several other agents in the same country to increase the possibility of export sales; he or she may also want to limit the agency agreement to a short period in order to test the market. The potential agent, on the other hand, may demand a higher percentage of sales than is being offered as commission, may insist on exclusivity within the country concerned, and may call for a contract of several years instead of a short trial period. In this situation, the exporter needs to know how to proceed in the talks to ensure that most of the firm's interests are covered in the final agreement.

The terms *clarification, comprehension, credibility,* and *creating value* are basic phrases in the negotiating process between the initial starting position and the point where both parties develop a common perspective. By applying each concept in sequence, one can follow a logical progression during the negotiation.

Clarification and comprehension are the first steps away from the situation of confrontation. In the case above, the exporter and the potential agent should clarify their views and seek the understanding of the other party about matters of particular concern. For instance, the parties may learn that it is important for the exporter to obtain a low commission rate and for the agent to have exclusivity in the territory concerned.

The next stages in business negotiation concern the concepts of credibility and creating value; i.e., the attitudes that develop as both parties discuss their requirements and the reasons behind them. In the example above, this may mean that the agent accepts as credible the exporter's need to reinvest a large portion of profits in order to keep the company competitive. The exporter, on the other side, has confidence that the agent will put maximum efforts into promoting the product, thus assuring the exporter that a long-term contract is not disadvantageous. As the negotiation proceeds, the two gradually reach a convergence of views on a number of points under discussion.

Following this is the stage of concession, counterproposals, and commitment. In this phase, the final matters on which the two parties have not already agreed are settled through compromises on both sides.

The final stage is conclusion; that is, agreement between the two parties. In the case of the exporter, this means a signed agreement with a new agent, incorporating at least some of the exporter's primary concerns (such as a low commission on sales) and some of the agent's main considerations (for instance, a two-year contract). The negotiation process, however, is not complete since circumstances may change that require renegotiation, a possibility both parties should keep in mind.

NEGOTIATION INFRASTRUCTURE

Before proceeding to negotiate, it is desirable to put the negotiation infrastructure in place. It makes the lives of negotiators easier and makes their jobs more rewarding. The infrastructure consists of assessing the current status of the company and establishing the BATNA; i.e., best alternative to a negotiated agreement.

Assessing Current Status

The current status can be assessed using the strengths, weaknesses, opportunities, and threats (or SWOT) method, a technique often used to assess business management situations. Although this is a well-known business management tool, insufficient attention has been given to linking the results of a SWOT analysis with the development of a business negotiation strategy.

The SWOT method as used for business management purposes consists, in simple terms, of looking at a firm's production and marketing goals and assessing the company's operations and management policies and practices in the light of these goals. The framework for this analysis is four key words: strengths, weaknesses, opportunities, and threats. All aspects of the company's activities are reviewed and classified under one of these terms.

This analysis is taken a step further when the SWOT results are applied to a negotiating plan. The strengths, weaknesses, opportunities, and threats identified are used to plan the negotiating strategy and tactics. Applying the SWOT technique to cross-border negotiations helps executives optimize their companies' strengths, minimize their weaknesses, be open to opportunities, and be ready to neutralize threats. On the basis of his or her company's strengths, a negotiator can obtain more support for the firm's proposals during the discussions. Similarly, to offset weaknesses, the negotiator can minimize their importance by focusing on other aspects of the talks or broadening the range of issues. With regard to opportunities, specific plans can be incorporated into the negotiating strategy for capitalizing on them. Finally, any threats to the company's business operations identified through the SWOT analysis can be countered in the negotiations through specific measures or proposals.

Depending on the nature of the negotiations, a negotiator can emphasize specific features or elements of the SWOT analysis in drawing up the strategy. If the aim is to enter into a joint venture, for instance, the SWOT analysis will be interpreted differently than if the goal is to find a new export agent. As an example, if a company, through the SWOT analysis, finds that one of its weak points is a lack of consumer familiarity with its products, the negotiator might overcome this weakness in negotiation with prospective agents in the target market by offering promotional allowance. At the same time, the negotiator may use one of the company's strengths identified through the SWOT analysis, that of the high quality of the firm's wooden cabinets, to convince the prospective agents to work with the firm on favorable terms.

Assessing BATNA

By assessing its BATNA (i.e., the best alternative to a negotiated agreement), a party can greatly improve the negotiation results by evaluating the negotiated agreement against the alternative.[9] If the negotiated agreement is better, close the deal. If the alternative is better, walk away.

The BATNA approach changes the rules of the game. Negotiators no longer see their role as that of producing agreements, but rather as making good choices. If an agreement is not reached, negotiators do not consider that a failure. If a deal is rejected because it falls short of a company's BATNA, the net result is a success, not a failure.

BATNA is affected by several elements; namely, alternatives, deadlines, interests, knowledge, experience, negotiator's resources, and resources of the other party. Any change in these elements is likely to change the BATNA. If, during the discussions, the negotiator obtains new information that influences the BATNA, he or she should take time to review the BATNA. BATNA is not static, but dynamic, in a negotiation situation.

The BATNA should be identified at the outset. This way an objective target that a negotiated agreement must meet is set, and negotiators do not have to depend on subjective judgments to evaluate the outcome. As the negotiation proceeds, the negotiator should think of ways to improve the BATNA by doing further research, by considering alternative investments, or by identifying other potential allies. The basic principle of BATNA is this: Never accept an agreement that is not at least as good as the BATNA.

GOING INTO NEGOTIATIONS

When conducting business negotiations, executives should keep in mind certain points that may arise as the discussions proceed.

- Situations to avoid during the negotiations: conflict, controversy, and criticism vis-à-vis the other party
- Attitudes to develop during the talks: communication, collaboration, and cooperation
- Goals to seek during the discussions: change (or, alternatively, continuity), coherence, creativity, consensus, commitment, and compensation

In business negotiations, particularly those between executives from different economic and social environments, introducing options and keeping an open mind are musts for establishing a fruitful, cooperative relationship. Experienced negotiators consider the skill of introducing options to be a key asset in conducting successful discussions. Giving the other party the feeling that new ideas proposed have come from both sides also contributes greatly to smooth negotiations.

The goal in such negotiations is to reach an agreement that is mutually beneficial to both parties, leading to substantive results in the long run. To negotiate mutually beneficial agreements requires a willingness to cooperate with others. The talks should, therefore, focus on common interests of the parties. If the discussions come to an impasse for any reason, it may be necessary to refocus them by analyzing and understanding the needs and problems of each party.

The approach to business negotiations is that of a mutual effort. In an international business agreement (whether it concerns securing an order, appointing a new agent, or entering into a joint venture), the aim is the creation of a shared investment in a common future business relationship.

PLAN OF THE BOOK

In today's global business environment, you must negotiate with people born and raised in different cultures. Global deal making has became a key element of modern business life. To compete abroad, you need skills to negotiate effectively with your counterparts in other countries. This book provides insightful, readable, well-organized material about the conceptual and practical essentials of international business negotiations.

The book is divided into five parts. Part 1 covers an overview of global negotiations organized as Chapter 1. Part 2, made up of Chapter 2 and Chapter 3, is devoted to the negotiation environment and setting.

Discussed in Chapter 1 are a number of variables relative to negotiation environment and negotiation setting. Of these, one environmental factor and one setting factor stand out as having the biggest effect in global negotiations. These are influence of culture and choice of proper negotiating style. Chapter 2 examines the important role of cultural differences in global negotiations, and Chapter 3 discusses the appropriate negotiation style for successful results.

The negotiation process is examined in Part 3. The subject is covered in Chapters 4 to 8. Chapter 4 deals with prenegotiation planning. Initiating global business negotiation and making the first move are covered in Chapter 5. Chapter 6 explores price negotiations. Closing negotiations is covered in Chapter 7. Chapter 8 focuses on renegotiations.

The two chapters (i.e., Chapter 9 and Chapter 10) in Part 4 deal with negotiation tools. The subject of Chapter 9 is communication skills for effective negotiations, while Chapter 10 is devoted to demystifying the role of power in negotiation.

Finally, Part 5 includes two chapters: Chapter 11 explores online negotiations, and Chapter 12 contains cases and exercises dealing with global business negotiations.

SUMMARY

For most companies, global business is a fact of life. That means executives must negotiate with people from to different cultures. This is more difficult than simply making deals with people who share one's own culture. Therefore, it is important to learn fundamental principles of global business negotiations.

This chapter introduces the global business negotiation architecture and its three aspects: negotiation environment, negotiation setting, and negotiation process. The environment defines the business climate in which negotiation takes place. The setting specifies the power, style, and interdependence of the negotiating parties. The negotiation process involves planning prenegotiation, initiating global business negotiation, negotiating price, closing negotiations, and renegotiating.

The next topic concerns negotiation infrastructure, which includes assessing the current status of a company from the viewpoint of global negotiation and assessing the BATNA (i.e., best alternative to a negotiated agreement).

NOTES

1. This and the following section draw heavily from Arrind V. Phatak and Mohammed M. Habib, "The Dynamics of International Business Negotiations." *Business Horizons*, May–June 1996, pp. 30–38.
2. Richard L. Hudson, "Apple Computer vs. French Chauvinism: Politics, Not Free Trade Wins in the End," *The Wall Street Journal*, February 22, 1985, p. 34.
3. *Business Week*, October 9, 1999, p. 61.
4. "Ultimatum for the Avon Lady," *Business Week*, May 11, 1998.
5. See Subhash C. Jain, *International Marketing*, 6th Edition (Cincinnati: South-Western College Publishing, 2001), Chapter 10.
6. Edward B. Taylor, *Primitive Culture* (London: John Murray, 1871), p. 1.
7. "Making Do Doing Ramadan," *Business Week*, April 8, 1991, p. 18A.
8. Kerry Petcher, "Can We Make a Deal?" *International Business*, March 1992, pp. 46–50.
9. Roger Fischer and William Ury, *Getting to Yes* (New York: Penguin Books, 1991).

2

Role of Culture in Cross-Border Negotiations

Merchants throughout the world have the same religion.
—Heinrich Heine

In a globalizing world, companies operate in a multicultural environment. While people from other nations may seem to present a perspective similar, they are different in many ways, defined by their cultures. Even if they speak English, they view the world differently. They define business goals, express thoughts and feelings, and show interest in different ways. Culture is a deep-rooted aspect of a person's life that is always present. No manager can avoid bringing his or her cultural assumptions, images, prejudices, and other behavioral traits into a negotiating situation.

Culture includes all learned behavior and values that are transmitted through shared experience to an individual living within a society. The concept of culture is broad and extremely complex. It involves virtually every part of a person's life and touches on virtually all human needs, both physical and psychological. A classic definition is provided by Sir Edward Taylor: "Culture is that complex whole which includes knowledge, belief, art, morals, law, custom, and any other capabilities and habits acquired by (individuals as members) of society."[1]

Culture, then, develops through recurrent social relationships that form patterns that are eventually internalized by members of the entire group. It is commonly agreed that a culture must have these three characteristics:[2]

1. It is *learned;* that is, people over time transmit the culture of their group from generation to generation.
2. It is *interrelated;* that is, one part of the culture is deeply connected with another part, such as religion with marriage or business with social status.
3. It is *shared;* that is, the tenets of the culture are accepted by most members of the group.

Another characteristic of culture is that it continues to evolve through constant embellishment and adaptation, partly in response to environmental needs and partly through the influence of outside forces. In other words, a culture does not stand still, but slowly, over time, changes.

EFFECT OF CULTURE ON NEGOTIATION

Culture is nonnegotiable. Deal or no deal, people do not change their culture for the sake of business. Therefore, it behooves negotiators to accept the fact that cultural differences exist between them and try to understand these differences. Cultural differences can influence business negotiations in significant and unexpected ways. Summarized below are the major effects of culture on cross-border negotiations.[3]

Definition of Negotiation

The basic concept of negotiation is interpreted differently from one culture to another. In the United States, negotiation is a mechanical exercise of offers and counteroffers that leads to a deal. It is a cut-and-dry method of arriving at an agreement. In Japan, on the other hand, negotiation is sharing information and developing a relationship that may lead to a deal.

Selection of Negotiators

The criteria for the selection of negotiators vary from culture to culture. Usually, the criteria include knowledge of the subject matter, seniority, family connections, gender, age, experience, and status. Different cultures assign different importance to these criteria in the choosing of negotiators. In the Middle East, for example, age, family connection, gender, and status count more; while in the United States, knowledge of the subject matter, experience, and status are given more weight.

Protocol

The degree of formality used by the parties in the negotiation is affected by their cultures. Culturally, the United States is an informal society, such that Americans like to address other people by their first name upon first meeting. Europeans, on the other hand, are highly title conscious. While in the United States, graduate students call their professor by his or her first name, in Germany, a professor with a Ph.D. is be addressed as Professor or Doctor.

Presentation of business cards at the beginning of a first meeting is normal protocol in Southeast Asia. As a matter of fact, the cards must be presented in a proper manner. In the United States, cards may or may not be exchanged and there is no cultural norm of presenting the cards. In many traditional cultures, when a man places the other person's business card in his wallet and then puts the wallet in his back pocket, this is considered an insult. (Women negotiators do not have this problem.) Likewise, methods of greeting as well as dress codes are impacted by one's culture. The way a person greets the other party or dresses for the occasion communicates his or her interest and intentions relative to the negotiation.

Communication

As noted in Chapter 1, culture plays a significant role in how people communicate, both verbally and nonverbally. Language as part of culture consists not only of the spoken word, but also of symbolic communication of time, space, things, friendship, and agreements. Nonverbal communication occurs through gestures, expressions, and other body movements.

The many different languages of the world do not translate literally from one to another, and understanding the symbolic and physical aspects of different cultures' communication is even more difficult to achieve. For example, the phrase *body by Fisher* translated literally into Flemish means "corpse by Fisher." Similarly, *Let Hertz put you in the driver's seat* translated literally into Spanish means "Let Hertz make you a chauffeur." *Nova* translates into Spanish as "it doesn't go." A shipment of Chinese shoes destined for Egypt created a problem because the design on the soles of the shoes spelled *God* in Arabic. Olympia's Roto photocopier did not sell well because *roto* refers to the lowest class in Chile, and *roto* in Spanish means "broken."[4]

In addition, meanings differ within the same language used in different places. The English language differs so much from one English-speaking country to another that sometimes the same word means something entirely different in another culture. *Table the report* in the United States means "postponement"; in England, it means "bring the matter to the forefront."

A case of nonverbal communication is body language. A certain type of body language in one nation may be innocuous, while in another culture, the same body language may be insulting. Consider the following examples.

Never touch a Malay on the top of the head, for that is where the soul resides. Never show the sole of your shoe to an Arab, for it is dirty and represents the bottom of the body, and never use your left hand in Muslim culture, for it is the hand reserved for physical hygiene. Touch the side of your nose in Italy, and it is a sign of distrust. Always look directly and intently into your French associate's eye when making an important point. Direct eye contact in Southeast Asia, however, should be avoided until the relationship is firmly established. If your Japanese associate has just sucked air in deeply through his teeth, that's a sign you've got real problems. Your Mexican associate will want to embrace you at the end of a long and successful negotiation; so will your Central and East European associates, who may give you a bear hug and kiss you three times on alternating cheeks. Americans often stand farther apart than their Latin associates but closer than their Asian associates. In the United States, people shake hands forcefully and enduringly; in Europe, a handshake is usually quick and to the point; in Asia, it is often rather limp. Laughter and giggling in the West indicates humor; in Asia, it more often indicates embarrassment and humility. Additionally, the public expression of deep emotion is considered ill-mannered in most countries of the Pacific Rim; there is an extreme separation between one's personal and public selves. The withholding of emotion in Latin America, however, is often cause for mistrust.[5]

Time

The meaning and importance of time vary from culture to culture. In Eastern cultures, time is fluid. It goes on forever. Therefore, if delay occurs in negotiation, it does not matter. In the United States, time is fixed and valuable. Time is money, which should not be wasted. For this reason, North Americans like to begin negotiation on time, schedule discussions from hour to hour to complete the day's agenda, and meet the deadline to close the negotiation. To a Chinese, however, the important thing is to complete the task, no matter how long it takes.

Risk Propensity

Cultures differ in their willingness to take a risk. In cultures where risk propensity is high, negotiators are able to close a deal even if certain information is lacking but the business opportunity otherwise looks attractive. The risk-prone cultures suggest caution. Negotiators belonging to risk-averse cultures demand additional information to carefully examine all sides of a deal before coming to a final agreement.

Groups versus Individuals

In some cultures, individuality is highly valued. In others, the emphasis is on the group. In group-oriented cultures, negotiation takes more time to complete since group consensus must be built. Compare that to the United States, where individuals can make decisions without getting approval from the group. For example, in a negotiation in China, a U.S. negotiator had to meet six different negotiators and interpreters going over the same material until the deal was completed.

Nature of Agreement

The nature of agreement also varies from culture to culture. In the United States, emphasis is placed on logic, formality, and legality of the agreement. For example, when a deal can be completed at a low cost, when all details of the agreement are fully spelled out, and when the agreement can be enforced in a court of law, it is satisfactory. In traditional cultures, a deal is struck depending on the family/political connections, even when certain aspects of the agreement are weak. Furthermore, an agreement is not permanent and is subject to change as circumstances evolve.

UNDERSTANDING CULTURE

The first step in gaining cultural understanding is to identify the group or community whose culture you want to study. Culturally, the world can be divided into a large number of groups, with each group having its own traditions, traits, values, beliefs, and rituals. People often speak in generalities, such as Asian culture, Latin culture, Western culture, and so on. With regard to negotiations, having a broad perspective about Asians is not sufficient since a Japanese negotiator may hold different values than a Chinese or a Korean. Similarly, a culture and a nationality are not always the same. In India, for example, Southern Indians may represent a different culture than Northern Indians. Indian Muslims are a different cultural group from Hindus. Thus, a country may have several distinct cultural groups.

Once a negotiator knows the cultural group to which the other party belongs, he or she should attempt to understand the history, values, and beliefs of the country. The best way to learn the culture of another group is to devote many years to studying the history, mastering the language, and experiencing the way of life by living among the people. For a prospective negotiator, however, this commitment is inconceivable. As an alternative, therefore, you should gain as much insight into the culture of the group as possible by reading books, talking to people who are knowledgeable about the group, and hiring consultants who specialize in conducting business deals with the group. In the summary section of this chapter, select books on cross-cultural business negotiations are mentioned, which provide deeper understanding of the subject matter.

As you undertake to understand the culture of the group, you may wonder what particular aspects you should concentrate on. This is important since culture per se is a broad field, and you may not learn much even after reading many books if you do not know what you are trying to achieve.[6] For negotiators, the relevant cultural knowledge can be divided into two categories: (1) traditions and etiquette and behavior of the group (which can be further split into protocols and deportment and deeper cultural characteristics) and (2) players and the process.

Before elaborating further on these categories, understand that cultural knowledge should be used with caution. You should avoid forming stereotypical notions about a group and considering them as universal truths. For example, not all Japanese avoid giving a direct negative answer. Not all Mexicans mind discussing business over lunch. Not all Germans make cut-and-dry comments about proposals. As a matter of fact, people are offended when you use stereotypes to describe their culture. A Latin executive would be offended if you said to him, "Although we plan to start the meeting at 9 A.M., I know you won't be here before 9:30 since Latinos are always late."

In addition to national cultures, negotiators need to be aware of professional and corporate cultures. Professional cultures refer to individuals who have studied a specific discipline, such as accounting, economics, engineering, and chemistry. As a result of their studies, these professionals have developed analytical skills, have acquired technical jargon, and tend to look at problems through their own professional interest (which sets them apart from their typical national culture).

Corporate cultures play a significant role in business negotiations. All companies over the years develop their own business culture, values, rules, and regulations. For example, an official from a state-owned enterprise or from a public utility has a different style than a manager from a high-tech start-up. An entrepreneur is likely to have a negotiating style different from that of a CEO of a multinational (see Figure 2-1).

Experience shows that these cultural traits are only indicative and must be taken with caution in view of two other factors influencing the behavior of negotiators. One is the age factor, and the other is multiculturalism. Today young professionals have more affinity among themselves. It is not uncommon to meet young executives who have studied abroad, who speak one or more foreign languages, and who have traveled extensively. These executives feel comfortable working outside their cultural environment and are no longer representatives of their own culture.

Similarly, executives with overseas experience have, over the years, developed greater understanding of foreign cultures while acquiring new values and tolerance for cultural diversity. Such executives are more multicultural-oriented. For these reasons, the wise negotiator finds out as much as possible about the background of the other party to avoid committing cultural

FIGURE 2-1
Cultural Differences among Managers Belonging to
Different Types of Companies

Cultural Trait	Type of Company		
	ENTREPRENEURS/ EXECUTIVES FROM START-UPS	MANAGERS FROM MULTINATIONALS	SENIOR OFFICIALS FROM PUBLIC/ STATE ENTERPRISES
Believes in	risk taking	calculated risks	avoiding risk
Seeks	high returns	high and sustainable profits	stable returns
Makes decisions	rapidly	decisively	after lengthy meetings
Sees himself or herself as a	doer	decision maker	policy maker
Concerned with	fast growth	reputation	stability/continuity
Responsible to	self/partners	stakeholders	public at large
Negotiates in	small teams/alone	multidisciplinary teams	large teams
Appreciates	self-realization	power	status/reputation
Communicates	using direct/ technical jargon	directly but cautiously	indirectly/ conservatively

blunders that can derail the discussions as well as lead to inferior outcomes.

PROTOCOL AND DEPORTMENT

Hundreds of articles and numerous books and manuals have been written about cultural traits of different groups, advising global businesspeople what to do or not to do in different matters. Consider the following cross-cultural negotiating behavior ascribed to different societies:

- English negotiators are very formal and polite and place great importance on proper protocol. They are also concerned with proper etiquette.
- The French expect others to behave as they do when conducting business. This includes speaking the French language.
- Protocol is important and formal in Germany. Dress is conservative; correct posture and manners are required. Seriousness of purpose goes hand in hand with serious dress.
- The Swedes tend to be formal in their relationships; dislike haggling over price; expect thorough, professional proposals without flaws; and are attracted to quality.
- Italians tend to be extremely hospitable but are often volatile in temperament. When they make a point, they do so with considerable gesticulation and emotional expression.
- The Japanese often want to spend days or even weeks creating a friendly, trusting atmosphere before discussing business.
- In China, the protocol followed during the negotiation process should include giving small, inexpensive presents. As the Chinese do not like to be touched, a short bow and a brief handshake are used during the introductions.
- Business is conducted in a formal yet relaxed manner in India. Having connections is important and one should request permission before smoking, entering, or sitting.
- Emotion and drama carry more weight than logic does for Mexicans. Mexican negotiators are often selected for their skill at rhetoric and for their ability to make distinguished performances.
- For Brazilians, the negotiating process is often valued more than the end result. Discussions tend to be lively, heated, inviting, eloquent, and witty. Brazilians enjoy lavish hospitality to establish a comfortable social climate.

The list can go on and on about the cultural differences between different groups. While such information might help a negotiator avoid certain mistakes, it is too general to be useful in

FIGURE 2-2
Cross-Cultural Etiquette

Greetings	How do people greet and address one another? What role do business cards play?
Degree of Formality	Will my counterparts expect me to dress and interact formally or informally?
Gift Giving	Do businesspeople exchange gifts? What gifts are appropriate? Are there taboos associated with gift giving?
Touching	What are the attitudes toward body contact?
Eye Contact	Is direct eye contact polite? Is it expected?
Deportment	How should I carry myself? Formally? Casually?
Emotions	Is it rude, embarrassing, or unusual to display emotions?
Silence	Is silence awkward? Expected? Insulting? Respectful?
Eating	What is the proper manner for dining? Are certain foods taboo?
Body Language	Are certain gestures or forms of body language rude?
Punctuality	Should I be punctual and expect my counterparts to be as well? Or are schedules and agendas fluid?

Source: James K. Sebenius, "The Hidden Challenge of Cross-Border Negotiations," *Harvard Business Review*, March 2002, pp. 76–89.

negotiations. Further, while culture does have a role in negotiation, other factors, such as personality of the negotiator and the culture of the organization to which the negotiator belongs, influence negotiation behavior. As a guide, therefore, a negotiator should seek answers to the questions about protocol and deportment shown in Figure 2-2. Sensitivity to these issues allows a negotiator to avoid being offensive, to demonstrate respect, to enhance cordial relationship, and to strengthen communication.

DEEPER CULTURAL CHARACTERISTICS

Two frameworks are presented for gaining deeper behavior knowledge of a culture: Hall's "Silent Language" and Hofstede's Cultural Dimensions.

Hall's Framework

According to Hall, the following aspects drive surface behavior, and their understanding can be of immense help in seeking cultural knowledge of a group.[7]

FIGURE 2-3
Low Context versus High Context Communication

Cultures can be predominantly verbal or nonverbal. In verbal communications, information is transmitted through a code that makes meanings both explicit and specific. In nonverbal communications, the nonverbal aspects become the major channel for transmitting meaning. This ability is called context. Context includes both the vocal and nonvocal aspects of communication that surround a word or passage and clarify its meaning—the situational and cultural factors affecting communications. High context or low context refers to the amount of information that is given in communication. These aspects include: the rate at which one talks, the pitch or tone of the voice, the fluency, expressional patterns, or nuances of delivery. Nonverbal aspects include eye contact, pupil contraction and dilation, facial expression, odor, color, hand gestures, body movement, proximity, and use of space.

The greater the contextual portion of communication in any given culture, the more difficult it is for one to convey or receive a message. Conversely, it is easier to communicate with a person from a culture in which context contributes relatively little to a message. In high context cultures, information about an individual (and consequently about individual and group behavior in that culture) is provided through mostly nonverbal means. It is also conveyed through status, friends, and associates. Information flows freely within the culture although outsiders who are not members of the culture may have difficulty reading the information.

In a low context communication, information is transmitted through an explicit code to make up for a lack of shared meaning—words. In low context cultures, the environment, situation, and nonverbal behavior are relatively less important and more explicit information has to be given. A direct style of communications is valued and ambiguity is not well regarded. Relationships between individuals are relatively shorter in duration and personal involvement tends to be valued less. Low context countries tend to be more heterogeneous and prone to greater social and job mobility. Authority is diffused through a bureaucratic system that makes personal responsibility difficult. Agreements tend to be written rather than spoken and treated as final and legally binding.

Low context countries include the Anglo-American countries and the Germanic and Scandinavian countries.

High context cultures can be found in East Asia (Japan, China, Korea, Vietnam), Mediterranean countries (Greece, Italy, Spain, to lesser extent France), the Middle East, and to a lesser extent Latin America.

Source: Excerpted from Donald W. Hendon, Rebecca A. Hendon, and Paul Herbig, *Cross-Cultural Business Negotiations* (Westport, CT: Quorum Books, 1996), pp. 65–67.

- Relationship: *Is the culture deal-focused or relationship-focused?* In deal-focused cultures, relationships grow out of deals; in relationship-focused cultures, deals arise from already developed relationships.
- Communication: *Are communications indirect and "high-context" or direct and "low-context"?* Do contextual, nonverbal cues play a significant role in negotiations, or is there little reliance on contextual cues (see Figure 2-3)? *Do communications require detailed or concise information?* Many North Americans prize

concise, to-the-point communications. Many Chinese, by contrast, seem to have an insatiable appetite for detailed data.

- Time: *Is the culture generally considered to be "monochronic" or "polychronic"?* In Anglo-Saxon cultures, punctuality and schedules are often strictly considered. This monochronic orientation contrasts with a polychronic attitude, in which time is more fluid, deadlines are more flexible, interruptions are common, and interpersonal relationships take precedence over schedules. For example, in contrast to the Western preference for efficient deal making, Chinese managers are usually less concerned with time.

- Space: *Do people prefer a lot of personal space, or are they comfortable with less?* In many formal cultures, moving too close to a person can produce extreme discomfort. By contrast, a Swiss negotiator who instinctively backs away from his up-close Brazilian counterpart may inadvertently convey disdain.

Hofstede's Cultural Dimensions

According to Hofstede, the way people in different countries perceive and interpret their world varies along four dimensions: power distance, uncertainty avoidance, individualism versus collectivism, and masculinity. Hofstede drew his conclusion based on his interviews with 60,000 IBM employees in over 40 countries.[8]

Power Distance (Distribution of Power): Power distance refers to the degree of inequality among people the population of a country considers acceptable (i.e., from relatively equal to extremely unequal). In some societies, power is concentrated among a few people at the top who make all the decisions. People at the other end simply carry these out decisions. Such societies are associated with high power distance levels. In other societies, power is widely dispersed and relations among people are more egalitarian. These are low power distance cultures. The lower the power distance, the more individuals expect to participate in the organizational decision-making process. The United States and Canada record a middle-level rating on power distance, but countries such as Demark and Austria exhibit much lower ratings. In these countries, leaders are more likely to give subordinates the initiative to participate. At the other extreme, employees in third-world countries generally have very limited input into decisions made by organizational leaders.

A somewhat higher power distance score is observed in Japan when compared to scores for the United States and Canada. With reference to negotiations, the relevant questions are these: Are significant power disparities accepted? Are organizations run mostly from the top down, or is power more widely and more horizontally distributed?

Uncertainty Avoidance (Tolerance for Uncertainty): Uncertainty avoidance concerns the degree to which people in a country prefer structured over unstructured situations. At the organizational level, uncertainty avoidance is related to such factors as rituals, rules orientation, and employment stability. As a consequence, personnel in less structured societies face the future as it takes shape without experiencing undue stress. The uncertainty associated with upcoming events does not result in risk avoidance behavior. To the contrary, managers in low uncertainty avoidance cultures abstain from creating bureaucratic structures that make it difficult to respond to unfolding events. But in cultures where people experience stress in dealing with future events, various steps are taken to cope with the impact of uncertainty. Such societies are high uncertainty avoidance cultures, whose managers engage in activities such as long-range planning to establish protective barriers to minimize the anxiety associated with future events. With regard to uncertainty avoidance, the United States and Canada score quite low, indicating an ability to be more responsive in coping with future changes. But Japan, Greece, Portugal, and Belgium score high, indicating their desire to meet the future in a more structured and planned fashion. The pertinent question for cross-cultural negotiations is this: How comfortable are people with uncertainty or unstructured situations, processes, or agreements?

Individualism versus Collectivism: Individualism denotes the degree to which people in a country learn to act as individuals rather than as members of cohesive groups (i.e., from collectivist to individualist). In individualistic societies, people are self-centered and feel little need for dependency on others. They seek the fulfillment of their own goals over the group's goals. Managers belonging to individualistic societies are competitive by nature and show little loyalty to the organizations for which they work. In collectivistic societies, members have a group mentality. They subordinate their individual goals to work toward the group goals. They are interdependent on each other and seek mutual accommodation to maintain group harmony.

Collectivistic managers have high loyalty to their organizations and subscribe to joint decision making. The higher a country's index of individualism, the more its managerial concepts of leadership are bound up with individuals seeking to act in their ultimate self-interest. Great Britain, Australia, Canada, and the United States show similar high ratings on individualism; Japan, Brazil, Colombia, Chile, Costa Rica, and Venezuela exhibit very low ratings. A negotiator should determine whether the culture of the other party emphasizes the individual or the group.

Masculinity (Harmony versus Assertiveness): Masculinity relates to the degree to which "masculine" values such as assertiveness, performance, success, and competition prevail over "feminine" values such as quality of life, maintenance of warm personal relationships, service, care for the weak, and solidarity. Masculine cultures exhibit different roles for men and women and perceive anything "big" as important. People in such societies have a need to be ostentatious. Feminine cultures value "small as beautiful" and stress quality of life and environment over materialistic ends. A relatively high masculinity index for the United States, Canada, and Japan is prevalent in approaches to performance appraisal and reward systems. In low-masculinity societies such as Denmark and Sweden, people are motivated by a more qualitative goal set as a means to job enrichment. Differences in masculinity scores are also reflected in the types of career opportunities available in organizations and associated job mobility. For cross-cultural negotiations, a negotiator should know if the culture emphasizes interpersonal harmony or assertiveness.

Managers negotiating in cross-cultural settings can use either of the two frameworks mentioned previously to gain deeper cultural understanding of the society in which they negotiate. Hall's and Hofstede's books, referred to here, are easy to read and are highly recommended for those who are negotiating globally.

PLAYERS AND PROCESS

Negotiators are the people who represent their organizations in striking business deals. While it is important to learn about culture and negotiating style, it may be more crucial to know about the organization that negotiators belong to and the process they must follow in seeking final approval of the agreement. A meaningful business agreement goes through a hierarchy of individuals in an organization before it is finalized. Therefore, it is useful to find out who the individuals are who might influence the negotiation outcome, what role each individual plays, and what the informal networking relationships are between the individuals that might affect the negotiation.[9]

Key Individuals

Key individuals refer to those people inside and outside the company whose approval must be sought before a negotiated deal is finalized. For example, in the United States, any large deal must be approved by the company's top officers and the board, as well as the Securities and Exchange Commission, the Federal Trade Commission, the Justice Department, and others. It is essential that the attitude of key individuals toward particular types of agreements be thoroughly examined before beginning to negotiate. Similarly, in Germany, labor unions must be taken into confidence before a deal goes through. In Europe, the European Union can become a stumbling block in many cases. For example, General Electric's management was shocked by the concerns raised by the EU about competition relative to the company's acquisition of Honeywell.

In developing countries, different government departments must clear a business deal before it is approved. In some cases, even nongovernment organizations (NGOs) can derail a deal. Thus, a negotiator should compile a list of all individuals who have a say in an agreement.

Decision Process

Equally important is the need to understand the role each individual is likely to play in the approval process. What particular aspects of the deal is an individual concerned with? Who has the authority to override the concerns a person might raise? What kind of information can be used to generate a favorable response from different individuals?

Informal Influences

Many countries have webs of influence that are more powerful than the formal bosses. These influences may not have formal standing, but they can make or break negotiations. A negotiator should determine the role of such influences and factor them into his or her negotiation approach.

The following illustration shows the significant role informal influences can play. A U.S. electrical goods manufacturer entered a joint venture with a Chinese company and hired a local manager to run the Chinese operation. The company tried to expand its product line, but the Chinese manager balked, insisting there was no demand for the additional products. The U.S. management team tried to resolve the dispute through negotiations. But when the Chinese manager would not budge, the team fired him; however, he would not leave. The local labor bureau refused to back the U.S. team, and when the U.S. executives tried to dissolve the venture, they discovered they could not recover their capital because Chinese law dictates that both sides need to approve a dissolution. A foreign law firm, hired at great expense, made no headway. It took some behind-the-scenes negotiation on the part of a local law firm to finally overcome the need for dual approval—an outcome that demanded local counsel well versed in the intricacies of Chinese culture.[10]

Simply knowing the individuals who are involved in the process is not enough. When negotiating with people, a negotiator is typically seeking to influence the outcome of an organizational process. The process takes different shape in different cultures. Besides, different processes call for radically different negotiation strategies. This means a negotiation approach should be carefully crafted depending on the individuals involved and the process they follow.

TRAITS FOR COPING WITH CULTURE

Knowledge about the culture of one's counterpart helps a negotiator to communicate, understand, plan, and decide the deal-making aspects effectively. But culture is a broad field, and there are hundreds of cultures in the world. No executive who negotiates internationally can cope with the cultural challenge no matter how skilled and experienced he or she is. To make the job easier, the following discussion presents the traits that are commonly faced in cross-cultural negotiations.[11] When a negotiator learns to deal with them, he or she can gain sufficient cultural training for the purpose of negotiating.

Negotiating Goal: Contract or Relationship

In some cultures, negotiators are more interested in short-term deals, such as in the United States. Therefore, for them, a signed contract is the goal. In other countries, the emphasis is on building long-term relationships. A case in point is Japan, where the goal of negotiation is not a signed contract, but a lasting relationship between the two parties.

A negotiator must determine if his or her goals match the goals of the other party. It is difficult to close a deal if the goals differ.

Negotiating Attitude

Basically, there are two approaches to negotiations: win-win and win-lose. If both parties view the negotiation as a win-win situation, it is easier to come to an agreement since both stand to gain. If one party sees the negotiation as a win-lose situation, it may be difficult to strike a deal because the weaker party believes its loss is the other party's gain. The stronger party can take the following steps to soften the attitude of the opponent: (1) Explain the perspectives of the transaction fully since the other party might lack the sophistication to understand the nitty gritty of the business deal being negotiated. (2) Determine the real interest of the other party through questioning. This may require the negotiator to understand the other's history and culture. (3) Amend the proposal it to satisfy the interest of the other party.

Personal Style: Informal or Formal

The negotiating style of the individuals can be informal or formal. Style here refers to the way a negotiator talks, uses titles, and dresses. For example, North Americans believe in informality, addressing people by their first name in an initial meeting. Germans, on the other hand, maintain a formal attitude. In this matter, the guest should adapt his or her attitude to be in line with the host.

Communication: Direct or Indirect

In cultures where communication is direct, such as Germany, a negotiator can expect direct answers to questions. In cultures that communicate indirectly (Japan, for instance), it may be difficult to interpret messages easily. Indirect communication uses signs, gestures, and indefinite comments, which a negotiator must learn to interpret.

Sensitivity to Time: High or Low

Some cultures are more relaxed about time than others. For North Americans, time is money, which is always in short supply. Therefore, they like to rush through a negotiation to obtain a signed contract quickly. Mexicans, as an example, are more relaxed about time. Thus, a Mexican dealing with a North American may view the latter's attempt to shorten the time as an effort to hide something. Thus, negotiation sessions should be planned and scheduled such that the pace of discussions runs smoothly.

Emotions: High or Low

Some negotiators are more emotional than others. A negotiator should establish the emotional behavior of the other party and make appropriate adjustments in negotiation tactics to satisfy such behavior.

Form of Agreement: General or Specific

Culture often influences the form of agreement a party requires. Usually, North Americans prefer a detailed contract that provides for all eventualities. Chinese, however, prefer a contract in the form of general principles. When a negotiator prefers a specific agreement while the other party is satisfied with general principles, the negotiator should carefully review each principle to make sure it is, in any event, not interpreted in such a manner that he or she stands to lose significantly.

Building an Agreement: Bottom-Up or Top-Down

Some negotiators begin with agreement on general principles and proceed to specific items, such as price, delivery date, and product quality. Others begin with agreement on specifics, the sum of which becomes the contract. It is just a matter of style. If a negotiator prefers a bottom-up approach and the other party is satisfied with general principles (i.e., a top-down approach), the negotiator should seek specific information about various aspects before closing the deal.

Team Organization: One Leader versus Consensus

In some cultures, one leader has the authority to make commitments. In other cultures, group consensus must be sought before agreeing to a deal. The latter type of organization requires more time to finalize an agreement, and the other party should be prepared for time it may take.

Risk Taking: High or Low

A negotiator must examine the attitude of the other party about risk. If the negotiator determines that the other party is risk-averse, he or she should focus the attention on proposing rules, mechanisms, and relationships that reduce the apparent risks in the deal.

SUMMARY

When people negotiate with someone outside their home country, culture becomes a significant factor. It is because people from different cultures present a different perspective in everything they do. Thus, their negotiating style, skills, and behavior vary. More specifically, culture affects the definition of negotiation, the selection of negotiators, protocol, communication, time, risk propensity, group versus individual emphasis, and the nature of agreement.

From the viewpoint of cross-cultural negotiator, the necessary cultural knowledge is grouped into two categories: (1) traditions and etiquette and group behavior (or protocols and deportment and deeper cultural characteristics) and (2) players and process.

Protocols and deportment deal with greetings, degree of formality, gift giving, touching, eye contact, deportment, emotions, silence, eating, body language, and punctuality. Two frameworks are suggested for deeper cultural understanding: one by Edward Hall and the other by Geert Hofstede. Either one can be used to gain deeper insights into a culture. Furthermore, it is important to know the players and to learn their negotiation process. This requires knowing the key individuals who can impact the negotiation; the role each individual plays; and the informal influences, those who carry weight in the negotiation process. Cultural traits that affect negotiations include negotiating goals, negotiating attitude, personal style of the negotiator, communication style, sensitivity to time, emotional makeup, form of the agreement, structure of the agreement, authority to commit, and risk taking.

For those readers interested in learning more about culture in the context of cross-border negotiations, the following sources are recommended:

- Robert T. Moran and William G. Stripp, *Successful International Business Negotiations* (Houston, TX: Gulf Publishing Company, 1991).
- Jeanne M. Brett, *Negotiating Globally* (San Francisco, CA: Jossey-Bass, 2001).
- Camille Schuster and Michael Copeland, *Global Business* (Orlando, FL: Harcourt Brace & Company, 1996).

NOTES

1. Edward B. Taylor, *Primitive Culture* (London: John Murray, 1871), p. 1.
2. Edward T. Hall, *Beyond Culture* (Garden City, NY: Anchor Books, 1977), p. 16.
3. Roy J. Lewicki, David M. Saunders, and John W. Minton, *Essentials of Negotiation*, 2nd Edition (New York: McGraw-Hill, 2001), pp. 196–200.
4. David A. Ricks, "International Business Blunders: An Update," *B&E Review*, January-March 1998, p. 11. Also see Dinker Raval and Bina Raval, "Cultural Shift in India Managers' Perceptions: Implications for MNCs' Negotiation Strategy," *ASC Annual Research Volume*, October 1998, pp. 337–345.
5. Dean Allen Foster, *Bargaining Across Borders* (New York: McGraw-Hill, 1992), p. 281.
6. Paul A. Herbig and Hugh E. Kramer, "Do's and Don'ts of Cross-Cultural Negotiations," *Industrial Marketing Management*, Vol. 21, 1992, pp. 287–298.
7. Edward T. Hall, *The Silent Language* (Garden City, NY: Anchor Books, 1973). Also see James K. Sebenius, "The Hidden Challenge of Cross-Border Negotiations," *Harvard Business Review*, March 2002, pp. 76–89.
8. Geert Hofstede, *Cultural Consequences: International Differences in World-Related Values* (London: Sage Publications, 1980).
9. This section draws heavily from James K. Sebenius, op. cit.
10. Charles Olivier, "Investing in China: 12 Hard Lessons," *Worldlink*, November, 1996.
11. Jeswald W. Salacuse, *Making Global Deals: Negotiating in the International Marketplace* (Boston: Houghton Mifflin, 1991), pp. 58–70.

Selecting Your Negotiating Style

*It's a well-known proposition that you know who's going to win a negotiation: it's he who pauses the longest.—**Robert Holmes***

Regardless of their past experiences, people have a preference for one approach or the other to negotiations. Over the years, they dealt with individuals who showed aggressive behavior, who displayed a cooperative attitude, who settled their differences through an exchange of concessions, and who withdrew from the discussion altogether. A negotiator must know his or her preferred style of negotiation as well as that of the other party. This knowledge allows the negotiator to improve his or her preparation, including selecting the most appropriate negotiation style for the situation. As every negotiation is unique, prior to entering into discussions, a negotiator should have identified the other party's style and adjusted his or hers in order to optimize mutual benefits.

STYLE DIFFERENCES AMONG NEGOTIATORS

Each negotiator applies a specific negotiating style. This depends on his or her cultural background, his or her professional responsibilities, and the context in which the discussions are taking place, as well as whether he or she is seeking a one-time deal or repeat business over the long term. Five distinct negotiation styles can be identified. These styles are influenced by two major forces; namely, relationship-oriented outcomes and substantive- or task-oriented outcomes. In most negotiations, there is a trade-off between these two orientations. Cultural characteristics play a significant role in determining the relative impact of these two orientations. In cultures where establishing and maintaining relationships is essential to carrying out business, the predominant negotiating style is more accommodation-oriented. In competitive cultures, where only the final outcome is considered important, the negotiation style is more task-oriented, relying on competitive and conflicting tactics.[1]

In terms of style, negotiations are grouped into five categories: dodgers, dreamers, hagglers, competitors, and problem solvers.

Dodgers

Generally, dodgers do not like facing situations where decisions must be made and risks assumed. In a negotiation, the dodger tries to postpone making decisions or, more likely, tries to find reasons for not getting involved at all. In other words, the dodger is a reluctant party who does not enjoy negotiating and who withdraws from the discussions or simply refuses to participate. These situations are not frequent, although they may be more common in certain cultures whereby an unwillingness to negotiate is seen as a lack of interest. In other situations, by the time the two sides meet, one party may no longer be interested in pursuing the negotiation due to a better offer received from a competitor; the party, therefore, adopts a dodging attitude. At times, executives doing business across cultural boundaries are likely to face dodgers and should decide early on whether to continue the discussions, ask for a recess, or deal only with negotiators who have decision-making responsibilities.

Dreamers

Dreamers approach negotiations with one major goal in mind; that is, to preserve the relationship even if it means giving up unnecessary concessions while reducing their own expectations. At times, they pretend to agree with the other party to maintain the relationship and goodwill, when in reality they have divergent views. In more traditional cultures, relationship plays a dominant role in negotiations. Without a relationship or without a trusted third party making an introduction, negotiations are unlikely to take place. In a competitive culture, dreamers are at a disadvantage, as their behavior is often interpreted as a sign of weakness. For example, face saving in Asian cultures is part and parcel of negotiations. Failing to take into consideration the role of relationship and face saving (or giving face) can result in negotiations that turn into deadlocks or that simply lead to breakdowns.

Dreamers are willing to accept lower outcomes on substantive issues for the sake of the relationship. Such negotiations often make sense to executives seeking entry into new markets by adopting an accommodating attitude in the hope of getting the business going. However, it is difficult to obtain a favorable agreement if concessions are given without obtaining similar ones in return.

Hagglers

Hagglers view negotiations as a give-and-take game. They are willing to lower their expectations provided they can obtain some benefits from the other party. Persuasion, partial exchange of information, and manipulation dominate the discussion. A short-term outlook and quick movements characterized with back-and-forth concessions prevail. Hagglers are flexible in their approach and seek instant compromises. As a result, hagglers fail to reach optimum outcomes, neglect details, and sometimes overlook long-term opportunities.

In their search for quick solutions, hagglers fail to identify the underlying needs of the other party. Hagglers build superficial relationships and are satisfied with splitting the difference to reach a final agreement.

This style is more suitable for one-time deals in domestic market situations. In international negotiations, where long-term relationships and trust are essential ingredients to successful implementation, haggling is not considered an effective approach that satisfies the interests of both parties.

Competitors

Competitors enjoy conflicts, feel comfortable with aggressive behavior, and employ hardball tactics. They enjoy struggling to meet their objectives, even at the cost of alienating the other side. Satisfying their own interests is their primary goal. Competitors use whatever power they have to win and fully exploit the other party's weaknesses. They are extremely persuasive in their discussions and persist in controlling the discussions. In this type of interaction, limited information is exchanged. Generally, such situations lead to win-lose agreements, where the competitor wins most of the benefits by obtaining the majority of concessions while giving few, if any, concessions in return. Frequently, these negotiations result in a breakdown when the weaker party decides to walk away. After all, no deal is better than accepting a bad deal.

Negotiators relying on competitive strategies and tactics are found everywhere, with a greater concentration in task-oriented cultures. In these cultures, only tangible results are considered worth negotiating for. Short-term benefits override long-term gains, and relationships are often considered marginal.[2] As a consequence, these negotiated agreements are unsustainable, often calling for renegotiations when the weaker party can no longer honor its commitments.

Problem Solvers

Problem solvers display creativity in finding mutually satisfying agreements. They take time to identify the underlying needs of the other party in order to explore how they can best meet their mutual interests jointly. In their search for a joint solution, they take into consideration the relationship as well as the substantive issues, since both are equally important to them. Problem solvers ask plenty of questions, share information openly, and suggest options and alternatives. During the discussions, they emphasize common needs and frequently summarize what has been agreed to so far. They tend to have long-term vision, sometimes at the cost of short-term benefits.

During the discussions, problem solvers exchange plenty of information in a cooperative and constructive environment. This style of negotiation requires more time to prepare and calls for face-to-face discussions. By exploring alternatives and developing multiple options, problem solvers are able to create optimum outcomes where both parties are winners, referred to as the win-win approach. This negotiating style is more conducive to international business deals, where implementation over the long run determines whether an agreement is profitable.

Figure 3-1 summarizes the strengths and weaknesses of each style.

APPROPRIATE NEGOTIATING STYLE

Of the five styles, problem solving is regarded as superior because it attempts to satisfy the needs of both parties. Problem solvers realize that a mutually agreeable outcome is the best insurance against the threat of competition or possible backlash from an unhappy party. This approach requires a negotiator to prepare thoroughly to identify his or her specific needs as well as the interests of the other party, to develop options, and to plan what concessions to make and what concessions to ask for. It also requires having an open and flexible mind, asking plenty of

FIGURE 3-1
Strengths and Weaknesses of Different Negotiation Styles

	STRENGTH	WEAKNESS	BEST FOR
Dodger	• Shows indifference • Will assess risk first • Has low needs	• Cannot make decisions • Dislikes negotiating • Fails to prepare • Is not comfortable with people • Is mainly inactive	• Avoiding entry into bad deals • Testing the market when issues are not important • Avoiding no-win situations
Dreamer	• Seeks relationships • Shows concern for others • Values friendship	• Wants to be well liked • Concedes easily • Preserves relationships at own expense • Gives away too much	• Seeking entry into new markets • Dealing in relationship-oriented markets
Haggler	• Makes quick decisions • Likes making deals • Has no strong positions • Is easy to deal with • Is open to counterproposals	• Is win-lose oriented • Accepts lower outcomes • Is satisfied with quick resuts • Is short-term oriented • Gives in easily	• Issues that are not considered important • Quick decisions • Breaking deadlocks • Restarting discussions
Competitor	• Is a risk taker • Cares for own needs • Controls discussions • Is persuasive/persistent • Enjoys pressure	• Is not interested in the other party • Is mostly short-term oriented • Is unwilling to shift positions • Is a poor listener • Leads to frequent breakdowns	• Quick decisions • Competitive markets • When similar styles are used
Problem Solver	• Shares information • Creates values • Is win-win oriented • Seeks win-win deals • Develops options • Has good listening skills • Asks a lot of questions	• Is a slow decision maker • Overlooks details • Can be unrealistic at times • Takes time • Requires thorough preparation	• Long-term deals • Repeat business • Complex negotiations • Important deals

FIGURE 3-2
Maximizing Joint Gains

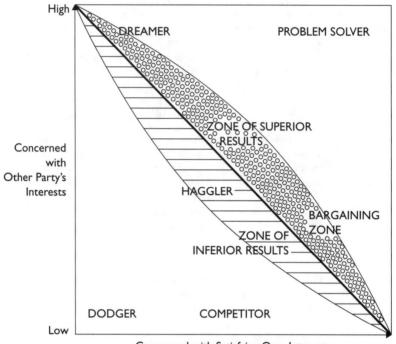

questions, and listening actively to fully understand the other party. In these discussions, useful information is exchanged, enabling each side to explore the full range of opportunities available to them. In the end, problem solvers place themselves in a position to improve on their expected results by enlarging the zone of agreement.[3] In other words, negotiators applying the problem-solving approach are most likely to achieve superior results (also known as the Pareto frontier, where there are no possible superior outcomes) in which each party gains without giving up more or taking more from the other side. Figure 3-2 shows how each style fits into the overall field of negotiation and how the problem-solving approach allows the negotiators to enter into the some of optimum outcomes: maximizing joint gains.

DETERMINING A NEGOTIATION STYLE

Having familiarized yourself with the five negotiating styles, you can identify your preferred style. In reality, most people rely on one or more styles depending on the situation they are in, although they probably have a predisposition for one specific negotiation style. A negotiator often adjusts the style as he or she interacts with the other party. If you are meeting a party who relies on competitive or aggressive tactics, you need to respond with appropriate tactics of your own to protect your interests. Equally, you need to project an image of self-confidence to the other party in order to send a message that such tactics are not conducive to satisfying both of your respective needs. In other words, despite having a tendency to use a certain style, you must modify it in light of the other party's behavior.

You can determine your preferred negotiating style by following the procedure discussed here. First, rate each of the 35 statements in Figure 3-3, Personal Assessment Inventory, on a five-point scale with 1 (strongly disagree), 2 (disagree), 3 (have no specific view), 4 (agree), or 5 (strongly agree).

Whenever possible, try to avoid using a rating of 3, as this rating will not reflect your true preferences. Further, bear in mind that there are no right or wrong answers. Just make sure your rating describes your preferred style when handling a negotiating situation.

Next, enter your ratings to all the 35 statements in Figure 3-4. Each column indicates where you should enter the ratings for the statements. For example, enter your responses to statements 1, 6, 11, 16, 21, 26, and 31 in The Dodger column.

The highest total score identifies your dominant style. In most negotiations, you are likely to use a mix of styles ranging from cooperation to competition. Your prevailing style is influenced by the importance you give to the relationship, the style of the other party, the degree of competition in the target market, and your wish to seek a one-time opportunity or repeat orders over the long term.

To get an overall view of your negotiation profile, plot your ratings in Figure 3-5. Any ratings near the top (35) mean that you tend to rely too much on that style in handling negotiations. If you have low ratings for Dodger and Dreamer and high ratings for the others, you have a good base for negotiations. A high rating for Competitor is good, but that style can backfire in some cultures. Ideally, a high rating for Problem Solver is considered the key ingredient for win-win solutions. You can repeat the exercise whenever you want to learn the style of the other party.

FIGURE 3-3
Personal Assessment Inventory

Rate each statement with a rating ranging from 1 (strongly disagree) to 5 (strongly agree) that best reflects your behavior when negotiating.

Your rating

1. (_)   I am not comfortable negotiating.
2. (_)   I push the other party toward my own positions/interests.
3. (_)   I avoid hurting people.
4. (_)   I try to learn the real needs of the other party before making a concession.
5. (_)   I enjoy making offers and counteroffers.
6. (_)   I don't like making difficult decisions.
7. (_)   Before negotiating, I know what results to expect and how to work to obtain them.
8. (_)   When negotiating, I like to make quick decisions to speed up the discussions.
9. (_)   I am willing to lower my expectations to save the relationship.
10. (_)   I encourage the other party to work with me in finding an acceptable solution.
11. (_)   I avoid getting involved in difficult situations.
12. (_)   I make sure I have power over the other party, and I use it to my advantage.
13. (_)   To advance the negotiations, I like to split the difference.
14. (_)   When negotiating, I make sure the other party feels comfortable.
15. (_)   I have no problem sharing information with the other party.
16. (_)   I don't negotiate when I have little chance of winning.
17. (_)   If necessary, I use threats to reach my goals.
18. (_)   I like to compromise to expedite the negotiations.
19. (_)   I make sure the other party explains his or her real needs.
20. (_)   I like to explore innovative approaches with the other party to achieve maximum outcomes.
21. (_)   I avoid taking risks.
22. (_)   To get what I want, I ask for more than what I am willing to settle for.
23. (_)   I look for a fair deal.
24. (_)   To me, personal relationships are vital to constructive discussions.
25. (_)   I frequently summarize issues we both agreed to.
26. (_)   I dislike dealing with difficult negotiators.
27. (_)   I try to create doubts in the mind of the other party.
28. (_)   To me, negotiating is a game of give and take.
29. (_)   I do not like to embarrass other people.
30. (_)   When I negotiate, I take a long-term outlook.
31. (_)   I avoid getting involved in controversies.
32. (_)   I do not give away information, but I try to obtain as much information as possible from the other party.
33. (_)   I look for a middle-of-the-road solution to close negotiations.
34. (_)   I avoid getting involved in nonessential details.
35. (_)   I enjoy meeting people.

FIGURE 3-4
Interpreting Your Scores

After completing the inventory, add your responses according to the following table:

The Dodger		The Dreamer		The Haggler		The Competitor		The Problem Solver	
S	R	S	R	S	R	S	R	S	R
1		3		5		2		4	
6		9		8		7		10	
11		14		13		12		15	
16		19		18		17		20	
21		24		23		22		25	
26		29		28		27		30	
31		35		33		32		34	
Total		Total		Total		Total		Total	

Legend: **S**: Statement
      R: Rating

For example, if you gave statement 17 in the inventory a score of 5, place 5 in The Competitor column next to 17.

FIGURE 3-5
Visualizing Negotiating Styles

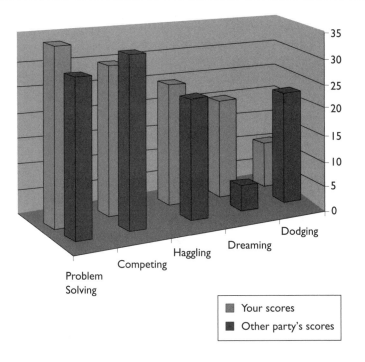

SUMMARY

A negotiator should know his or her negotiation style as well as the style of his or her counterpart. The negotiator can then adjust his or her style to match the style of the other party, ensuring smooth negotiations.

The five different negotiation styles are dodgers, dreamers, hagglers, competitors, and problem solvers. Among these, the problem solver is considered the best style because it satisfies the needs of both parties.

A negotiator can determine his or her negotiation style by following the procedure discussed in the chapter. The same procedure can be utilized to figure out the negotiation style of the other party. Each style is influenced by one of two forces: task orientation or relationship orientation. A method for computing your orientation is suggested.

NOTES

1. Stephen E. Weiss, "Negotiation with 'Romans'—Part 1," *Sloan Management Review,* Winter 1994, pp. 51–61.
2. Paul A. Herbig and Hugh E. Kramer, "Do's and Don'ts of Cross-Cultural Negotiations," *Industrial Marketing Management,* Vol. 21, 1992, pp. 287–298.
3. See Dean Allen Foster, *Bargaining Across Borders* (New York: McGraw-Hill, 1992), Chapter 8.

4

Prenegotiations Planning

*By failing to prepare, you are preparing to fail.—**Benjamin Franklin***

It is widely recognized that systematic planning and preparation are critical elements of successful business negotiations. Experienced executives devote substantial time to these functions before sitting down at the negotiating table. As a general rule, the more complex the transaction to be negotiated, the longer the planning period. The preparatory phase is also more lengthy for international transactions than for domestic ones because of the difficulty of gathering all necessary preliminary information.

The most common business negotiation mistakes, shown in Figure 4-1, reflect insufficient preparation. A majority of these errors can be eliminated or greatly reduced when adequate attention is given to doing the background work.

FIGURE 4-1
Most Common Negotiation Errors

- Unclear objectives
- Inadequate knowledge of the other party's goals
- An incorrect view of the other party as an opponent
- Insufficient attention to the other party's concerns
- Lack of understanding of the other party's decision-making process
- Nonexistence of a strategy for making concessions
- Too few alternatives and options prepared beforehand
- Failure to take into account the competition factor
- Unskillful use of negotiation power
- Hasty calculations and decision making
- A poor sense of timing for closing the negotiations
- Poor listening habits
- Too low of an aim
- Failure to create added value
- Insufficient time
- Uncomfortable negotiations
- Overemphasis of the importance of price

KEY FACTORS

Preparing for negotiations is time-consuming, demanding, and often complex. The following factors are considered critical for the prenegotiation phase. Failure to prepare on these points may result in a less-than-satisfactory outcome. A golden rule of negotiations is this: *Do not negotiate if you are unprepared.*

- Define the issues.
- Know the other party's position.
- Know the competition.
- Know the negotiations limits.
- Develop strategies and tactics.
- Plan the negotiation meeting.

DEFINING THE ISSUES

The first step in prenegotiation planning is to identify the issues to be discussed. Usually, a negotiation involves one or two major issues (e.g., price, commission, and duration of agreement) and a number of minor issues. For example, in the appointment of a distributor in a foreign market, the major issues would be the commission on sales, duration of the agreement, and exclusivity. Other issues could include promotional support provided by the agent, sales training, information flow, and product adaptation. In any negotiations, a complete list of issues can be developed through (a) analysis of the situation at hand, (b) prior experience on a similar situation, (c) research conducted on the situation, and (d) consultation with experts.

After listing all of the issues, the negotiator should prioritize them.[1] He or she must determine which issues are most important. Once negotiations begin, parties can easily become overwhelmed with an abundance of information, arguments, offers, counteroffers, trade-offs, and concessions. When a party is not clear in advance about what it wants, it can lose perspective and agree to suboptimal issues. A party must decide what is most important, what is second most important, and what is least important or group the issues into three categories of high, medium, or low importance. A negotiator should set priorities for both tangible and intangible issues. In addition, the negotiator needs to determine whether the issues are connected or separate. When the issues are separate, they can easily be added later or put aside for the time being. When they are linked to each other, settlement on one involves the others as well. For example, making concessions on one issue is inevitably tied to other issues.

After prioritizing the list of issues, a negotiator should touch base with the other party to determine his or her list of issues. The two lists are combined to arrive at a final list of issues that form the agenda. In other words, before the negotiation starts, both sides should firmly agree on the issues they are deliberating.[2] There should be no disagreement about the issues to be negotiated.

Each party can develop and prioritize his or her issues and share them with each other. At a prenegotiation meeting or through phone/fax/e-mail communication, the two lists can be combined to develop a common list of issues. This combined list is often called a bargaining list.

KNOWING ONE'S POSITION

After issue development, the next major step in preparing for business negotiation is to determine one's goals, a clear understanding of what one is planning to achieve, and an understanding of one's strengths and weaknesses.

Goals

Goals are usually tangibles such as price, rate, specific terms, contract language, and fixed package. But they can also be intangible, such as maintaining a certain precedent, defending a principle, or getting an agreement regardless of cost. An intangible goal of an automobile parts manufacturer might be to acquire recognition as a reliable supplier of quality products to major car producers.

Negotiators should clearly define their goals. This requires stating all of the goals they wish to achieve in the negotiation, prioritizing the goals, identifying potential multigoal packages, and evaluating the possible trade-offs among them.

Goals and issues are closely related, and they evolve together, impacting each other. What a negotiator wants to achieve through a negotiation can dramatically impact the issues he or she raises at the negotiation. Likewise, how a negotiatior sees an issue has an effect in communicating what he or she wants to achieve from an upcoming negotiation. Goals and issues are interactive; the existence of one quickly produces evidence of the other.

It is important to understand the four aspects of how goals affect negotiation.[3]

- *Wishes are not goals:* Wishes may be related to interests or needs that motivate goals themselves. A wish is a fantasy, a hope that something might happen. A goal, however, is a specific, realistic target that a person can plan to realize.

- *One party's goals are permanently linked to the other party's goals:* The linkage between the two parties' goals defines the issue to be resolved. An exporter's goal is to give the distributor a low commission on sales, while the distributor's goal is to settle for the highest commission. Thus, the issue is the rate of commission. Goals that are not linked to each other often lead to conflict.

- *Goals have boundaries:* Goals have boundaries, set by the ability of the other party to meet them. Thus, if a negotiator's goals exceed the boundary, he or she must either change the goals or end the negotiation. Stated differently, goals must be realistic; i.e., reasonably attainable.

- *Effective goals must be concrete and measurable:* The less concrete and measurable a person's goals are, the more difficulty the person will have communicating what he or she wants to the other party, understanding what the other party wants, and determining whether an outcome meets the goals of both parties.

Strengths and Weaknesses

Knowing one's negotiating position also implies an understanding of the company's strengths and weaknesses. When analyzing strengths, a person should consider those that are real and those that are perceived. For instance, if you are an exporter from a country with an international reputation for producing high-quality goods, you may be perceived as having an advantage over other suppliers. You should identity your firm's strengths so you can bring them to the forefront when you need them during the negotiations.

A negotiator also needs to identify his or her company's weaknesses and take corrective measures to improve the deficiencies when possible. The other party is likely to bring the firm's weak points into the open at a critical moment in the negotiations to obtain maximum concessions. Some weaknesses cannot be eliminated, but others can be reduced or turned into strengths.

Small- and medium-sized exporters often view themselves as being in a weak position with buyers from larger organizations. If you are negotiating on behalf of a small export firm with limited production capacity, you can turn this perceived weakness into a strength by stressing low overhead costs, flexibility in production runs, minimal delays in switching production lines, and a willingness to accept small orders. Too often small- and medium-size firms fail to recognize that many of their perceived weaknesses can become strengths in different business situations.

Small suppliers who are highly committed to their specific transactions are likely to increase their strength with larger buyers. Large companies that deal with smaller ones may be overconfident, thereby coming to the negotiating table poorly prepared. In negotiation, highly committed companies that do their background work prior to the talks improve their chances of achieving desired outcomes.

KNOWING THE OTHER SIDE'S POSITION

Just as important as knowing what one's company wants from the forthcoming negotiation is understanding what the other party hopes to obtain. This information is not always available, particularly when the discussions are with a new party. A negotiator may need to make assumptions about the other party's goals, strengths and weaknesses, strategy, and so on. Whatever assumptions are made, they should be verified during the negotiations. Usually, a negotiator attempts to obtain the following information about the other party: current resources, including financial stability; interests and needs; goals; reputation and negotiation style; alternatives; authority to negotiate; and strategy and tactics.

Current Resources, Interests, and Needs

A negotiator should gather as much information as possible about the other party's current resources, interests, and needs through research. What kind of facts and figures makes sense depends on what type of negotiation will be conducted and who the other party is. A negotiator can draw useful clues from the history of the other party and from previous negotiations the party might have conducted. In addition, the negotiator might gather financial data about the other party from published sources, trade associations, and research agencies. Interviewing people who are knowledgeable about the party is another way the negotiator can acquire information. Furthermore, where feasible, a great deal of information can be sought by visiting the other party.[4] Additionally, the negotiator can explore the following ways to learn the perspectives of the other party: (a) by conducting a preliminary interview or discussion in which the negotiator talks about what the other party wants to achieve in the upcoming negotiation; (b) by anticipating the other party's interests; (c) by asking others who have negotiated with the other party; and (d) by reading what the other party says about itself in the media.

Goals

After determining the other party's resources, interests, and needs, the next step for a negotiator is to learn about the party's goals. It is not easy to pinpoint the other party's goals with reference to a particular negotiation. The best way for the negotiator to figure out the other party's goals is to analyze whatever information he or she has gathered about the party, make appropriate assumptions, and estimate the goals. After doing this groundwork, the negotiator can contact the other party directly to share as much information about each other's perspectives as is feasible. Because information about the other party's goals is so important to the strategy formulation of both parties, professional negotiators are willing to exchange related information or initial proposals days (or even weeks) before the negotiation. The negotiator should use the information gleaned directly from the other party to refine his or her goals.

When identifying the goals of the other party, a negotiator must not assume stereotypical goals. Similarly, the negotiator should not use his or her own values and goals as a guide, assuming the other party wants to pursue similar goals. A negotiator must not judge others by his or her own standards/values.

Reputation and Style

A negotiator wants to deal with a dependable party with whom it is a pleasure to do business. Therefore, he or she must seek information about the reputation and style of the other party. There are three different ways to determine that reputation and style: (a) from one's own experience, either in the same or a different context; (b) from the experience of other firms that have negotiated with the other party in the past; and (c) from what others, especially business media, have said about the other party.

While past perspectives of the other party provide insight into how it conducts negotiations, provision must be made about management changes that might have taken place, which can affect the forthcoming negotiations. Furthermore, people do change over time. Thus, what they did in the past might not be relevant in the future.

Alternatives

In the prenegotiation process, a negotiator must work out the alternatives. The alternatives offer a viable recourse to pursue if the negotiation fails. Similarly, the negotiator must probe into the other party's alternatives. When the other party has an equally attractive alternative, it can participate in the negotiation with a great deal of confidence, set high goals, and push hard to realize those goals. On the other hand, when the other party has a weak alternative, it is more dependent on achieving a satisfactory agreement, which might result in the negotiator driving a hard bargain.

Authority

Before beginning to negotiate, a negotiator must learn whether the other party has adequate authority to conclude negotiations with an agreement. If the other party does not have the authority, the negotiator should consider the negotiation as an initial exercise.

A negotiator should be careful not to reveal too much information to someone who does not have the authority to negotiate. The negotiator does not want to give up sensitive information that should have been used only with someone with the authority to negotiate.

A negotiator should plan his or her negotiation strategy, keeping in mind that no final agreement will result. Otherwise, he or she may become frustrated dealing with someone with little or no authority who must check every point with superiors at the head office. The negotiator may, therefore, indicate how far he or she is willing to negotiate with someone without the proper authority.

Strategy and Tactics

A negotiator can find it helpful to gain insights into the other party's intended negotiation strategy and tactics. The other party will not reveal the strategy outright, but the negotiator can infer it from the information he or she already gathered. Thus, reputation, style, alternatives, authority, and goals of the other party can throw a light on his or her strategy.

Information about the other party is helpful in drawing up a negotiating strategy, tactics, and counteroffers. Skill in using positions of strength is an essential aspect of negotiation. Generally, the person with the most strong points leads the negotiation toward its final outcome at the expense of the other party.

KNOWING THE COMPETITION

In addition to the above considerations, it is important to know who the competition will be in a specific transaction. Negotiators often prepare for business discussions without giving much attention to the influence of competition. During marketing negotiations between two sides, an invisible third party consisting of one or more competitors is often present that can influence the outcome. As shown in Figure 4-2, competitors, although invisible, are key players in such discussions.

For example, how many times has a supplier been asked to improve an offer because he or she is told by the other party that competitors can do better? Unless a negotiator plans for such situations in advance and develops ways to overcome them, he or she may find it difficult to achieve the desired outcome in the negotiations.

A negotiator must conduct research about the competition in order to identify the relative strengths and weaknesses of such third parties for the discussions ahead. A competitor may be able to offer better terms than the negotiator's company, but because the competitor is currently working to full capacity, it may not be in a position to accept additional orders. Such information, if known, can help a negotiator resist requests to improve his or her offer. When gathering information, the negotiator should address such questions as who the competitors are

FIGURE 4-2
Competitors—The Third Party in Negotiations

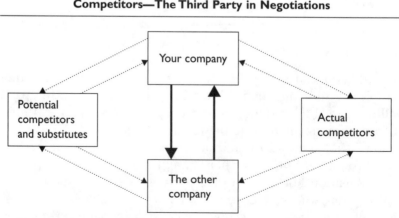

for this transaction, what his or her company's strengths are versus the competition, what his or her company's weaknesses are versus the competition, and how competition can affect his or her company's goals in this negotiation.

Essentially, knowledge about competitors includes their size, growth, and profitability; the image and positioning of their brands; objectives and commitments; strengths and weaknesses; current and past strategies; cost structure; exit barriers limiting their ability to withdraw; and organization style and culture. The following procedure can be adopted to gather competitive intelligence:[5]

- Recognize key competitors.
- Analyze the performance record of each competitor (i.e., sales growth, market share, profitability).
- Study how satisfied each competitor appears to be with its performance. (If the results of a product are in line with expectations, the competitor will be satisfied. A satisfied competitor is likely to follow its current strategy, while an unsatisfied competitor is likely to come out with a new strategy.)
- Probe each competitor's marketing strategy (i.e., different moves in the areas of product, price, promotion, and distribution).
- Analyze current and future resources and competencies of each competitor.

KNOWING ONE'S NEGOTIATION LIMITS

A crucial part of preparation is setting limits on concessions—the minimum price as a seller and the ceiling price as a buyer. During the prenegotiation phase, each party must decide on the boundaries beyond which there are no longer grounds for negotiation. For example, as a seller, you should know at which point a sale becomes unprofitable, based on a detailed costing of your product and other associated expenses. Similarly, as a buyer, you must determine in advance the maximum price and conditions that are acceptable. The difference between these two points is the bargaining zone. Generally, it is within this range that a negotiator and the other party make concessions and counterproposals.

A negotiator's opening position as a supplier should, therefore, be somewhere between the lowest price he or she would accept for his or her goods and the highest price he or she perceives to be acceptable by the other party (the buyer). It is important that the initial offer be realistic, credible, and reasonable in order to encourage the other party to respond. An opening position highly favorable to the negotiator cannot be justified, for example, if it is likely to send a negative message to his or her counterpart, resulting in a lack of trust and possibly more aggressive tactics by the other party.

Target and Reservation Points

A target point refers to a negotiator's most preferred point, an ideal settlement. The target point should be based on a realistic appraisal of the situation. For example, an exporter wants to pay as little sales commission to an overseas distributor as possible, but that does not mean the distributor is willing to represent the exporter for a meager commission of 1 percent. Thus, the exporter may set his or her target point for distributor commission at 6 percent, but not 2 percent.

A reservation point represents a point at which a negotiator is indifferent between reaching a settlement and walking away from negotiation. The outcome of negotiation depends more on the relationship between parties' reservation points than on their target points. A method of determining one's reservation point is to utilize one's BATNA, best alternative to a negotiated agreement.

BATNA

The term *BATNA*[6] refers to the best alternative to a negotiated agreement. Although it appears simple, BATNA has developed into a strong and useful tool for negotiators. This concept was initially introduced by Fisher and Ury while associated with the Harvard Negotiation Project.

BATNA is the standard against which a proposed agreement should be evaluated. It is the only standard that can protect a negotiator from accepting terms that are too unfavorable and from rejecting terms that are in his or her best interest to accept.

Assessment of BATNA requires the following steps:

- *Brainstorm alternatives:* The negotiator should brainstorm to generate alternatives if the overseas distributor refuses to accept 6 percent commission on sales. The alternatives should be realistic and based on reliable information. For example, the negotiator may consider distributing in the overseas market through a home-based company (e.g., in the United States through an Export Management Company). Another alternative may be to utilize the Internet to participate in the overseas market. A third alternative may be to increase the commission of the distributor.

- *Evaluate each alternative:* The negotiator should evaluate each alternative identified above for its attractiveness or value. If an alternative has an uncertain outcome, such as the amount of sales that can be generated through a home-based company, the negotiator should determine the probability of sales outcome. Consider the following three alternatives:

    Alternative 1: Distribution through a home-based company
    Alternative 2: Distribution on the Net
    Alternative 3: Increase foreign distributor's commission to 10 percent

Assume the sales potential in the market is $20 million. The probability of reaching that level under the three alternatives is 0.5, 0.2, and 0.3, respectively. The commission and sales expense vary as follows: Alternative 1, 7 percent; Alternative 2, 4 percent; Alternative 3, 10 percent.

Thus, the expected value of sales is as follows:

Alternative 1: $20 million $\times$ .5 = $10 million
Alternative 2: $20 million $\times$ .2 = $4 million
Alternative 3: $20 million $\times$ .3 = $6 million

Sales commission under the three alternatives will be:

Alternative 1 = $10 million $\times$ 7% = $700,000
Alternative 2 = $4 million $\times$ 4% = $160,000
Alternative 3 = $6 million $\times$ 10% = $600,000

Based on the above information, the best alternative among the three options is Alternative 1, and it should be selected to represent the negotiator's BATNA.

Determining Reservation Point

To determine the reservation point, compute the value of distribution under the three alternatives.

Value of distribution through
home-based company where $7\% \times 0.5 = 3.5\%$
commission is 7 percent of sales

Value of distribution on the Net where the selling expenses are 4 percent of sales		$4\% \times 0.2 = 0.8\%$
Value of increasing the distributor's commission to 10 percent		$10\% \times 0.3 = 3\%$
$.5\,(7\%) + .2\,(4\%) + .3\,(10\%)$	or	$3.5 + .8 + 3.0 = 7.3\%$

Thus, 7.3% is the reservation price. It means the negotiator should not give more than 7.3 percent commission for distribution in the overseas market.

Bargaining Zone

The bargaining zone refers to the region between parties' reservation points.[7] The final settlement, using the above example, falls somewhere above the commission offered by the exporter and below the commission demanded by the overseas distributor.

The bargaining zone serves a useful purpose since it determines whether an agreement is feasible and whether it is worthwhile to negotiate. To establish the bargaining zone, a negotiator needs not only his or her reservation point, but also the reservation point of the other party. Needless to say, determining the other party's reservation point is not easy. However, based on the available information, the reservation point must be established, even if it is a mere guess.

The bargaining point can be positive or negative. In a positive bargaining zone, parties' reservation points overlap. This means it is possible for the parties to reach an agreement. For example, in Figure 4-3, the exporter's reservation point is 7.3 percent and the overseas distributor's reservation point is 6 percent. The exporter is willing to pay, at the most, 1.3 percent more commission. If the two parties reach an agreement, the settlement will be between 6 percent and 7.3 percent. If the parties fail to reach an agreement, the outcome is an impasse and is insufficient since both parties are worse off by not coming to some kind of agreement.

The bargaining zone can be negative, where the reservation points of the parties do not overlap, as shown in Figure 4-4. The reservation point of the exporter is 7.3 percent commission, while the reservation point of the distributor is 8 percent commission. In other words, the maximum that the exporter is willing to pay as commission does not meet the minimum requirements of the overseas distributor. In this situation, it is advantageous for both parties to give up and call off the negotiation.

FIGURE 4-3
Positive Bargaining Zone

Overseas Distributor's Bargaining Range

Positive Bargaining Zone

Exporter's Bargaining Range

3   4   5   6   7   7.3   8   9   10   11   12

ET—
Exporter's
Target Point

DR—
Distributor's
Reservation
Point (6%)

ER—Exporter's
Reservation
Point (7.3%)

DT—
Distributor's
Target Point

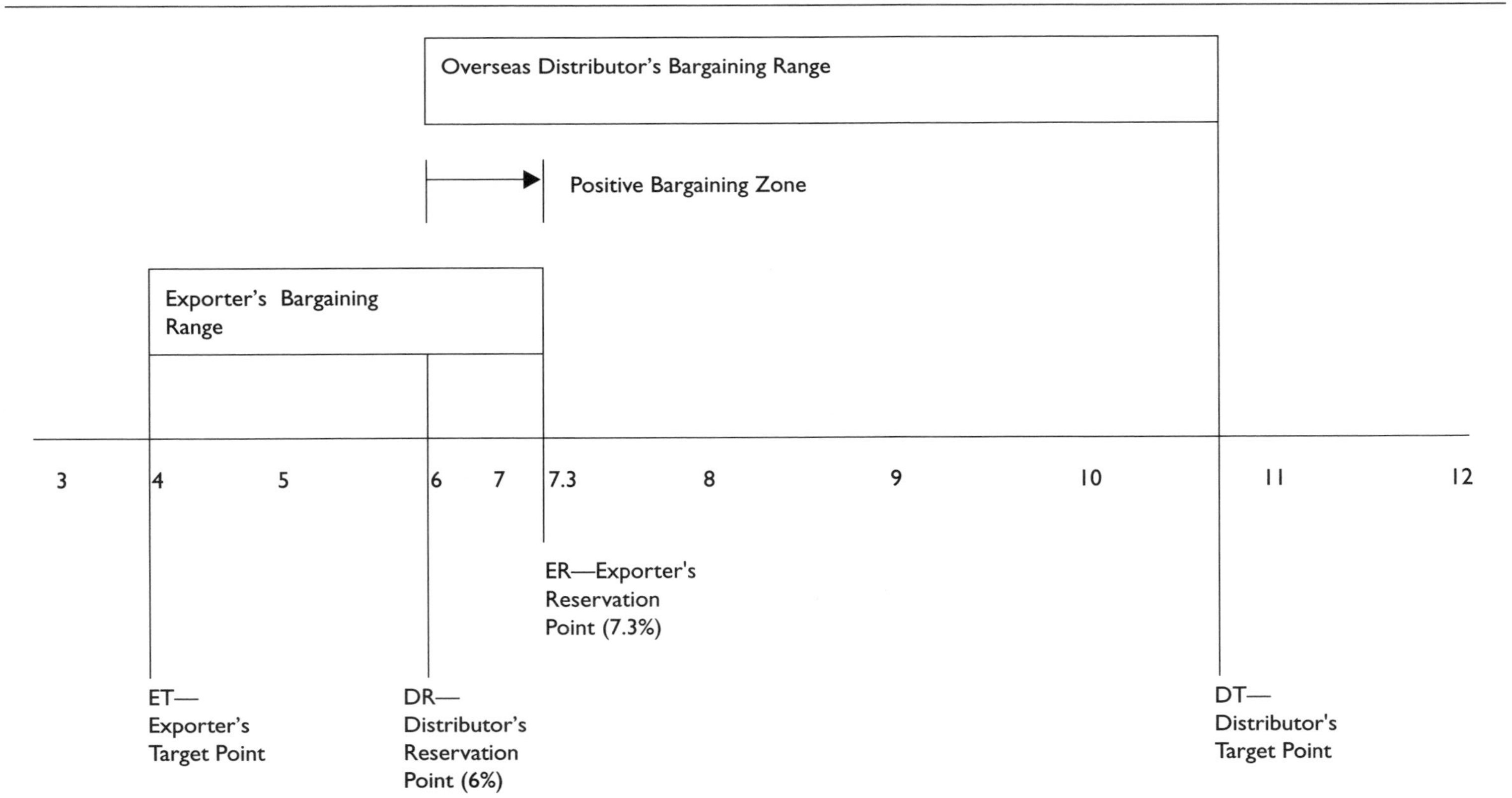

FIGURE 4-4
Negative Bargaining Zone

Distributor's Bargaining Range

Negative Bargaining Zone

Exporter's Bargaining Zone

3 4 5 6 7 7.3 8 9 10 11 12

ET—
Exporter's
Target Point

ER—
Exporter's
Reservation
Point (7.3%)

DR—
Distributor's
Reservation
Point (8%)

DT—
Distributor's
Target Point

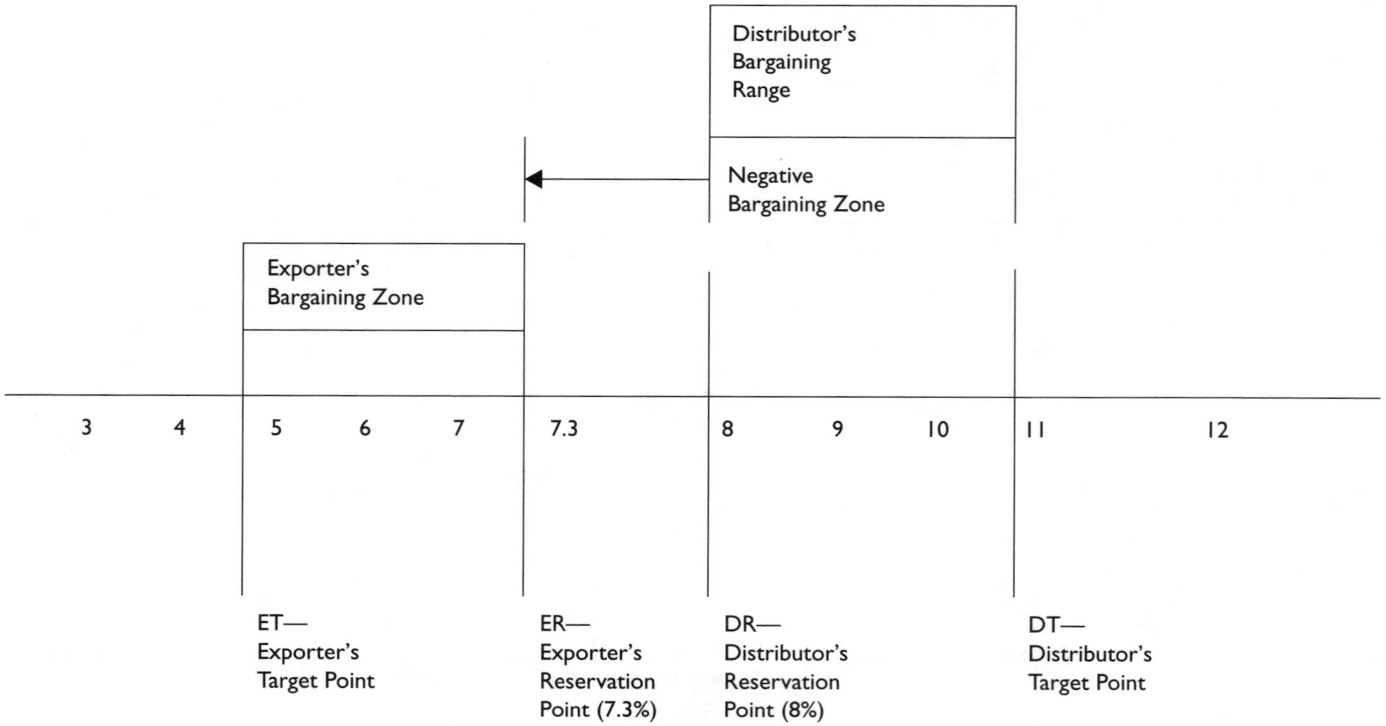

Power

Power plays a distinctive role in negotiations. Power in negotiations can be of different forms: reward, coercive, legitimate, referent, and expert. *Reward power* is attributable to a person's ability to influence the behavior of another person by giving or taking away rewards. Rewards can be tangible (e.g., money) or intangible (e.g., praise and recognition). *Coercive power* is related to a person's ability to influence the behavior of another person through punishment. Punishment can be tangible (e.g., a fine) or intangible (e.g., faint praise). *Legitimate power* refers to a person's authority to demand obedience (e.g., authority of a senior military officer over a lower-ranking officer). *Referent power* is based on a person's respect and admiration of another, which may be related to one's position, money, or status. Finally, *expert power* is attributable to a person's knowledge, skills, or abilities.

With regard to negotiations, no single type of power is more or less effective. However, reward (and punishment) power is less stable since it requires perpetual maintenance. In comparison, status, attraction, and expertise are more intrinsically based forms of power.

DEVELOPING STRATEGIES AND TACTICS

A negotiator should prepare strategies based on his or her company's goals in the forthcoming negotiation, knowledge about the other firm's goals and position, the presence and strength of competition, and other relevant information. A negotiator has several strategies to choose from, ranging from a competitive to a cooperative stance. The approach he or she selects will probably be a mix of both.

Each negotiation is a separate situation requiring specific strategies and appropriate tactics. For example, in some cases, the negotiator who concedes first is considered to be in a weak position, encouraging the other party to press for more concessions; an early concession in other circumstances is sometimes regarded as a sign of cooperation, inviting reciprocity.

The long-term implications of one's actions should be taken into consideration when designing strategies and corresponding tactics. For example, if you have been doing business with the same buyer for some years and are generally satisfied with the business relationship, you are likely to adopt a cooperative strategy in negotiations with that buyer. This means both of you are willing to share information, reciprocate concessions, and seek a mutually beneficial result. In contrast, an inexperienced negotiator is generally more interested in short-term gains and often uses more competitive tactics.

Competitive versus Cooperative Strategies

Negotiating strategies are broadly categorized as competitive and cooperative.[8] Competitive strategies are followed when the resources, over which negotiations are to be conducted, are finite. Strategies are developed with the objective of seeking the larger share of the resources.

Competitive strategies require making high initial demands and convey the impression of firmness and inflexibility. Under this strategy, the concessions are made grudgingly and in small quantities. A negotiator using a competitive strategy likes to convince the other party that he or she cannot accommodate any more and if agreement is to be reached, the latter must concede. Competitive negotiators speak forcefully, appearing to be making threats and creating a chaotic scenario that intimidates the other party, thereby putting him or her on the defensive.

Competitive strategies are common in circumstances where the negotiation involves a one-time deal and where a future relationship is meaningless. Further, when there is a lack of trust, negotiating parties resort to competitive strategies. Sometimes a negotiator switches to a competitive strategy when the negotiations are not progressing well or when a deadlock occurs.

Overall, competitive strategies do not make sense since they fail to create harmony between the parties and focus on a one-time deal. The emphasis of this strategic posture is a win-lose situation; emphasis is not about enlarging the size of the outcome.

Cooperative (or collaborative) strategies refer to a win-win situation where negotiators attempt to strike a mutually satisfying deal. Cooperative negotiators are willing to work with each other, sharing information and understanding each other's point of view. The emphasis of cooperative negotiations is on understanding the perspectives of the other party and developing strategies that benefit both. Cooperative strategies lead to creative solutions that enlarge the outcome, whereby both parties get more than what they aspired to initially.

Choice of a Negotiation Strategy

In international business, it is in the interest of both parties to a transaction to consider cooperative strategies that are conducive to the establishment of sound business relationships and in which each side finds it beneficial to contribute to the success of the negotiated deal. A purely cooperative strategy may be impractical, however, when the other side seeks to maximize its own interests, leading to competitive tactics. Therefore, a combination of cooperative and competitive strategies is advisable (with cooperative moves prevailing during most of the discussions and with some competitive moves used to gain a share of the enlarged outcome).

A negotiator must consider alternative competitive strategies in advance, in case the other party interprets an willingness to cooperate as a sign of weakness. Similarly, if the other party becomes unreasonable and switches to more competitive moves to extract extra concessions, the negotiator may need to change his or her negotiating approach.

Other Strategic Aspects of Negotiations

A number of other strategic issues must be determined and analyzed before the negotiations begin. These include setting the initial position, making concessions, and developing supporting arguments.

Setting the Initial Position. An important issue in any negotiations is to set the initial position. When a negotiator does not know much about the other party, he or she should begin with a more extreme position. Since the final agreements in negotiations are more strongly influenced by initial offers than by subsequent concessions of the other party, particularly when issues under consideration are of uncertain or ambiguous value, it is better to begin with a high position, provided it can be justified. Further, response to an extreme offer gives it some measure of credibility, which can highlight the dimensions of the bargaining zone.

In the context of international business, a negotiator should base his or her decision about initial position in reference to the culture of the other party. In some cultures, negotiators begin with extreme positions, leaving enough room for maneuvering. In Asia and the Middle East, bargaining is commonly employed in business deals. Therefore, a negotiator must start with a high position in order to become fully involved in the bargaining. In most Western societies, negotiators are less inclined to haggle; therefore, a negotiator should set the initial position close to the terms he or she is willing to accept.

Making Concessions. A business negotiator must plan in advance which concessions to make, if necessary; calculate their cost; and decide how and when to make them. Successful executives consider the timing and the manner in which they make concessions just as important as the value of the concessions. For instance, a small concession can be presented in such a way that the other party believes it is a major gain. When the other party sees that worthwhile concessions are being made, he or she becomes more cooperative and reciprocates with better offers too.

The consequences of concessions are important in international business negotiations. For instance, in some cultures, negotiators make small or no concessions in the early stage of the session and wait until the end to make major trade offers. In other cultures, frequent concessions are presented in the opening phase, with fewer trade-offs offered in the closing period. For this reason, a negotiator most plan in advance a few inexpensive yet high-value concessions for emergency purposes, in case further offers are expected or necessary to close the deal. Last-minute concessions are anticipated by many negotiators when a transaction is nearing completion. In fact, in some countries, this practice is interpreted as a sign of cooperation and a willingness to find a mutually agreeable outcome.

The identification of concessions is, therefore, a critical element in negotiation preparation. In addition to determining which concessions are relevant for the negotiations, a negotiator must also estimate their value, establish their order of importance, determine what is expected in exchange, and plan when to offer them.

Developing Supporting Arguments. An important aspect of conducting successful negotiations is the ability to argue in favor of one's position, duly supported by facts and figures, and to refute the points made by the other party through counterarguments. This requires prior preparation through the analysis of collected information from various sources. In this process, seeking answers to the following questions can help:

- What kind of factual information would support and substantiate the argument?
- Whose help might be sought to clarify the facts and elaborate on them?
- What kind of records, databases, and files exist in public domain that might support the argument?

- Has anybody negotiated before on similar issues? What major arguments were successfully used?
- What arguments might the other party make, and how might he or she support them? How can those arguments that go further in addressing both sides' issues and interests be refuted and advanced?
- How can the facts be presented (e.g., using visual aids, pictures, graphs, charts, and expert testimony) to make them more convincing?

PLANNING THE NEGOTIATION MEETING

A variety of logistical details should be worked out before the negotiations begin so the meeting runs smoothly. These include planning the agenda, choosing the meeting site, setting the schedule, and deciding the order of formal introductions.

Agenda

The agenda of each meeting of the negotiations should be carefully set to decide what topics will be discussed and in what order. When the other party shares his or her agenda, the negotiator should reconcile the two, making sure critical issues are adequately addressed.

Opinions differ about the order in which the issues should be discussed. Some suggest the issues should be taken up according to the difficulty involved in resolving them. Thus, the parties begin with the easiest issue, followed by the next issue (which may be a little more involved), and so on, with the most complex issue coming up last. This way the parties strengthen their confidence in each other so that by the time a complex issue is examined, they have developed a relationship of harmony and trust. In contrast, many negotiators recommend resolving the most difficult issue first, believing which less important issues will fall in place on their own without the parties needing to expend much effort. According to these negotiators, this method is more efficient than spending time on insignificant issues first.

Further, the parties need to decide whether to tackle one issue at a time or to discuss the issues randomly, jumping from one issue to the next. Culturally speaking, Americans prefer the one-issue-at-a-time approach. In other societies, all of the issues are examined together. The latter approach is preferred particularly by the Japanese. They discuss issues one after the other without settling anything. Toward the end, however, concessions are made to come to mutually agreeable solutions.[9] This disorganized approach is resented by Westerners, particularly North Americans, since they must wait until the end to find out whether an issue has been resolved.[10]

Meeting Site

Many negotiators believe that the site of the meetings has an impact on the outcome. Therefore, a negotiator should choose a site where he or she might have some leverage. Basically, there are three alternatives to site selection: (1) negotiator's place, (2) other party's place, or (3) a third place (i.e., neutral territory).[11]

The home place gives the negotiator a territorial advantage. Psychologically the negotiator is more comfortable in familiar surroundings, which boosts his or her confidence in dealing with the visiting party. Further, negotiating at home obviates the need for travel and, thus, saves money. The negotiator is closer to his or her support system; i.e., home, family, and colleagues. Any information needed becomes readily available. In addition, playing host to the other party enables the negotiator to enhance the relationship and potentially obligates the other party to be more reasonable.

On the other hand, the home site can put the other party at a disadvantage. He or she is away from home, is probably jet-lagged, and runs the risk of culture shock. All of this is beneficial to the negotiator.

Choosing the other party's place as the site has merits and demerits as well. A negotiator can see the actual facilities of the other party. Simply being told the party has a large factory may not mean much since concept of size varies from nation to nation. The negotiator can also meet all of the people involved and has the opportunity to assess their connections in the business community and government. Of course, the negotiator must travel to the other party's site, incurring expenses; suffers from jet lag; and must negotiate in an unfamiliar environment.

The third alternative is to choose a neutral place. For example, Geneva could be a central site for parties from the United States and Singapore. However, if the other party has been there before and speaks French, the negotiator is no longer negotiating in a neutral place. Negotiators often alternate sites. The first meeting may be held at the negotiator's place, while the next meeting is scheduled at the other party's place. This ensures that neither party has a territorial advantage.

A survey of U.S. professional buyers dealing with foreign suppliers showed that 60.5 percent prefer negotiating in their offices compared to only 6.7 percent in the supplier's premises and 17.5 percent at a neutral site. Of the buyers, 20.9 percent considered the impact of the negotiation site on the outcome significant; 49.8 percent, moderate; and 26.9 percent, slight.[12]

Schedule

A schedule allocates time to different items on the agenda. The schedule must be realistic and flexible. Enough time must be budgeted for all contingencies. Introductions may take more time than planned. Coffee breaks/lunches do not always coincide with the time allocated. Further, it is difficult to anticipate how many questions each side will raise and how long it will take to answer each question.

In many nations, the tempo is slow and people move at ease. They are not under any time pressure. But if a negotiator comes from a country where time is money and every minute counts, he or she would be frustrated. A negotiator should not force his or her own values in developing the schedule.

The party that has traveled a long distance from a different time zone needs time to relax. A negotiator should also value the party's desire to see cultural and historic places and to shop. In any event, the schedule must remain flexible so the parties can remain responsive to changing situations.

Introductions

Some societies are very formal; others are not. For example, in the United States and Australia, addressing each other on a first-name basis is readily accepted. But overseas, people are often conscious about their status and title. Therefore, they want to be introduced with their appropriate title. Further, there is the question of protocol; i.e., who should be addressed first, next, and last. Making a mistake in identifying someone and mispronouncing a person's name are social blunders to avoid. It is important that attention be devoted to all of these minute details.

The following episode shows how a simple error in addressing someone can become an embarrassing situation. Such a situation can be avoided with a little bit of homework.

Sam Perry was the assistant director of a corporate team investigating the prospects of a manufacturing venture in a small Caribbean country. After six weeks in the field, the team received a request from the government to address the head of state and his cabinet about their proposal. The team spent several days preparing a presentation. At the last minute, the project director was called away; she assigned Sam to address the assembled leaders in her place.

Sam had spent enough time helping to prepare the presentation that he felt comfortable with it. He even practiced his introduction to the prime minister—the honorable Mr. Tollis—and to the prime minister's cabinet. Finally, the day arrived for the address. Sam and the team were received at the governmental palace. Once settled into the prime minister's meeting room, Sam opened the presentation. "Honorable Mr. Tollis," he began, "and esteemed members of the cabinet, . . ."

Abruptly, the prime minister interrupted Sam. "Won't you please start over?" he asked with a peeved smile.

Sam was taken aback. He hadn't expected his hosts to be so formal. They always seemed so casual in their open-necked short-sleeved shirts, while Sam and his team sweated away in their suits. But Sam soon regained his composure. "Most Honorable Tollis and highly esteemed members of the cabinet, . . ."

"Be so kind as to begin again," said the prime minister, now visibly annoyed.

"Most esteemed and honorable Mr. Tollis, . . ."

"Perhaps you should start yet again."

Shaken, Sam glanced desperately at his team, then at the government officials surrounding him. The ceiling fans rattled lightly overhead.

One of the cabinet ministers nearby took pity on Sam. Leaning over, the elderly gentleman whispered, "Excuse me, but Mr. Tollis was deposed six months ago. You are now addressing the honorable Mr. Herbert."[13]

SUMMARY

In any negotiations, the actual interface between the two parties is only one phase of the negotiation process, representing the tip of the iceberg. The most crucial element is the planning and preparatory phase. Yet negotiators, particularly those who are new to the game, often neglect it. Experienced executives know that one can be overprepared, but not underprepared. Each party has its own strengths and weaknesses, but the party that is more committed and works harder for its goals achieves the best results. Being prepared is probably the best investment a business executive can make before entering into international marketing negotiations.

Prenegotiation planning requires defining the issues, knowing the other side's position, knowing the competition, knowing one's negotiation limits, developing strategies and tactics, and planning the negotiation meeting. Among these factors, one stands out and that is knowing one's negotiation limits. This factor deals with determining BATNA; i.e., the best alternative to a negotiated agreement. BATNA is the standard against which any negotiated agreement is evaluated.

NOTES

1. Roy J. Lewicki, David M. Saunders, and John W. Minton, *Essentials of Negotiation*, 2nd Edition (New York: McGraw-Hill Irwin, 2001), Chapter 2.
2. Jeffrey Z. Rubin and Burt R. Brown, *The Social Psychology of Bargaining and Negotiation* (New York: Academic Press, 1975).
3. Lewicki, et al. op. cit.
4. Henry H. Calero and Bob Oskam, *Negotiate the Deal You Want* (New York: Dodd, Mead & Company, 1983).
5. Subhash C. Jain, *Marketing Planning and Strategy*, 6th Edition (Cincinnati: South-Western College Publishing, 2000), Chapter 4.
6. See Roger Fisher and William Ury, *Getting to Yes* (New York: Penguin Books, 1991).
7. See Leigh Thompson, *The Mind and Heart of the Negotiator* (Upper Saddle River, NJ: Prentice Hall, 1998).
8. Michael Kublin, *International Negotiating* (Binghamton, NY: The Haworth Press, Inc., 1995).
9. John L. Graham, "Across the Negotiating Table from the Japanese," *International Marketing Review*, Autumn 1986, pp. 58–70.
10. Stewart J. Black and Mark Mendenhall, "Resolving Conflicts with the Japanese: Mission Impossible," *Sloan Management Review*, Spring, 1993, pp. 49–53.
11. See Donald W. Hendon, Rebecca Hendon, and Paul Herbig, *Cross-Cultural Business Negotiations* (Westport, CT: Quorum Books, 1996).
12. Hokey Min and Williams Galle, "International Negotiations Strategies of U.S. Purchasing Professionals," *International Journal of Purchasing and Materials Management*, Summer 1993.
13. Charles F. Valentine, *The Arthur Young International Business Guide* (New York: John Wiley and Sons, 1988), p. 400.

5

Initiating Global Business Negotiations: Making the First Move

This estimable merchant so had set his wits to work, none knew he was in debt.—**Geoffrey Chaucer**

The way a person opens business negotiations influences the entire process, from the initial offer to the final agreement. For first-time negotiations, especially between different cultures, these opening moments are even more critical.

Doing business in the global arena is a long-term prospect, where personal relationships are essential. Skilled negotiators create a favorable atmosphere that has a positive impact on the tone, style, and progress of negotiations, as well as on the final agreement.

Once made, first impressions are difficult to change, particularly if they are negative. People tend to have quicker, stronger, and longer-lasting reactions to bad impressions than to positive ones. Thus, extra care is needed when formulating opening statements. For fruitful negotiations, the opening offer should (a) stress mutual benefits, (b) be clear and positive, (c) imply flexibility, (d) create interest, (e) demonstrate confidence, and (f) promote goodwill.

MAKING THE FIRST OFFER

If a negotiator wishes to take the initiative and set the tone of the discussions, he or she should make the first offer. The negotiator gains a tactical advantage by submitting his or her position first by establishing a reference or anchor point.

A person's anchor point can influence the other party's response. When the other party knows the negotiator's *position*, he or she either rejects the offer or requests a counteroffer. The other party may also revise its acceptance limits in light of the opening offer.

At this point, the negotiator should not make unnecessary concessions; he or she should seek clarification instead. This approach assumes that the initial offer was based on recent market information, was credible, and was presented with conviction. In other words, when a negotiator is highly confident of the other party's reservation point, making the first offer is to the negotiator's advantage. The ideal first offer should barely exceed the other party's reservation point. The other party will consider such an offer to be serious and respectable because it is within the bargaining zone. If the other party accepts the offer, the negotiator can keep a big share of the bargaining surplus.

In most international business deals, sellers are expected to make the first offer since buyers consider themselves in a position of power. In some markets, buyers dictate and control the discussions from the beginning of the negotiations to the final agreement. If a negotiator is not familiar with the market in which he or she is trying to do business, making an offer without adequate information or a clear understanding of what the other side wants places him or her in a risky position. For example, having the first offer immediately accepted means the negotiator underestimated the market; he or she experienced the winner's curse. If the negotiator must make the first offer, he or she can avoid the winner's curse by making the offer so low or so high (depending on his or her role as buyer or a seller) that it is virtually impossible for the other party to accept. But the danger is that a ridiculous offer can create an unfavorable impression and may jeopardize the relationship. Thus, as a rule, a negotiator should not make the first offer if the other party has more information.

OPENING HIGH/LOW

As the negotiations begin, a negotiator faces a dilemma about whether the opening offer should be high or low. If the negotiator makes a high offer, he or she may lose the business. Alternatively, a low offer might mean giving up profits, since an offer seen as modest by the other party probably could have been higher. If a negotiator has accurate knowledge about the reservation point of the other party, the offer could be within the bargaining zone, suggesting a cooperative stance. Unfortunately, in most cases, negotiators possess limited information about the perspectives of their counterparts; thus, the perplexing question of high or low remains unresolved.

Empirical work on the subject shows that negotiators who make extreme opening offers achieve higher settlements than those who make low or modest opening offers.[1] An initial high price is suggested for three reasons. First, it allows the negotiator to gather and exchange information without making early concessions. Second, it communicates to the other party that the negotiation process is going to be time-consuming—and that the other party must be prepared to grant more concessions than it initially intended. Third, it allows the negotiator to continue discussions, despite the rejection of a high initial offer.

An extreme opening presents two problems. One, it might be summarily rejected by the other party. Two, it shows an attitude of toughness, which is not conducive to a long-term relationship.

Any objections to a high offer should be dealt with through questions and answers, not through concessions. The negotiator should determine which parts of the proposal are acceptable and which areas are problematic. Based on this knowledge, the negotiator can justify his or her initial offer or eventually make a counterproposal. Proposals and counteroffers should be handled step by step, with repeated questioning, as shown in Figure 5-1. This allows the negotiator to gather and exchange information without making early concessions.

Starting high is common in markets where business executives rate their superior negotiating skills by how many concessions they obtain. For example, a high initial offer is expected in many countries in Latin America and the Middle East. In highly competitive markets, frequently found in Southeast Asia, North America, and Nordic Europe, opening offers are slightly above the bottom line.

The main mistake to avoid with the high-offer strategy is to present an offer considered so high by the other party that it results in a deadlock. Another common pitfall is to start with a high offer and not be prepared to justify it. To overcome the lack of justification, negotiators wrongly begin to make concessions immediately, without asking for reciprocity.

Skilled negotiators sometimes make a low initial offer near the bottom line, not so much to get the business, but to be invited to the negotiation. They intend to improve their offer on the basis of new information gathered during the discussions. In some industries and markets, a product is sold at a going price and at predetermined conditions, leaving the negotiator with little choice in setting an opening offer. In such a situation, your

FIGURE 5-1
Negotiate Successfully through Repeated Questioning

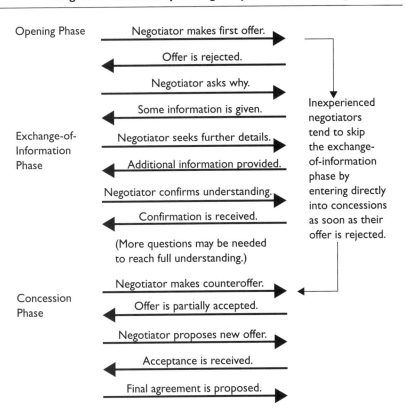

Source: Claude Cellich, "Business Negotiations: Making the First Offer," *International Trade FORUM*, 2/2000, p 15.

offer must be more or less in line with that of the competition. An advantage of having an opening offer close to the competition's is that it allows the negotiator to remain in contention for the business. To increase his or her chances of being retained, the negotiator's proposal must address the specific needs of the other party and demonstrate how the offer best meets the party's requirements.

When a negotiator enters a new market or wants to get a foot in the door with a new customer, he or she should open with a proposal that is close to, or at times below, the bottom line. In such cases, the negotiator must explain that the offer is valid for a limited time only. For example, an exporter may be faced with extra production capacity during the last quarter of the year. In this situation, the exporter could propose a limited business deal at a one-time price preferential in order to utilize the extra capacity and thus recover the fixed costs and part of the variable costs.

At times, a negotiator may wish to make a low offer in order to secure business with well-known global firms. This strategy is common among small- and medium-sized firms seeking business deals from world-class companies. Advantages of being associated with large international firms often override the need for immediate profits. However, such a negotiation strategy places the negotiator in a weak position from the beginning and often results in unprofitable agreements. To avoid being caught in this situation, the negotiator should shift the discussions away from the initial offer to the needs of the other party. The negotiator should take charge of the discussion through questions and make sure he or she has a clear understanding of the real needs of the other party. Once the negotiator knows exactly what the other party's requirements are, he or she can propose additional features such as better quality, faster delivery, individual versus bulk packaging, short and flexible production runs, and other intangibles to improve profit margins. By managing successfully even with a low-offer strategy, he or she can obtain a profitable agreement. Professional buyers are known to seek the best-quality products or services from the most reputable firms at the lowest possible price. In the end, these same buyers often end up paying a premium price to avoid the risk of getting inconsistent quality or receiving late deliveries.

There are times when entrepreneurs from small or midsized firms propose very low offers in the hope of receiving large orders at higher prices in the future. Too often, promises for future business opportunities remain just that—promises. Negotiating deals at low prices in the hope of recovering lost profits from future orders is a dangerous strategy. Wise negotiators avoid such a strategy because of the high risks involved. The moment they raise the price (with or without justification), the buyer is likely to shift business away, to a competitor.

MAKING CONCESSIONS

The question of making concessions arises after the first offer has been made and rejected. But a negotiator should not resort to concessions right away. Experienced negotiators expect objections. They turn objections into opportunities, without taking a defensive attitude and getting into concessions. They consider such reactions as an ideal opportunity to start an information exchange through questioning.

Before the negotiator justifies the initial proposal, he or she should ask the other party what part of the offer is acceptable. This information allows the negotiator to initiate discussions in a positive manner and to reintroduce the proposal, stressing those features considered best by the other party. By not giving in to pressure, the negotiator gains a psychological advantage in the early round of discussions. The exchange of information between both parties is necessary to identify common grounds and to explore new interests in order to reach a better agreement.

Figure 5-2 provides a summary of the most common objections in the opening phase of the face-to-face discussions and appropriate responses. These objections are generally meant to put the negotiator on the defensive. By taking charge of discussions through repeated questioning until he or she has a clear understanding of what the other party really wants, the negotiator can successfully overcome these early objections and be in a favorable position to steer the negotiation toward his or her goals.

After gathering enough information, the negotiator is ready to make a counteroffer. The counteroffer may mean holding on to the original position or making some concessions. Holding on to the original offer implies a position of firmness, which does not go far and might lead to a breakdown of the negotiations because the negotiator appears to capture most of the bargaining range. The other party may adopt a similar posture and reciprocate with firmness. The parties may become disguised or disillusioned and withdraw completely.[2]

The other alternative is to adopt a flexible position, establishing a cooperative rather than a combative relationship.[3] This shows there is room for maneuvering and the negotiations continue.

Concessions are an essential part of negotiations. Studies have shown that parties feel better about an agreement if it involves a progression of concessions. Concession making shows an acknowledgment of the need of the other party and an attempt to reach the position where that need is at least partially met.[4] Three aspects of flexibility in negotiation are reciprocity, size, and pattern.

Reciprocity

An important aspect of concession making is reciprocity. If a negotiator makes a concession, he or she expects the other party

FIGURE 5-2
Reasons for Rejection of the First Offer

Your offer is too expensive.
- Ask what is meant by "too expensive."
- Find out what is considered acceptable and on what basis.
- Respond by providing justification.
- Avoid lowering your price until you learn more about what the other party is looking for.
- Find out if the objection is due to your price offer or if it reflects other factors.
- Ask yourself: If I'm too expensive, why is the other party negotiating with me?

We don't have that kind of budget.
- Find out how large the budget is and for what time frame.
- Explore whether your offer can fit within the overall budget by checking whether the other party can combine several budget lines.
- Propose deferred payment schedules.
- Confirm the order and postpone deliveries until a new budget allocation is confirmed.

- Split the order into smaller units or mini orders to meet current budget limitations.

That's not what we are looking for.
- Ask what they are looking for and insist on specifics.
- Find out which aspects of your offer they like best.
- Keep asking questions until you have a clear understanding of the other party's real needs.
- Repackage your offer in light of the new information received.

Your offer is not competitive.
- Ask what is meant by "not competitive."
- Find out if your competitors' offers are comparable to yours.
- Look for weaknesses in the other offers and stress your strengths.
- Reformulate your offer by avoiding direct comparison with the competition. Stress the unique features of your products/services.

Source: Claude Cellich, "Business Negotiations: Making the First Offer," *International Trade FORUM*, 2/2000, p. 16.

to yield similar ground. As a matter of fact, sometimes a negotiator seeks reciprocity by making his or her concessions conditional. For example, I will do A and B for you if you do X and Y for me.[5]

Size

The size of concession is also important. In the initial stages, a higher-level concession is feasible, but as a negotiator gets closer to his or her reservation point, he or she tends to make the concession smaller. Suppose a supplier is setting the price of her product with the agent and makes the first offer $100 below the other party's target price. A concession of $10 would reduce the bargaining by 10 percent. When negotiations reach within $10 of the other party's target price, a concession of $1 gives up 10 percent of the remaining bargaining range. This example shows how the other party might interpret the meaning of concession size.

Pattern

The pattern of concession is significant as well. To illustrate the point, assume a company in California and a company in South Korea are negotiating the unit price of a chemical. Each company is dealing with a difficult customer. As shown in Figure 5-3, the California company makes three concessions, each worth $4 per unit for a total of $12. On the other hand, the South Korean company makes four concessions, worth $4, $3, $2, and $1 per unit for a total of $10. Both companies tell their counterpart they have reached a point where no more concession is feasible. The South Korean company's claim is more believable because the company communicated through its pattern of concession making that it has nothing more to concede. The California company's claim, however, is less believable because the company's pattern (three concessions) implies there is room for additional concession. In reality, though, the California company conceded more than the South Korean company. This example illustrates the importance of the pattern of concessions.[6]

FIGURE 5-3
Pattern of Concession Making for Two Negotiators

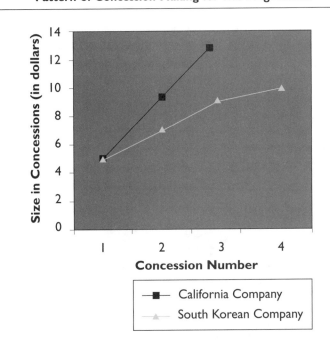

Source: Based on Roy J. Lewicki, David M. Saunders, and John W. Minton, *Essentials of Negotiation*, Second Edition (New York: McGraw-Hill, Irwin, 2001). p. 72.

INFLUENCING NEGOTIATION

Influence refers to tactics negotiators use to utilize their power with the intention of seeking a favorable outcome of negotiations for themselves. Cialdini has identified six different categories of influence: reciprocity, consistency, social proof, liking authority, and scarcity.[7]

Either party to the negotiation can use influence to its advantage. A negotiator should attempt to influence the outcome of negotiation in a way that is favorable to him or her. At the same time, the negotiator should be sensitive to the use of influence by the other party.

Reciprocity

The principle of reciprocity means that if someone does a person a favor, that person must return the favor, since he or she feels obligated to do so. In negotiation, reciprocity is often used by one party to seek concessions from the other. A negotiator feels indebted to the other party to make concessions because the party did something for the negotiator in the past. The other party will tactfully remind the negotiator that he or she owes the party the concessions.

Basically, there is nothing irrational or illogical about reciprocity in negotiation. However, a negotiator should be careful not to yield too much ground in the name of reciprocity. In other words, the negotiator does not want to be victimized or exploited by the other party. The negotiator must weigh what the other party did for him or her and what he or she might do for the party to repay the favor. Nothing should be conceded beyond that. A situation to avoid is to give away concessions now with the promise of receiving concessions in future deals. Unfortunately, concessions received in the past are easily forgotten, and the future deal never materializes.

Consistency

Psychologically, people like to be consistent in their behavior since inconsistency is a sign of irrationality.[8]

Following on the consistency principle, a negotiator should not agree to terms he or she cannot and/or do not want to follow through on. For example, an exporter is negotiating with an overseas distributor on commission on sales. The distributor accepts the exporter's terms on the condition that the exporter make adaptations to the product to be shipped. The exporter agrees to such product adaptation, probably without thinking about what it might entail, and the negotiations are successfully completed. Now, to be consistent, the exporter must comply with the product adaptation even if it costs him more than he had anticipated. The principle of consistency influences him to make the agreed-upon adaptation.

Social Proof

People often justify their behavior based on what others have done or might do under similar circumstances. In business negotiation, the other party may ask for concessions using the principle of social proof. For example, the overseas distributor may influence the exporter to pay for the transportation costs of defective products that are returned, citing the example of other foreign companies the distributor represents. The distributor convinces the exporter using the behavior of other companies as proof that it is the exporter's responsibility to absorb the transportation costs of returns. If the exporter's information shows that statement to be untrue, the only way he can counter the social proof advanced by the other party is to demand evidence of the proof. If the exporter's knowledge of the industry practice shows that the transportation costs of returns are absorbed by the distributor, the exporter should obtain some proof to support it. He can then submit his own social proof and discount the distributor's argument.

Liking

Generally speaking, people are more agreeable with those they like. A negotiator is more likely to make concessions to those of the other party he or she likes. Thus, the other party in negotiations can take steps to make the negotiator like him or her, which leads the negotiator to making the concessions the party desires.

A negotiator can use the liking principle to his or her advantage in negotiation by making the other party like him or her. This can be achieved in various tangible and intangible ways. For example, the negotiator can present the other side with a gift or talk positively about the other party's country; for example "You have a wonderful country with a long history and a rich culture." Once the negotiator has created an atmosphere in which the other party likes him or her, the negotiator will find it easier to seek concessions in negotiation. Savvy negotiators go a long way in making themselves likable, humorous, knowledgeable, and friendly so the other party likes them.[9] By the time negotiation begins, the other party believes he or she is dealing with an accomplished friend. This influences the other party's behavior favorably.

Authority

Behaviorally speaking, people accept the opinions, views, and directions of those they consider an authority on the subject. When people are sick, they accept the advice of a doctor because they consider the doctor an authority on health matters. Similarly, in negotiation, the other party will accept a negotiator's offer without much questioning if the negotiator is considered an authority.

It is important, therefore, that people assigned to negotiate on one's behalf are capable, are fully knowledgeable about the details of the situation, and can present themselves as authoritative. A weak person lacking the necessary authority might give in too soon, providing more concessions to the other party than necessary.

Authority has another connotation in negotiations. It has to do with the authority of the negotiators to finalize the agreement on behalf of his or her organization. If the negotiator does not have the authority to make a deal, he or she will be considered by the other party as a go-between, and the other party will be less willing to strike a deal. For example, if the other party is seeking concessions and the negotiator has no authority to make concessions, the other party might as well end the negotiations. In the other party's eyes, the negotiator has no credibility. Whoever is responsible for handling negotiations must be equipped with adequate authority.

Scarcity

It is human nature to want things that are rare, are hard to get, or are in great demand. This tendency applies to negotiations as well. In accordance with the principle of scarcity, a negotiator should make different attributes of an offer seen rare and scarce, which would result in the other party wanting them. A negotiator may be willing to include those attributes in his or her first offer but should hold them back, emphasizing that such attributes cannot be provided.

Since the negotiator makes the attributes seen scarce, the other party wants them at all costs. The negotiator then makes them available, grudgingly, as negotiations advance. Such concessions will be valued highly by the other party, and the negotiator might obtain additional concessions in return.

COMMON CONCERNS

Frequently, negotiators face many questions to which there are no easy answers. While the negotiators must address these questions on their own based on the environment in which they are placed, guidelines are examined here.[10]

Sharing Information about Reservation Price

The previous chapter discussed the term *bargaining zone*, which is the final price agreed upon between the reservation points of the two parties. Each party seeks as much portion of the bargaining zone as it can. And the parties negotiate for that. If one party reveals its reservation point, that strengthens the bargaining position of the other party. Thus, it is not a good idea to share information about one's reservation point with a counterpart.

Some negotiators believe the task becomes easier when both the parties trust each other and reveal their reservation points. Thus, they can negotiate to share the surplus in a rational fashion. However, the problem in negotiations is not a matter of trust, but strategy. The strategy calls for maximizing the surplus. Therefore, trusting the other party will only cause conflict.

Lying about Reservation Point

Lying about one's reservation point is dysfunctional for several reasons. First, it shortens the bargaining zone, which renders the making of concessions difficult. The negotiations may end in impasse. Further, lying can impact the negotiator's reputation negatively in the marketplace. People often talk about their negotiation endeavors, and a lying negotiator would be mentioned as an undependable party. Remember, good news travels fast, but bad news travels faster.

Catching the Liar

A negotiator should make sure the other party is not lying. Three strategies can be used to catch a lie in negotiation. First, test the consistency in the other party's statements. Negotiations involve asking each other a variety of questions. One should watch for any inconsistencies in the answers the other party supplies. Of course, questions should be adequately designed so that inconsistencies show up if an opponent is lying. Second, enrich the mode of communication by adopting a multichannel strategy. For example, if a person suspects the other party is lying and the person has been negotiating by phone, written correspondence, or e-mail, he or she should ask the other party for a face-to-face meeting. It becomes difficult for liars to monitor themselves when communicating through different channels. Signs of lying are often revealed through nonverbal communication, such as gestures and eye contact. Third, ask the other party to support what he or she said by providing tangible proof or evidence.

Determining the Reservation Point of the Other Party

As a negotiator should not reveal his or her reservation point for the reasons examined previously, it would be counterproductive for the negotiator to ask the other party for his or her reservation point. The other party might lose respect and withdraw from the negotiation. Frankly, it is unethical for a negotiator to probe into the other party's reservation point while not wanting to reveal his or her own.

Choosing between Tough and Soft Negotiation Stance

A tough negotiator is inflexible, demands much, yields few concessions, and holds out. Tough negotiators are stubborn and do not hesitate to walk away from negotiations that might be highly rewarding. A soft negotiator, on the other hand, reveals his or her reservation point, makes too many generous concessions, and attempts to make the other party feel good.

Neither of the two approaches mentioned above—tough or soft—works well from the perspective of global negotiation. The best approach for successful negotiations is strategic creativity. This approach suggests the use of strategies to seek the larger proportion of the bargaining zone through sharing information, making select concessions, and creating a lasting relationship.

Playing a Fair Game

Conceptually, it is appealing if both parties play a fair game. The negotiations are finalized quickly, and both parties end up as winners. Unfortunately, in practice, this ideal approach may not work. First, what is fair and what is not fair is difficult to define. The concept of fairness is vague, and different people define it differently. Thus, even though, in their estimation, both parties are playing a fair game, they may be far apart from each other. Further, while parties desire a fair outcome, their ideas about how to achieve fairness can vary. Thus, negotiations cannot be conducted on the basis of fairness alone.

Making the Final Offer

A negotiator should not rush into making a final offer, an irrevocable commitment, until he or she is ready. Once the negotiator reaches the point at which he or she is comfortable walking away from the negotiations, only then should he or she take the stance of final offer. This happens when his or her BATNA represents a more attractive option.

SUMMARY

For every negotiation, a negotiator's initial offer should stand on its own merit within the prevailing context surrounding the discussions. Entering the negotiation under false pretenses or unfounded premises can prove costly or result in a deadlock. A negotiator must make the first offer competitive in the eyes of the other party and be ready to defend it with valid arguments.

The worst-case scenario is to make concessions immediately following objections to an initial offer. Unskilled or unprepared negotiators frequently face this dilemma in their business dealings. Asking questions, listening actively, and being patient go a long way in conquering this tendency. A negotiator should anticipate the typical objections he or she is likely to face, prepare appropriate replies in advance, and formulate information-seeking questions before meeting the other party.

One' knowledge of the market, a clear assessment of the competition, and an understanding of the other party's real needs should help in this crucial initial phase. As the opening offer shapes the outcome of the negotiation, a negotiator's ability to make a good impression from the outset is critical. He or she may not be given a second chance to make a good first impression.

Although it is better to place an initial offer slightly higher in order to reach a better outcome, a negotiator may lower it if he or she is doing business in highly competitive markets. In more traditional and less competitive markets, offers should be on the higher side with plenty of built-in concessions available to the other party.

An initial offer should be presented with confidence and conviction, yet imply flexibility. The issue is not to have an offer accepted or rejected or to be the first to make an offer, but to be in a position to start strong and maintain control of the discussions. Only through a series of high-yield questions can a negotiator learn what the other partly really requires, enabling the negotiator to reformulate the offer to meet the party's specific needs.

The initial phase of the negotiation should be regarded as an opportunity to create an atmosphere of trust, leading to an exchange of strategic information. It is not the time to begin making concessions. Executives from certain corporations consider this initial phase a waste of time and begin trading away concessions immediately. Successful negotiators know better. They invest their time by finding out the real needs of the other party and by determining how they can best satisfy those needs in an acceptable package. In other words, a negotiator's first offer should reflect the best-case scenario, supported by first-class justification.

NOTES

1. Roy J. Lewicki, David M. Saunders, and John W. Minton, *Essentials of Negotiation*, 2nd Edition (New York: McGraw-Hill, 2001), pp. 67–68.
2. Deepak Ghosh, "Nonstrategic Delay in Bargaining: An Experimental Investigation," *Organizational Behavior and Human Decision Processes*, Vol. 67, No. 4, 1996, pp. 312–325.
3. Mary Olekalns, Peter L. Smith, and Thomas Walsh, "The Process of Negotiating: Strategy and Timing as Predictors of Outcomes," *Organizational Behavior and Human Decision Processes*, Vol. 68, No. 1, 1996, pp. 68–77.
4. Charles L. Gruder and Robert J. Duslak, "Elicitation of Cooperation by Retaliatory and Non-retaliatory Strategies in a Mixed Motive Culture," *Journal of Conflict Resolution*, Vol. 17, No. 2, 1973, pp. 162–174.
5. Dean G. Pruitt, "Strategic Choice in Negotiation," *American Behavioral Scientist Negotiation Journal*, Vol. 10, No. 3, 1994, pp. 217–230.
6. George Yukl, "Effects of the Opponent's Initial Offer, Concession Magnitude, and Concession Frequency on Bargaining Behavior," *Journal of Personality & Social Psychology*, Vol. 30, No. 4, 1974, pp. 323–335.
7. Robert B. Cialdini, *Influence: Science and Practice* (New York: Harper Collins, 1993).

8. Norman Eyuboglu and Anthony Buja, "Dynamics of Channel Negotiations: Contention and Reciprocity," *Psychology & Marketing*, Vol. 10, 1993, pp. 47–65.

9. Kirk O'Quin and John Aronoff, "Humor as a Technique of Social Influence," *Social Psychology Quarterly*, Vol. 44, No. 4, pp. 349–357.

10. Leigh Thompson, *The Mind and Heart of the Negotiator* (Upper Saddle River, NJ: Prentice-Hall, 1998), pp. 38–42.

6

Price Negotiations

As I hurtled through space, there was only one thought on my mind—that every part of the capsule was supplied by the lowest bidder.—John Glenn

---

Firms entering new markets, particularly small- and medium-size firms, often face problems in initial negotiations with importers, agents, and buyers in the target markets. These difficulties generally center on pricing questions, particularly the fact that their prices may be too high. Although price is only one of many issues that must be discussed during business negotiations, too frequently it tends to influence the entire negotiation process. New exporters may be inclined to compromise on price at the beginning of the discussions, thereby bypassing other negotiating strengths they may have, such as the product's benefits, the firm's business experience, and the firm's commitment to providing quality products.

As pricing is often the most sensitive issue in business negotiations, it should be postponed until all of the other aspects of the transaction have been discussed and agreed upon.[1] Decisions involving a long-term commitment to place export orders are, in any case, rarely made on the basis of price alone, but rather on the total export package. This is particularly so in markets where consumers are highly conscious of quality, style, and brand names; where marketing channels are well structured, and where introduction of the product in the market is time-consuming and expensive.

By presenting a more comprehensive negotiating package in a well-planned and organized manner, exporters should be able to improve the effectiveness of their negotiation discussions and, in the long term, the profitability of their export operations.

PRICING FACTORS

As a prelude to undertaking the negotiation, a negotiator should analyze his or her flexibility in negotiating on price. This requires examining the factors that influence the pricing decision.[2] The factors to consider in international pricing exceed those in strictly domestic marketing not only in number, but also in ambiguity and risk. Domestic price is affected by such considerations as pricing objectives, cost, competition, customers, and regulations. Internationally, these considerations apply at home and in the host country. Further, multiple currencies, trade barriers, and longer distribution channels make the international pricing decision more difficult. Each of these considerations includes a number of components that vary in importance and interaction in different countries.

Pricing Objectives

Pricing objectives should be closely aligned to the marketing objectives. Essentially, objectives can be defined in terms of profit or volume. The profit objective takes the shape of a percentage markup on cost or price or a target return on investment. The volume objective is usually specified as a desired percentage of growth in sales or as a percentage of the market share to be achieved.

Cost Analysis

Cost is one important factor in price determination. Of all the many cost concepts, fixed and variable costs are most relevant to setting prices. Fixed costs are those that do not vary with the scale of operations, such as number of units manufactured. Salaries of staff, office rent, and other office and factory overhead expenses are examples of fixed costs. On the other hand, variable costs, such as costs of material and labor used in the manufacture of a product, bear a direct relationship to the level of operations.

It is important to measure costs accurately in order to develop a cost/volume relationship and to allocate various costs as fixed or variable. Measurement of costs is far from easy. Some fixed short-run costs are not necessarily fixed in the long run; therefore, the distinction between variable and fixed costs matters only in the short run. For example, in the short run, the salaries of salespeople would be considered fixed. However, in the long run, the sales staff could be increased or cut, making sales salaries a variable instead of fixed expense.

Moreover, some costs that initially appear fixed are viewed as variable when properly evaluated. A company manufacturing different products can keep a complete record of a sales manager's time spent on each product and, thus, may treat this salary as variable. However, the cost of that record keeping far exceeds the benefits derived from making the salary a variable cost. Also, no matter how well a company maintains its records, some variable costs cannot be allocated to a particular product.

The impact of costs on pricing strategy can be studied by considering the following three relationships: (1) the ratio of fixed costs to variable costs, (2) the economies of scale available to a firm, and (3) the cost structure of a firm with regard to competitors. If the fixed costs of a company in comparison with variable costs form the higher proportion of its total costs, adding sales volume will be a great help in increasing earnings. Such an industry would be termed *volume-sensitive.* In some industries, variable costs constitute the higher proportion of total costs. Such industries are *price-sensitive,* because even a small increase in price adds a lot to earnings.

If substantial economies of scale are obtainable through a company's operations, market share should be expanded. In considering prices, the expected decline in costs should be duly taken into account; that is, prices may be lowered to gain higher market share in the long run. The concept of obtaining lower costs through economies of scale is often referred to as the *experience effect,* which means that all costs go down as accumulated experience increases. Thus, if a company acquires a higher market share, its costs will decline, enabling it to reduce prices. If a manufacturer is a low-cost producer, maintaining prices at competitive levels will result in additional profits. The additional profits can be used to promote the product aggressively and increase the overall scope of the business. If, however, the costs of a manufacturer are high compared with competitors, prices cannot be lowered in order to increase market share. In a price-war situation, the high-cost producer is bound to lose.

Competition

The nature of competition in each country is another factor to consider in setting prices. The competition in an industry can be analyzed with reference to such factors as the number of firms in the industry, product differentiation, and ease of entry. Competition from domestic suppliers as well as other exporters should be analyzed.

Competitive information needed for pricing strategy includes published competitive price lists and advertising, competitive reaction to price moves in the past, timing of competitors' price changes and initiating factors, information about competitors' special campaigns, competitive product line comparison, assumptions about competitors' pricing/marketing objectives, competitors' reported financial performance, estimates of competitors' costs (fixed and variable), expected pricing retaliation, analysis of competitors' capacity to retaliate, financial viability of engaging in a price war, strategic posture of competitors, and overall competitive aggressiveness.

In an industry with only one firm, there is no competitive activity. The firm is free to set any price, subject to constraints imposed by law. Conversely, in an industry comprising a large number of active firms, competition is fierce. Fierce competition limits the discretion of a firm in setting price. Where there are a few firms manufacturing an undifferentiated product (such as in the steel industry), often only the industry leader has the discretion to change prices. Other industry members tend to follow the leader in setting price.

A firm with a large market share is in a position to initiate price changes without worrying about competitors' reactions. Presumably, a competitor with a large market share has the lowest costs. The firm can, therefore, keep its prices low, thus discouraging other members of the industry from adding capacity, and further its cost advantage in a growing market.

When a firm operates in an industry that has opportunities for product differentiation, it can exert some control over pricing even if the firm is small and competitors are many. This latitude concerning price occurs when customers perceive one brand to be different from competing brands. Whether the difference is real or imaginary, customers do not object to paying a higher price for preferred brands. To establish product differentiation of a brand in the minds of consumers, companies spend heavily for promotion. Product differentiation, however, offers an opportunity to control prices only within a certain range.

Customer Perspective

Customer *demand* for a product is another key factor in price determination. Demand is based on a variety of considerations, price being just one. These considerations include the ability of customers to buy, their willingness to buy, the place of the product in the customer's lifestyle (whether a status symbol or an often-used product), prices of substitute products, the potential market for the product (whether the market has an unfulfilled demand or is saturated), the nature of non-price competition, consumer behavior in general, and consumer behavior in segments in the market. All of these factors are interdependent, and it may not be easy to understand their relationships accurately.

Demand analysis involves predicting the relationship between price level and demand, simultaneously considering the effects of other variables on demand. The relationship between price level and demand is called *elasticity of demand*, or *sensitivity of price*, and it refers to the number of units of a product that would be demanded at different prices. Price sensitivity should be considered at two different levels: the industry and the firm.

Industry demand for a product is elastic if demand can be substantially increased by lowering prices. When lowering price has little effect on demand, it is considered inelastic. Environmental factors, which vary from country to country, have a direct influence on demand elasticity. For example, when gasoline prices are high, the average consumer seeks to conserve gasoline. When gasoline prices go down, people are willing to use gas more freely; thus, the demand for gasoline can be considered somewhat elastic. In a developing country such as Bangladesh, where only a few rich people own cars, no matter how much gasoline prices change, total demand is not greatly affected, making demand inelastic.

When the total demand of an industry is highly elastic, the industry leader may take the initiative to lower prices. The loss in revenues from a decrease in price will presumably be more than compensated for by the additional demand generated, thus enlarging the total market. Such a strategy is highly attractive in an industry where economies of scale are possible. Where demand is inelastic and there are no conceivable substitutes, prices may be increased, at least in the short run. In the long run, however, the government may impose controls or substitutes may develop.

An *individual firm's demand* is derived from the total industry demand. An individual firm seeks to find out how much market share it can command in the market by changing its own prices. In the case of undifferentiated, standardized products, lower prices should help a firm increase its market share, as long as competitors do not retaliate by matching the firm's price. Similarly, when business is sought through bidding, lower prices should help. In the case of differentiated products, however, market share can actually be improved by maintaining higher prices (within a certain range).

Products can be differentiated in various real and imagined ways. For example, a manufacturer in a foreign market who provides adequate warranties and after-sale service might maintain higher prices and still increase market share. Brand name, an image of sophistication, and the impression of high quality are other factors that can help differentiate a product and hence afford a company an opportunity to increase prices and not lose market share. In brief, a firm's best opportunity lies in differentiating its product. A differentiated product offers more opportunity for increased earnings through premium prices.

Government and Pricing

Government rules and regulations pertaining to pricing should be taken into account when setting prices. Legal requirements of the host government and the home government must be satisfied. A host country's laws concerning price setting can range from broad guidelines to detailed procedures for arriving at prices that amount to virtual control over prices.

Although international pricing decisions depend on various factors (such as pricing objective, cost competition, customer demand, and government requirements), in practice, total costs are the most important factor. Competitors' pricing policies rank as the next important factor, followed by the company's out-of-pocket costs, the company's return-on-investment policy, and the customer's ability to pay.

ASPECTS OF INTERNATIONAL PRICE SETTING

The impact of such factors as differences in costs, demand conditions, competition, and government laws on international pricing is figured in by following a particular pricing orientation.[3]

Pricing Orientation

Companies mainly follow two different types of pricing orientation: the cost approach and the market approach. The *cost approach* involves computing all relevant costs and adding a desired profit markup to arrive at the price. The cost approach is popular because it is simple to comprehend and use and it leads to fairly stable prices. It has two drawbacks though. First, definition and computation of cost can become troublesome. Should all (both fixed and variable) costs be included or only variable costs? Second, this approach brings an element of inflexibility into the pricing decision because of the emphasis on cost.

A conservative attitude favors using full costs as the basis of pricing. On the other hand, incremental-cost pricing would allow for seeking business otherwise lost. It means as long as variable costs are met, any additional business should be sought without any concern for fixed costs. Once fixed costs are recovered, they should not enter into the equation for pricing later orders. Figure 6-1 illustrates this point. The Natural Company would not be able to conduct its foreign business if it insisted on recovering the full unit cost of $11.67. If the full-costing method were the decision criterion, the company would actually pass up the opportunity to add $3,000 to profit.

The profit markup applied to the cost to compute final price can simply be a markup percentage based on industry practice. Alternatively, the profit markup can represent a desired percentage return on investment. For example, if the total investment in a business is $20 million and the total cost of annual output (averaged over the years) is $25 million, the *capital turnover ratio* will be $20,000,000/$25,000,000, or 0.8. Multiplying the capital turnover ratio, 0.8, by the desired return on investment (say, 20 percent) would give a markup of 16 percent (0.8 × 0.2) on standard cost. It can be shown as follows:

$$\frac{Percentage}{markup\ cost} = \frac{Total\ invested\ capital}{Standard\ cost\ of\ annual\ normal\ production} \times \frac{Percentage\ desired}{return\ on\ investment}$$

This method is an improvement over the pure cost-plus method because markup is derived more scientifically. Nonetheless, the determination of *rate of return* poses a problem.

Under the *market approach*, pricing starts in a reverse fashion. First, an estimate is made of the acceptable price in the target country segment. An analysis should be performed to determine if this price meets the company's profit objective. If not, the alternatives are to give up the business or to increase the price. Additional adjustments in price may be required to cope with competitors, the host country government, an expected cost increase, and other eventualities. The final price is based on the market rather than estimated production costs.

Essentially, the cost and market approaches consider common factors in determining the final price. The difference between the two approaches involves the core concern in setting prices. The market approach focuses on pricing from the viewpoint of the customer. Unfortunately, in many countries, it may not be easy to develop an adequate price-demand relationship;

FIGURE 6-1
Example of Full Costing versus Incremental Costing

The Natural Company has a production capacity of 20,000 units per year. Presently the company is producing and selling 15,000 units per year. The regular market price is $15 per unit. The variable costs are as follows:

Material	$5/unit
Labor	$4/unit
Total Variable Cost	$9/unit

The fixed cost is $40,000 per year.
The income statement reflecting the preceding situation appears as follows:

Income Statement

Sales (15,000@$9)		$225,000
Cost: Variable Cost (15,000@$9)	$135,000	
Fixed Cost	40,000	175,000
Profit		$50,000

Now suppose the company has the opportunity to sell an additional 3,000 units at $10 per unit to a foreign firm. This is a special situation that will not have an adverse effect on the price of the product in the regular market.

If Natural Company uses the full-costing method to make its decision, the offer will be rejected. The reasoning behind this rejection is that the price of $10.00/unit does not cover the full cost of $11.67/unit (175,000/15,000 = $11.67). Using the full-costing method as a decision criterion, the company will actually give up $3,000 in additional profits.

If the incremental-costing method is used, this offer will be accepted, and a gain of $3,000 in profits will be realized. The incremental-costing method compares additional costs to be incurred with the additional revenues received if the offer is accepted.

Additional Revenue (3,000@$10)	$30,000
Additional Costs (3,000@$9)	27,000
Additional Income	$3,000

The difference between the two decision methods results from the treatment of fixed costs. The full-costing method includes the fixed cost per unit calculation. The incremental-costing method recognizes that no additional fixed costs will be incurred if additional units are produced. Therefore, fixed costs are not considered in the decision process.

Following is an income statement comparing the results of the company with and without the acceptance of the foreign offer.

Income Statement

	Rejecting the Offer	Accepting the Offer
Sales (15,000@$15)	$225,000	$225,000
(3,000@$10)		30,000
Total Sales	$225,000	$255,000

FIGURE 6-1
Example of Full Costing versus Incremental Costing (Contd.)

Costs: Variable (@$9/unit)	$135,000	$162,000
Fixed	40,000	40,000
Total Cost	$175,000	$202,000
Net Income	$50,000	$53,000

Note: An important factor in such a decision is considering what the effects of accepting the offer will be on a regular market price. If the additional sales were made in the regular market at the $10 price, it could depress the regular market price below $15, which would severely hamper operations in the future.

therefore, implementation of the market approach can occur in a vacuum. It is this kind of uncertainty that forces exporters to opt for the cost approach.

Export Pricing

Export pricing is affected by three factors:

1. The price destination (that is, who it is that will pay the price—the final consumer, independent distributors, a wholly owned subsidiary, a joint venture organization, or someone else.)
2. The nature of the product (that is, whether it is a raw or semiprocessed material, components, or finished or largely finished products or whether it is services or intangible property—patents, trademarks, formulas, and the like).
3. The currency used for billing (that is, the currency of the purchaser's country, the currency of the seller's home country, or a leading international currency).

The price destination is an important consideration since different destinations present different opportunities and problems. For example, pricing to sell to a government may require special procedures and concessions not necessary in pricing to other customers. A little extra margin might be called for. On the other hand, independent distributors with whom the company has a contractual marketing arrangement deserve a price break. Wholesalers and jobbers who shop around have an entirely different relationship with the exporter than the independent distributors.

As products, raw materials and commodities give a company very little leeway for maneuvering. Usually, a prevalent world price must be charged, particularly when the supply is plentiful.

However, if the supply is short, a company may be able to demand a higher price.

Escalation of Export Prices

The retail price of exports is usually much higher than the domestic retail price for the same product. This escalation in foreign price can be explained by costs such as transportation, customs duty, and distributor margins, all associated with exports. The geographic distance those goods must travel results in additional transportation costs. The imported goods must also bear the import taxed in the form of customs duty imposed by the host government. In addition, completion of the export transaction can require passage of the goods through many more channels than in a domestic sale. Each channel member must be paid a margin for the service it provides, which naturally increases cost. Also, a variety of government requirements, domestic and foreign, must be fulfilled, resulting in further costs.

The process of price escalation is illustrated in Figure 6-2. It is evident that the retail price for exported goods is about 60 percent more than the domestic retail price. For example, about $90 (transportation to point of shipment: $5 more than domestic transportation; export documentation handling and overseas freight: $65; handling and transportation overseas: $20) more is spent on the transaction alone. An additional $90 is accounted for by the import tariff. Finally, the agent costs for the exported goods amount to about $371.40 (importer margin: $56.00; wholesale margin: $49.28; retail margin: $266.12), compared with $194.56 (wholesale margin: $30.40; retail margin: $164.16) for domestic distribution.

Export Price Quotation

An export price can be quoted to the overseas buyer in any one of several ways. Every alternative implies mutual commitment by the exporter and importer and specifies the terms of trade. The price alters according to the degree of responsibility the exporter undertakes, which varies with each alternative.

There are five principal ways of quoting export prices: ex-factory free alongside ship (FAS); free on board (FOB); cost, insurance, and freight (CIF); and delivered duty-paid. The ex-factory price represents the simplest arrangement. The importer is presumed to have bought the goods at the exporter's factory. All costs and risks from thereon become the buyer's problem.

FIGURE 6-2
A Example of Price Escalation: Export from the United States to Africa

	DOMESTIC TRANSACTIONS	AFRICAN TRANSACTIONS
Manufacturing price in the United States	$362.00	$362.00
Transportation to wholesaler/point of shipment	18.00	23.00
	$380.00	$385.00
Export documentation (i.e., bill of lading, Consular's invoice)		4.00
Handling for overseas shipping		2.50
Overseas freight and insurance		58.50
		450.00
Import tariff: 20 percent of landed cost		90.00
		540.00
Handling in foreign port of entry		3.00
		543.00
Transportation from port of entry to importer		17.00
		560.00
Importer margin (on sale to wholesaler): 10 percent		56.00
		616.00
Wholesale margin: 8 percent	30.40	49.28
	410.40	665.28
Retail margin: 40 percent	164.16	266.12
Final retail price	$574.56	$931.40

The ex-factory arrangement limits the exporter's risk. However, an importer may find an ex-factory deal highly demanding. From another country, a company could have difficulty arranging transportation and taking care of the various formalities associated with foreign trade. Only large companies, such as Japanese trading companies, can smoothly handle ex-factory purchases in another country.

The *FAS* contract requires the exporter to be responsible for the goods until they are placed alongside the ship. All charges incurred up to that point must be borne by the seller. The exporter's side of the contract is completed upon receiving a clean wharfage receipt indicating safe delivery of goods for foreign embarkation. The FAS price is slightly higher than the ex-factory price because the exporter undertakes to transport the goods to the point of shipment and becomes liable for the risk associated with the goods for a longer period.

The *FOB* price includes the actual placement of goods aboard the ship. The FOB price may be changed by the FOB inland carrier or the FOB foreign carrier. If it is an FOB inland carrier, the FOB price will be slightly less than the FAS price. However, if it is an FOB foreign carrier, the price will include the FAS price plus the cost of transportation to the importer's country.

Finally, the delivered duty-paid alternative imposes on the exporter the complete responsibility for delivering the goods at a particular place in the importer's country. Thus, the exporter makes arrangements for the receipt of the goods at the foreign port, pays necessary taxes/duties and handling, and provides for further inland transportation in the importer's country. Needless to say, the price of delivered duty-paid goods is much higher than goods exported under the CIF contract.

PLANNING FOR PRICE NEGOTIATION

To achieve a favorable outcome from a negotiation, an exporter should draw up a plan of action beforehand, which addresses a few key issues. Experienced negotiators know that as much as 80 percent of the time they devote to negotiations should go to such preparations. The preliminary work should be aimed at obtaining relevant information about the target market and the buyers of the product. Preparation should also include developing counterproposals in case objections are raised on any of the exporter's opening negotiating points. Thus, the preparations should involve formulating the negotiating strategy and tactics.

Knowing what a buyer wants or needs requires advance research. In addition to customers' preferences, an exporter should assess the competition from domestic and foreign suppliers and be familiar with the prices they quote. The exporter should also examine the distribution channels used for the product and the promotional tools and messages required. Such information will be valuable when negotiating with buyers. The more the exporter knows about the target market and the buyers for the products concerned, the better able he or she is to conduct the negotiations and match an offer to the buyer's needs. On the other hand, making counterproposals requires that the buyer know detailed information about the costs of the exporter's production operations, freight insurance, packaging, and other related expenses. An exporter should carry out a realistic assessment of the quantities his or her company can supply and the

FIGURE 6-3
Potential Price Objectives

Importer's Reaction to the Price Offer	Exporter's Possible Response
1. The initial price quoted is too high; a substantial drop is required.	Ask the buyer what is meant by "too high"; ask on what basis the drop is called for; stress product quality and benefits before discussing price.
2. Lower offers have been received from other exporters.	Ask for more details about such offers; find out how serious such offers are; convince the buyer that your firm has a better offer.
3. A counteroffer is required; a price discount is expected	Avoid making a better offer without asking for something in return, but without risking loss of interest; when asking for something in return, make a specific suggestion, such as "If I give you a 5 percent price discount, would you arrange for surface transport, including storage costs?"
4. The price of $.... is my last offer.	Avoid accepting such an offer immediately; find out the quantities involved; determine whether there will be repeat orders; ascertain who will pay for storage, publicity, after-sales service, and so on.
5. The product is acceptable, but the price is too high.	Agree to discuss details of the costing; promote product benefits, reliability as a regular supplier, timely delivery, unique designs, and so on.
6. The initial price quoted is acceptable.	Find out why the importer is so interested in the offer; recalculate the costing; check the competition; contact other potential buyers to get more details about market conditions; review the pricing strategy; accept a trial order only.

Source: Claude Cellich, "Negotiating Strategies: The Question of Price," *International Trade FORUM*, April–June 1991, p. 12.

schedule for supplying them. Every effort should be made to match the export firm's size, financial situation, production capacity, technical expertise, organizational strength, and export commitment with compatible buyers.

As part of the preparations for negotiations, the negotiator should list the potential price objections the buyer may have toward the offer, along with possible responses. Some of the most common price objections, together with suggested actions,

FIGURE 6-4
Check Readiness to Undertake Price Negotiations

Question	Action Required
1. Am I well prepared?	Undertake thorough research about target markets and buyers.
2. Do I know the nonprice benefits of my products?	Develop a list of product benefits to use to counter price objections.
3. Do I know my best markets and buyers?	Obtain detailed information about market and buyer requirements; be ready with options.
4. Will the buyer listen to me and take me seriously?	Practice projecting confidence and maintaining two-way communication.
5. Am I ready to make concessions?	Decide on the maximum concessions you can make; list concessions you wish to receive; prepare several negotiating options.
6. Will I be in a position to accept the negotiated deal?	Determine what is considered a sustainable sales agreement; decide ahead of time not to enter into a transaction simply for the sake of exporting; remember that no deal is better than a bad deal.

Source: Claude Cellich, "Negotiating Strategies: The Question of Price," *International Trade FORUM,* April–June 1991, p. 12.

are listed in Figure 6-3. Sellers should adapt this list to their own product, the particular competitive situation, and specific market requirements.

Finally, the negotiator should test his or her readiness to undertake price negotiations. Such testing can be conducted using the questions listed in Figure 6-4.

INTO NEGOTIATIONS

The preliminary groundwork should provide a negotiator with enough information to initiate the price negotiation. He or she should know the needs and requirements of the other party. If the subject of price is raised at the outset, the negotiator should avoid making any commitments or concessions at this point. The proceeding talks should include the following substantive topics.

Emphasize the Firm's Attributes

A negotiator should promote the strength of his or her firm as a reliable commercial partner who is committed to a long-term business relationship. The other party should be convinced that the negotiator is capable of supplying the type of goods needed on acceptable terms. This can be accomplished by stressing the following aspects of a firm's operations:

- Management capability
- Production capacity and processes: quality control system
- Technical cooperation, if any, with other foreign firms
- Export structure for handling orders
- Export experience, including types of companies dealt with
- Financial standing and references from banking institutions
- Membership in leading trade and industry associations, including chambers of commerce

Highlight the Product's Attributes

Once the other party is convinced he or she is dealing with a reliable firm, negotiations can be directed toward the product and its benefits. The attributes of a product tend to be seen differently by different customers. Therefore, a negotiator must determine whether his or her product fits the need of the other party.

In some cases, meeting the buyer's requirements is a simple process. For example, during sales negotiations, a Thai exporter of cutlery was told by a U.S. importer in a major market that the price was too high, although the quality and finish of the items met market requirements. In the discussions, the exporter learned that the importer was interested in bulk purchases rather than prepackaged sets of 12 in expensive teak cases, as consumers in the United States purchase cutlery either as individual pieces or in sets of eight. The exporter then made a counterproposal for sales in bulk at a much lower price based on savings in packaging, transportation, and import duties. The offer was accepted by the importer, and both parties benefited from the transaction. This example illustrates that knowing what product characteristics the importer is looking for can be used to advantage by the exporter.

An exporter may not have a unique product, but by stressing the product attributes and other marketing factors in the negotiation, he or she can offer a unique package that meets the need of the importer.

Maintain Flexibility

In the negotiation process, the buyer may request modifications in the product and its presentation. The exporter should show a willingness to meet such a request if possible. The exporter should analyze whether the product adaptation would allow him or her to run a profitable export business. For example, in one case, negotiation on the export of teak coffee tables was deadlocked because of the high price of the tables. During the discussions, the exporter realized that the buyer was interested primarily in the fine finish of the tabletop. Therefore, the exporter made a counterproposal to supply the coffee table at a lower price, using the same teak top but with table legs and joineries made of less expensive wood. The importer accepted the offer, and the exporter was able to develop a profitable export business.

Offer a Price Package

After covering all of the nonprice issues, the exporter can shift the discussion in the final phase of the talks to financial matters that have a bearing on the price quotation. This is the time to come to an agreement on issues such as credit terms, payment schedules, currencies of payment, insurance, commission rates, warehousing costs, after-sales servicing responsibilities, costs of replacing damaged goods, and so on. Agreement reached on these points constitutes the price package. Any change in the buyer's requirements after his agreement should be reflected in a new price package. For example, if the buyer likes the product but considers the final price to be too high, the exporter can make a counterproposal by, for example, cutting the price, but asking the buyer to assume the costs of transportation, to accept bulk packaging, and to make advanced payment.

Differentiate the Product

In some cases, price is an all-important factor in sales negotiation. The most obvious situation is when firms are operating in highly competitive markets with homogeneous products. Bypassing the pricing issue at the outset of negotiations is difficult when buyers are interested only in the best possible price, regardless of the source of supply. In such a situation, the negotiator should consider differentiating the product from those of the competition in order to shift the negotiations to other factors, such as product style, quality, and delivery.

GUIDELINES FOR PRICE NEGOTIATIONS

An importer may reject an exporter's price at the outset of the discussion simply to get the upper hand from the beginning of the negotiation, thereby hoping to obtain maximum concessions on other matters. The importer may also object to the initial price quoted to test the seriousness of the offer, to find out how far the exporter is willing to lower the price, to seek a specific lower price because the product brand is unknown in the market, or to demonstrate a lack of interest in the transaction as the product does not meet market requirements.

If the importer does not accept the price, the exporter should react positively by initiating discussions on nonprice questions, instead of immediately offering price concessions or taking a defensive attitude. Widening the issues and exploring the real reasons behind the objections to the price quoted will put the talks on a more equal and constructive footing. Only by knowing the causes of disagreement can an exporter make a reasonable counteroffer. This counteroffer need not be based merely on pricing; it can also involve related subjects.

To meet price objections, some suppliers artificially inflate their initial price quotations. This enables them to give price concessions in the opening of the negotiation without taking any financial risk. The danger of this approach is that it immediately directs the discussion to pricing issues at the expense of other important components of the marketing mix. Generally, such initial price concessions are followed by more demands from the buyer that can further reduce the profitability of the export transaction. For instance, the buyer may press for concessions on the following:

- Quantity discounts
- Discounts for repeat orders
- Improved packaging and labeling (for the same price)
- Tighter delivery deadlines, which may increase production and transportation costs
- Free promotional materials in the language of the import market
- Free after-sales servicing
- A supply of free parts to replace those damaged from normal wear and tear
- Free training of staff in the maintenance and use of the equipment
- Market exclusivity

- A long-term agency agreement
- Higher commission rates
- Better credit and payment terms

To avoid being confronted by such costly demands, an exporter should from the outset try to determine the buyer's real interest in the product. This can be ascertained by asking appropriate questions but must also be based on research and other preparations completed before the negotiations. Only then can a suitable counterproposal be presented.

SUMMARY

Prices determine the total revenue and, to a large extent, the profitability of a business. When making pricing decisions, the following factors deserve consideration: pricing objective, cost, competition, customer, and government regulations. In price negotiations, these factors must be examined in reference to one's own country and the other party's country. Each factor is made up of a number of components that vary in each nation, both in importance and in interaction.

Price negotiations follow either a cost approach or a market approach. The cost approach involves computing all relevant costs and adding a profit markup to determine the price. The market approach examines price setting from the customer's viewpoint. Export price negotiation is affected by three additional considerations: the price destination, the nature of the product, and the currency used in completing the transaction. Price escalation is an important consideration in export retail pricing. The retail price of exports usually is much higher than the domestic retail price for the same goods. This difference can be explained by the added costs associated with exports, such as transportation, customs duty, and distributor margin.

Satisfactory price negotiations require a negotiator to draw up a plan of action ahead of time with regard to buyer wants, willingness and/or ability to pay, and objections likely to be raised on initially quoted price. The negotiator must prepare responses to the objections and decide whether he or she is willing to make a counterproposal on pricing.

While negotiating price, a negotiator should emphasize his or her firm's attributes, highlight his or her product's attributes, maintain flexibility, offer a price package, and attempt to differentiate his or her products from those of the competition.

NOTES

1. Kerry Pechter, "Can We Make a Deal." *International Business,* Vol. 5, No. 3, pp. 46–50.
2. The discussion on pricing factors draws heavily from: Subhash C. Jain, *International Marketing,* 6th Edition (Cincinnati, Ohio: South-Western College Publishing, 2001), Chapter 13.
3. Ibid.

7

Closing Business Negotiations

*In closing, timing is everything.—**Anonymous***

Bringing business negotiations to a close requires special skills and techniques. As no two negotiations are alike, no single approach to closing is better than another. Negotiators must use their own judgment in selecting the most appropriate method to close the negotiations.

METHODS OF CLOSING NEGOTIATIONS

A wide range of methods exists for closing the negotiations.[1] Choice of the appropriate method depends on the existing relationship between the parties, the objectives of the negotiation, the cultural environment, the negotiating styles of the participants, the state of the discussions, and the goal of whether the talks concern new business opportunities or the extension of existing contracts. The following are common methods of closing.

Alternative

Also known as the 'either-or' technique, in this approach, one party makes a final offer consisting of a choice for the other side. For example, one party is willing to lower his or her commission rate if the other agrees to deliver the goods to the warehouse at its own cost.

Assumption

With this method, the negotiator assumes the other side is ready to agree and to proceed with detailed discussions of delivery dates, payment schedules, and so on. Sellers use this method frequently to rush buyers into agreement. It is a useful approach when the initiating party has more than one option to offer the other side.

Concession

This method is characterized by the negotiator keeping a few concessions in reserve until the end of the talks to encourage the other party to come to an agreement. It is particularly effective in situations in which concessions are expected as a sign of goodwill before final agreement is given. These last-minute concessions should not be overly generous; they should, however, be significant enough to encourage the other party to finalize the talks.

Incremental

Another approach is for the negotiator to propose agreement on a particular issue and then proceed to settle other issues until accord is reached on all pending matters. This method is used when the negotiation process follows an orderly sequence of settling one issue after another.

Linkage

Another approach is linking a requested concession to another concession in return. Linkage is usually most effective when both sides have already agreed on the outstanding issues and need to settle remaining ones prior to reaching consensus.

Prompting

Prompting is used to obtain immediate agreement by making a final offer with special benefits if the offer is accepted immediately. The purpose of prompting is to overcome all objections by offering special incentives such as free installation and maintenance, no price increase for next year's deliveries, and free training if the other party agrees to conclude the transaction on the spot.

Summarizing

This method requires one negotiator to summarize all of the issues being discussed, to emphasize the concessions made, and to highlight the benefits the other party gains by agreeing to the proposal. As the discussions near the deadline and consensus is reached on all outstanding issues, one party summarizes the points and asks the other party to approve them. The summaries should be short and should accurately reflect what has been discussed. This approach can be applied in any cultural environment or business situation.

Splitting the Difference

A useful closing method is "splitting the difference," in which both parties are close to agreement and the remaining difference is minimal. At this point, it may be preferable to split the difference rather than continue endless discussion on minor issues that may be secondary to overall negotiation objectives and possibly jeopardize the relationship.[2] Splitting the difference supposes that both sides started with realistic offers; otherwise, this method would give an unfair advantage to the party with an extremely low offer (from the buyer) or a very high offer (from the seller). This is a common method that can expedite closure, but negotiators must ensure that it does not result in an unbalanced agreement.

Trial

Trial is a method used to test how close the other side is to agreement. In a trial offer, one party makes a proposal, giving the other party an opportunity to express reservations. Objections to the trial offer indicate the areas requiring further discussion. By making a trial offer, the initiating party is not committing itself, and the other party is not obligated to accept. Generally, a trial offer results in a constructive discussion on remaining issues while maintaining a fruitful dialogue between the parties until a consensus is reached.[3] This technique is useful to determine what remaining matters need to be clarified.

Ultimatum/or Else

Another method is to force the other party to make a decision on the last offer. If the other party fails to respond or accept the offer, the initiating party walks away from the negotiation. The "or else" method, also known as an ultimatum, is generally not recommended for negotiations in which trust and goodwill are required to execute the agreement.

CHOOSING A CLOSING METHOD

The closing method should be selected during the prenegotiation phase. Once chosen, it must be carefully understood to ensure its mastery. The method selected should fit the environment in which the discussions take place and should match the overall objectives of the negotiations. With experience, negotiators can shift from one method to another or combine one or more as part of their negotiation strategy.[4]

Overall, experienced negotiators prefer either the concession, the summarizing, or the splitting the difference method, although the other methods (assumption, prompting, linkage, and trial closings) are effective in certain types of negotiations and cultures.

TIME TO CLOSE

As nearly every negotiation is different, the time to bring the discussion to a close varies greatly from one situation to another. Timing is also influenced by the cultural background of the negotiators, the complexity of the deal, the existing relationships, and the degree of trust between the parties. For example, when two companies have been doing business for years and are discussing repeat orders, they are likely to arrive at a settlement rather rapidly. Discussions concerning the setting up of a joint venture, however, may take months or years to finalize.

When making a final offer, a negotiator must ensure that the other party has the authority to decide; otherwise, the party may need additional time to discuss the offer within his or her organization. In some countries, where decisions are made by consensus, closing is time-consuming, as negotiators are required to consult other members of the organization for approval. These additional discussions can result in delays as well as further demands for last-minute concessions. To counter such demands, the initiating party must clearly state when making the final offer that any further changes requested will call for a review of all issues on which agreement has been reached.[5]

Clues

A few clues can help experienced negotiators detect when it is time to close the talks. The most obvious one is when the concessions by one party become less important and less frequent and are given more reluctantly. Generally, this is a sign that no further compromises are possible. Any concessions beyond that point may lead to a breakdown of the negotiations.

In nearly all negotiations, a time comes when both parties have met most of their objectives and are ready to concede on some lesser issues to reach agreement. Up to this point, both sides exchanged views to determine their respective needs, validated their assumptions, and estimated the negotiating range and type of concessions required. Most concessions are made toward the end of the discussions, particularly as the deadline approaches. As much as 80 percent of all concessions are exchanged in the closing phase of the talks. By this stage, the parties have become familiar with each other's interests, tend to take a problem-solving attitude, and usually consider making concessions to reach agreement.

Another clue that it is time to close the discussions is when one party decides he or she has reached a maximum outcome and makes a final offer. This final offer must be made with conviction and must be followed by a request for a firm commitment from the other party. It is sometimes difficult to determine whether the party making the final offer is trustworthy or is simply employing a closing tactic to arrive at a settlement in his or her favor.

Again, a great deal depends on the relationship and trust between the two parties, as well as the cultural environment in which the negotiation is taking place. In some countries, a final offer is considered final; while in others, it conveys a willingness to reach agreement. When making a final offer, the party initiating the proposal must be willing to terminate negotiations if the other side refuses to accept. To avoid breaking the negotiation process, however, the party making the final offer can introduce a deadline for the other side to consider the "final" offer. This gives the receiving side more time to reexamine the proposal and/or to obtain additional facts to make the continuation of the negotiation possible.

In some countries, such as France, negotiators begin the discussions with general principles followed by more specific issues.[6] The party shifting to specific issues is usually expressing its interest in bringing the discussions to a close. In the United States, however, negotiators begin to compromise on specific issues one by one until all outstanding matters have been agreed to. These different approaches illustrate the influence cultural background has on business negotiations and the need for executives to be flexible in concluding international negotiations.

It is widely accepted that negotiators, before agreeing to a final offer, ask for last-minute concessions. Such requests are expected and are part of the negotiating process. To be prepared to respond to last-minute requests, negotiators should keep a few concessions in reserve to maintain the momentum and to encourage the other party to close. These concessions should be valued and appreciated by the requesting party, yet not be too costly to provide. For this reason, negotiators should identify the real needs of the other party and the likely concessions they must make before closing and build them into the overall package.

Before applying any of the closing methods, the negotiators should ask themselves the following questions:

- Does the agreement meet our goals?
- Will we be able to fulfill the agreement?
- Do we intend to commit the resources required to implement the agreement?
- Do we consider the other party capable of meeting its commitment to the agreement?

Only when each question is answered with a "yes" can both parties be ready to bring the discussions to a close.

Deadline

The most obvious sign that it is time to close discussions is when the deadline approaches. Both parties should agree to the deadline in advance, at the initial stage of the negotiation or when setting the agenda. A deadline arbitrarily set by one party in the course of the talks can lead to undue pressure on the other side to close.

Deadlines should, however, be flexible. They can be renegotiated to allow the discussions to proceed until agreement is reached. In particular, when negotiators enter into complex talks in different cultural environments, they should allow for the possibility of extra time when planning the discussions.

Final Points

When a deal is about to be concluded, negotiators need to ask themselves certain questions in order to avoid unpleasant experiences in the implementation phase. In most cases, agreements that run into problems do not suddenly become difficult to implement. Instead, it is generally minor issues that are unattended to or left to degenerate over time that lead to major crises.[7] To ensure smooth implementation, negotiators should ask themselves the following questions:

- Have all the essential issues been discussed?
- Is the agreed-upon proposal workable by both parties?

FIGURE 7-1
Closing a Negotiation: Some Dos and Don'ts

Do:
- Anticipate last-minute demand when planning your negotiating strategy and tactics.
- Agree to an agenda that reflects your objectives and set realistic deadlines.
- Listen to the other party's objections and ask why he or she is not agreeing.
- Emphasize the benefits to be gained by the other party's acceptance of your proposal.
- Look for a change in the pattern, size, and frequency of the other party's concessions.
- Overcome objections by giving clear explanations.
- Take notes throughout the discussions, including your concessions and the ones made by the other party.
- Make your "final" offer credible and with conviction.
- Examine the draft agreement and clarify any points that you do not understand before signing.

Don't:
- View the closing as a separate step in the negotiations.
- Be in a hurry to close.
- Make large concessions at the last minute.
- Rush into costly concessions because of deadlines.
- Push your advantage to the point of forcing the other side to leave the negotiations.
- Lose sight of your long-term objectives when getting blocked on minor issues.
- Become too emotional when closing. (You need to think as clearly as possible during the closing.)
- Discuss the deal with the other party once you have agreed. (You run the risk of reopening negotiations.)

Remember:
- Flexibility is the heart of closing a deal.
- Experienced negotiators plan their closing tactics during their preparations for the negotiation.
- Successful negotiators follow their preset goals and concentrate their efforts on essential issues.
- Successful negotiators encourage the other party to close when the time is appropriate because many negotiators are afraid of closing or do not know how and when to close.
- The best time to close is when both sides have achieved their expected goals.
- Successful negotiators close only when the deal is good, not only for themselves but for the other party as well.
- The notion of closing varies in different parts of the world because of cultural factors requiring different closing methods.
- Closing is not done in a hurry.
- Overcoming objections is a part of getting approval of proposals.
- Successful closers seek consensus.
- Buyers often say "no" one more time before saying "yes."
- Nothing is agreed to until everything is agreed to.
- Not all negotiations lead to the closing of a deal. Sometimes no deal is better than a bad deal.

Source: Claude Cellich, "Closing Your Business Negotiations," *International Trade FORUM*, 1/1997, p. 16.

- Does the agreement clearly specify what is to be done by both sides, including payment terms, delivery schedules, product specifications, and so on?
- Have the major barriers to implementing the deal been identified and the means to overcome them agreed to?
- In case of potential disputes during implementation, what mechanisms have been instituted to resolve them?
- If either of the parties needs to renegotiate the terms, what procedures should be followed?

The executives engaged in the talks should remain involved in the implementation phase. Each party should monitor the execution of the contract through the agreed procedures by periodic visits and ongoing communications. By maintaining regular contact, keeping accurate records of all transactions, and paying attention to minor details, the parties can help ensure a smooth business relationship. Figure 7-1 lists some dos and don'ts and points to remember about closing.

SUMMARY

Many negotiators do not know how to bring business talks to a successful close. They should be thoroughly prepared, including knowing when and how to apply appropriate methods and how to respond to the other party's use of closing tactics. By mastering closing techniques, negotiators can achieve agreements that both parties can implement smoothly throughout the life of the agreed-upon transaction. When closing a deal, negotiators should remember that negotiations based on trust and fair play may lead to repeat business and referrals. As it is expensive and time-consuming to find new business partners, negotiators should retain existing ones by agreeing to terms and conditions with which both sides feel comfortable.

NOTES

1. Robert Moran and William G. Stripp, *Successful International Business Negotiations* (Houston, TX: Gulf Publishing Co., 1991).
2. John Riley and Richard Zeckhauser, "When to Haggle, When to Hold Firm," *Quarterly Journal of Economics*, May 1983, pp. 267–289.
3. Dean Allen Foster, *Bargaining Across Borders* (New York: McGraw-Hill, 1992).
4. Pervez Ghauri, "Guidelines for International Business Negotiations," *International Marketing Review*, Autumn 1986, pp. 72–82.

5. John L. Graham, "Across the Negotiating Table from the Japanese," *International Marketing Review*, Autumn 1986, pp. 58–70.
6. Nigel Campbell, John L. Graham, Alain Jolibert, and Haus Meissur, "Marketing Negotiations in France, Germany, the United Kingdom and the United States," *Journal of Marketing*, April 1988, pp. 49–62.
7. Roger Axfel, *Dos and Taboos Around the World* (New York: John Wiley, 1985).

8

Undertaking Renegotiations

Contract is an agreement that is binding on the weaker party.
—Frederick Sawyer

Today's business executives are finding it more and more difficult to negotiate 'static' agreements that withstand the pressure of change. As a result, renegotiations are a growing trend in international business. Every day, companies operating in the global arena sign agreements expected to be mutually beneficial and long-lasting. Despite good intentions and ironclad contracts, unexpected difficulties do arise once contracts are under way, making renegotiations essential.

Too often, at the time of closure, parties assume that the negotiations are over and that both sides can look forward to a successful outcome. In reality, negotiations are only the beginning. A negotiation is not complete until the agreement is fully implemented. With so many unexpected changes occurring in the global marketplace, smooth implementation is the exception rather than the rule.

Although the main purpose of entering into a business deal is to make a profit, frequently contracts turn out to be unprofitable. The parties may also have different interpretations about their respective responsibilities. Thus, continuous monitoring of an agreement is important. And when difficulties arise, parties should not hesitate to undertake renegotiations.

REASONS FOR RENEGOTIATION

Anecdotal evidence shows that renegotiations are more prevalent in international business than in domestic deals. This is because international business negotiation involves situations not present in domestic settings. When one party believes the deal has become overly burdensome or unreasonable due to changes beyond his or her control, the party considers renegotiation as a distinct possibility over outright rejection. The situations that can lead to renegotiations are examined below.[1]

Dimensions of International Business Environment

International business deals are susceptible to political and economic changes, which are different from those that result when business is conducted at home. Politically, a country may face internal strife, such as civil war, a coup, or a radical shift in policy. On the economic front, currency devaluation or a natural calamity can create conditions highly inconducive to fulfilling a negotiated deal.

Mechanisms for Settling Disputes

If the other party to the negotiation does not have effective access to the legal system in the negotiator's country, the negotiator may believe he or she has little to lose by not implementing a burdensome deal. Under such circumstances, renegotiation is a satisfactory solution in order to keep the deal alive.

Involvement of Government

In developing countries in particular, international business often entails dealing with government departments or with a public sector corporation, a company that is owned and operated by a government. Governments may refuse to abide by a contract, which they, at a later date, consider burdensome. They may force renegotiation for the sake of the welfare of their people or in the name of their national sovereignty.

Cultural Differences between Nations

Doing business with diverse cultures requires extra care in ensuring full understanding of an agreement's content. For instance, in countries where contracts are lengthy and detailed, little or no flexibility is allowed. In such cases, all possible events that could affect the deal over the period of the contract are identified and appropriate clauses are included in the agreement. To avoid deviations, penalties for noncompliance are built in to ensure strict adherence.

Some cultures are more likely to consider the contract as the beginning of a business relationship. In these cultures, the possibility of reopening the discussions is rather high. Because interpretations can vary due to different cultural views of the negotiation process, negotiators doing business with a different culture seriously consider the follow-up phase and eventual post-negotiation discussions. Consider the following example:

An American company in a transaction with a Japanese firm may view their signed contract as the essence of the deal and the source of rules governing their relationship in its entirety. The Japanese, however, see the deal as a partnership that is subject to reasonable changes over time, a partnership in which one party ought not to take unfair advantage of purely fortuitous events like radical and unexpected movements in exchange rates or the price of raw materials. Ironically, as a result of the rise in value of the Japanese yen, certain American companies, tied to long-term supply agreements payable in yen for components and materials produced in Japan, relied upon this distinctly un-American approach to contracts to seek renegotiation of payment terms that unanticipated monetary changes had made unprofitable.[2]

REDUCING THE NEED TO RENEGOTIATE

In today's dynamic global market, it is difficult to avoid renegotiating business agreements. Negotiators can, however, reduce the frequency and extent of renegotiations by clarifying all major issues, introducing penalties for noncompliance, insisting on regular meetings to monitor implementation, and explaining the negative impact problems can have on future business opportunities. Doing this should alert both parties to their responsibilities and risks.

Conducting business in different parts of the world requires alternative negotiating approaches. In some cultures, negotiations do not end with the signing of an agreement, but continue throughout the duration of the relationship. So business can take place in these environments, the contract should include built-in early warning signals to detect the presence of problems. Instead of insisting on a detailed, lengthy contract leaving nothing to chance, a shorter agreement acknowledging the possibility of eventual amendments may be more appropriate. Penalties or similar deterrents should be included, however, to avoid potential abuses in critical areas of the agreement.

For instance, when a manufacturer requests an order of spare parts that is larger than the supplier expects, the supplier should consider it a warning signal. Perhaps the equipment is not being used properly or maintenance is inadequate. In this example, the supplier can review clauses concerning warranty, responsibility for repairs, supplying of spare parts, and other matters relating to equipment breakdown. The manufacturer can offer to train operators on proper use of the equipment, adapt the operations manual to local conditions, translate the manual into the language of the user, or agree to participate in the maintenance of the equipment during the initial installation phase. By taking these additional precautions, both parties can look forward to the execution of the contract with minimum difficulty.

A question most experienced international negotiators ask themselves at the time of closing is, "What does the contract mean to the other party?" In other words, is it the beginning or end of negotiations? Another key question to be raised toward closing is, "How much is the other party committed to the agreement?" Answers to these and other questions can alert the negotiator to potential problems likely to arise during the life of the contract. Such probing at "closing" should help reduce the need for renegotiation. A more thorough examination is presented in Figure 8-1.

FIGURE 8-1
Reducing the Need to Renegotiate

If you can safely answer yes to most of the questions below, you are close to entering into an agreement that is unlikely to require serious renegotiation. For those questions where the answer is no, however, you need to conduct additional discussions. When you can answer all the questions with a yes, you can be fairly certain that renegotiation will not be needed.

- Does the agreement fit the overall long-term business strategies of both parties?
- Will both parties benefit from the agreement? (Is it a win-win business deal?)
- Are you convinced the other party is fully committed to implementing the agreement?
- Will management support you unconditionally in executing the contract?
- Are you sure the other party has the capacity (managerial, technical, and financial) to fulfill its obligations?
- Have all major potential problems been identified, discussed, and resolved?
- Do you consider the agreement fully enforceable?
- Are the penalties for noncompliance sufficient to ensure fiull adherence to the contractual terms?
- Has a feedback mechanism been put in place to monitor execution of the agreement?

Source: Claude Cellich, "Contract Renegotiations," *International Trade FORUM*, 2/1999, p. 13.

Prevent Renegotiation

Renegotiation can be prevented (or at least avoided) if both parties anticipate the problem ahead of time and make due provision. Another underlying principle relative to renegotiation is this: If costs to the other party of rejecting an agreement are less than fulfilling, the risk of repudiation and renegotiation goes up. Thus, as a matter of strategy, to give stability to an agreement, a negotiator should make sure that sufficient benefits accrue to the other party in order to keep the deal alive. To implement this strategy, a negotiator should follow these steps:

- *Lock the other party in.* This is accomplished by including detailed provisions and guarantees for proper implementation. The agreement should have built-in mechanisms to reduce the likelihood of rejection and renegotiation. These mechanisms either raise the cost to the other party for not fulfilling his or her obligations under the contract or provide compensation for the negotiator for having lost the benefit of the agreement he or she made. The two popular mechanisms for this purpose are performance bond and linkage. Under the performance bond, the other party or some reliable third party (multinational bank, investment house) allocates money or property that is turned over to the negotiator if the other party fails to perform. The linkage mechanism involves increasing the costs of noncompliance to the party failing to implement the deal. An example of linkage is the formation of an alliance of several banks to finance a project in a developing country. The developing country may find it difficult to go against the entire alliance group by noncompliance of the agreement. The country will find the cost of losing its credibility detrimental to future development plans.
- *Balance the deal.* A successful deal is one that benefits both of the parties. Thus, a negotiator should make sure the deal leads to a win-win agreement. If the agreement is mutually beneficial, neither party will consider noncompliance. A balanced deal allocates risks according to the strengths of the parties and not merely on the basis of bargaining power. In addition, unexpected windfalls or losses should be shared by both parties.
- *Control the renegotiation.* This amounts to specifying a clause in the agreement for periodically undertaking intradeal renegotiation on issues that are susceptible to change. In other words, a negotiator should have a provision in the

negotiated deal for opening up the deal and undertake negotiations at defined intervals. It is better to recognize the possibility of renegotiation at the outset and specify a procedure for conducting it. An intradeal negotiation is examined later in this chapter.

Build in Renegotiation Costs

Experienced international business executives include potential renegotiation costs in their final offer. Renegotiations can be costly in time and money; therefore, there are ways to build additional costs into the original offer to absorb such future expenses.

One possibility is to separate implementation into several stages, with payment made after successful execution of each stage. This type of agreement is appropriate for lengthy and complex contracts, such as initiating a joint venture. The most effective preparation requires access to accurate information of all past transactions. This helps parties eliminate time blaming each other for deviating from the agreed-upon terms.

The introduction of penalties for noncompliance is another way to discourage the other party from deviating from the initial agreement. One party giving excessive attention to penalties, however, may indicate his or her lack of confidence in the other party, which could lead to mistrust and resentment. This is hardly the basis for developing a stable business relationship in an ever-changing competitive environment. The key points for dealing with renegotiations are summarized in Figure 8-2.

FIGURE 8-2
Renegotiation: Key Points to Remember

Before the contract begins
- Consider negotiations as a dynamic process, requiring constant monitoring of the agreement.
- Build extra costs into the contract to cover future expenses related to renegotiations.
- Make the implementation phase an integral part of the overall negotiation strategy.
- Encourage a healthy relationship between the parties, as it is the best guarantee for a lasting agreement.

During the contract
- Prepare for the possibility of renegotiations—maintain records of all transactions, from initial discussions to the actual execution of the agreement.
- Remember that agreements mean different things to different cultures, requiring flexibility, understanding, and patience.

FIGURE 8-2
Renegotiation: Key Points to Remember (Contd.)

- Do not blame the other party of any wrongdoing until you know all of the facts.
- Do not wait for minor problems to develop into major ones before considering renegotiations.

If renegotiations appear possible
- Before beginning renegotiations, consult everyone involved in the original negotiation, as well as those responsible for implementation.
- Be sure you clearly understand the factors that trigger the reopening of negotiations.
- Foster constructive discussions between concerned parties, which is preferable to legal recourse.
- Keep long-term business objectives in mind when renegotiating.
- Encourage steps that ensure that all parties are satisfied, even if it means renegotiations. Higher profits come from satisfied parties through repeat business and referrals.

Source: Claude Cellich, "Contract Renegotiations," *International Trade FORUM*, 2/1999, p. 15.

OVERCOMING FEAR TO REOPEN NEGOTIATIONS

More often than not, companies underestimate potential problems that call for renegotiating specific terms contained in an agreement. When something goes wrong, it is only natural that parties get together to resolve the problem. Surprisingly, the party who is the source of the problem is generally reluctant to seek changes or revisions. Often the people in charge of implementation are afraid to address the issue for fear of rejection.

When a business deal is developed in a spirit of cooperation, one party may consider it inappropriate to ask the other party for special conditions, which may be interpreted as taking advantage of the relationship. Fear of receiving a negative answer can lead to missed opportunities for improving the business relationship and fulfilling the agreed-upon terms.

In some cultures, fear of embarrassment is so great that indirect "signals" are sent to indicate the need for revisions. For instance, a sudden lack of communication, vague answers, or an inability to contact the other party, including periods of prolonged silence, may suggest a problem.

As soon as one party sees a problem (for example, products of inferior quality or inability to meet delivery dates), it should take the initiative to contact the other party. It is much easier to take corrective action from the outset by recognizing the problem and suggesting ways of resolving it. Sometimes lack of international business experience or insufficient knowledge of stringent market specifications means suppliers are not fully aware of what is required to produce top-quality products.

Strict adherence to delivery is another sensitive issue, with firms relying on just-in-time inventory. Concerns with delivery are likely to increase in the years ahead, as more and more enterprises outsource some of their production and/or services. To minimize problems, executives must maintain open communication lines, make contact early, and be willing to discuss problems openly should they arise.

A real-life example is the case of a furniture importer, who received a large shipment in December that exceeded the contract agreement. This unexpected shipment resulted in extra storage costs and handling charges and other indirect expenses. Instead of lodging a complaint or sending back the extra goods, the importer contacted the supplier immediately. It turned out that this huge shipment was initiated by the export manager since this would have given him a large Christmas bonus. After hearing the views of the supplier, the importer explained the economic hardship caused by this shipment and requested compensation on future orders. By doing so, the importer did not antagonize or criticize the other party, but tried to find a workable solution, while expressing a commitment to continue the business relationship over the long term.

TYPES OF RENEGOTIATION

It is unrealistic to assume stability of a contract in a rapidly changing global setting. Although negotiators attempt to anticipate the future and make provisions in the contract for eventualities that may arise later on, it is virtually impossible to foresee every possibility. Therefore, business executives negotiating international contracts realize that ongoing discussions and consultations are necessary ingredients to successful outcomes. Thus, renegotiations are unavoidable.

Four different types of renegotiation are used: preemptive, intradeal, extradeal, and postdeal. Each type is relevant under particular circumstances, raises different problems, and demands varying solutions. In any renegotiation, open communications and continuous monitoring are critical to success. Flexibility, commitment, and recognition that renegotiation may be necessary should be part and parcel of a negotiator's strategy.

Preemptive Negotiation

After a deal has been struck but before it is implemented, unforeseen events may take place that make it difficult to fulfill the negotiated agreement. Shrewd negotiators control the situation by resorting to preemptive negotiation; i.e., renegotiation before the disturbing event happens. Preemptive negotiation requires (a) searching for potential problems, (b) creating a mechanism to manage voluntary change, and (c) establishing a mechanism to settle differences and disputes that threaten relations between the two parties.[3]

From a business standpoint, the problems fall mainly into three categories: late performance, defective performance, and nonperformance.

- *Late performance:* Meeting a deadline is the accepted norm in modern-day commerce. Goods must be delivered on the appointed day; defects must be corrected promptly; payment must be made on time. But if a company cannot meet a deadline because of unexpected events at its end (for example, a labor strike) or in the external environment (for example, unavailability of a component), the firm must renegotiate with the other party for late performance.
- *Defective Performance:* Suppose you negotiated to custom-design furniture and deliver it to an overseas buyer. Subsequently, you ordered components and parts to complete the order. As the product was readied to be shipped, you found problems with one of the components. This forces you to renegotiate with the part supplier to correct the defect or give you a price break on the product with the defective component or to undertake to supply a new product at a later date.
- *Nonperformance:* A furniture factory is not able to fulfill an agreement because of a fire at its warehouse. This requires renegotiation with the other party to invalidate the agreement. The renegotiation may nullify the deal, with no compensation due to the other party, or the firm may become liable for damages due to nonperformance.

Intradeal Renegotiation

The most common type of renegotiation occurs within the life of the contract due to the failure of one party to fulfill its obligations. In such cases, known as intradeal, one party seeks relief of its commitments. Another example of intradeal negotiation is when one party wishes to withdraw from the agreement due to its inability to meet the commitments. This type of renegotiation is often found in small- and medium-sized firms entering foreign markets for the first time. Their limited capacity to meet high-quality standards, to produce large quantities, and to meet strict delivery dates forces them to renegotiate the contract or to request cancellation.

Intradeal renegotiations run smoother when the initial agreement contains a clause that permits them. Acceptance at the outset that specific clauses may need to be renegotiated due to unforeseen events goes a long way toward reducing tensions and misunderstandings. In such cases, renegotiation is regarded as a legitimate activity in which both parties can engage in good faith.

The opportunity to renegotiate also arises when both parties establish specific dates or time frames to review an agreement. For example, when a long-term agreement is put in place, both parties may decide to meet at specified times on a regular basis to review the deal based on the experience gained so far. These meetings also identify issues that arise from changing market conditions.

Intradeal renegotiations are used particularly in countries where an agreement is considered to be more of a relationship than just a business deal. Inclusion of intradeal provisions formalizes their way of doing business; i.e., during times of change, parties to a negotiation should meet to decide how to cope with the change.

While periodic renegotiation is worthwhile, where deals extend over a length of time, it does have its downside. First, periodic renegotiation increases uncertainty of the terms agreed upon. Second, it raises suspicion that one of the parties might demand renegotiation using changed circumstances as the excuse to gain better terms for itself. Finally, it questions the validity of the agreement since it is open to renegotiation.

Postdeal Renegotiation

Renegotiations can also take place after an agreement expires. There are instances when one or both parties may decide to wait for the expiration of the contract before reentering into new negotiations. Postdeal negotiations may reflect a change in existing business strategies or may indicate that one party is no longer convinced of the benefits in continuing the business relationship.

In a way, the postdeal renegotiation is similar in process to the initial negotiation although there are some crucial differences. First, the two parties have a shared experience of knowing each other. Each party understands the other's goals, methods, intentions, and reliability, which become a significant input in renegotiation. Second, many concerns relative to risks and opportunities of the deal have been examined and need not be revisited in renegotiation. Third, parties have made investments in money, time, and commitment and are eager to continue the relationship if the result has been mutually satisfying.

Extradeal Renegotiation

This type of renegotiation amounts to dropping the existing agreement and inviting the other party to renegotiate. Generally, there is no provision in the agreement to resort to renegotiation, but if one party claims it is unable to implement the agreement, it may suggest renegotiations. The other party finds accepting renegotiation to be emotionally disturbing because its hopes of expected benefits are shattered. Furthermore, extradeal renegotiations often begin with a feeling of pessimism. In circumstances where renegotiation is the only viable option, parties reluctantly participate as unwilling partners. The environment surrounding extradeal renegotiation is marked with bad feelings and mistrust.

Both parties to the negotiation feel offended. One party thinks the other should appreciate its difficulties and, thus, fully cooperate in renegotiating the deal. The other party feels deprived of the profits expected from the agreement and believes it is being asked to give up something to which it had legal and moral right.

The extradeal renegotiation has a variety of implications for both parties. The party seeking renegotiation may lose credibility in the business community. On the contracts it renegotiates, the other party may demand stricter terms or penalties for noncompliance. The party yielding to renegotiation may gain the reputation of being weak and susceptible to pressure. This can encourage other parties on other agreements to demand renegotiation and better terms. The ripple effect of renegotiation can weaken the yielding party with regard to future deals with other parties.

APPROACHES TO RENEGOTIATION

The following approaches are available for conducting renegotiation.[4]

- *Clarify ambiguities in the existing agreement.* This approach entails appending clarification to ambiguities in the existing agreement rather than creating a new agreement. It accepts the validity of the current agreement, but changes are made in it to accommodate an emerging situation. For example, assume an exporter has negotiated to pay for air transportation of goods to a foreign destination. After a few months, there is a worldwide energy crisis, with the price of crude oil doubling every two weeks. The exporter finds that transportation costs have wiped out her profits, and she cannot afford to continue in business unless the importer agrees to renegotiation to relieve her from excessive air transportation costs. An amendment to the main contract is added with the importer absorbing part of the extra cost of airfreight. This nominal change is agreed upon without questioning the validity of the original contract.

- *Reinterpret key terms.* Sometimes terms in an agreement lead to different interpretations based on the background of the parties involved. Under this approach, renegotiation amounts to redefining these terms such that both parties attach the same meaning to them. For example, an exporter agreed to service the machines he supplied to an Asian importer free of charge for defects in manufacturing. The exporter was surprised to find that virtually all of the products sent to an Asian country were found to be defective, and he was obliged to service them, incurring a huge cost. Probing the problem, the exporter discovered that the machines were not adequately used, which resulted in frequent breakdowns. The basic product had no defects; it was the misuse that made them break down so frequently. The renegotiation made the change in the agreement, with the exporter remaining responsible for servicing defective machines as long as customers followed the instructions properly.

- *Waiver from one or more requirements of the agreement.* As a part of renegotiation, the burdened party is relieved from fulfilling some aspect of the agreement. For example, suppose the commission margin of a foreign deal is based on booking a minimum amount of business. Due to difficult economic conditions in the market, the "minimum amount of business" requirement may be waived for a year so the dealer can earn the commission.

- *Rewrite the agreement.* If all else fails, the parties may be forced into invalidating the existing agreement and renegotiating a new deal.

SUMMARY

With intense competition, greater outsourcing, and the increase of electronic commerce, renegotiating business contracts is likely to become the norm rather than the rule. Instead of looking at the implementation stage as a separate entity, successful business executives consider the follow-up phases to be an integral part of negotiating strategies.

Renegotiation of business deals may be necessary and can prove to be more profitable in the long term even if renegotiation offers some temporary disadvantages. Global managers know that relying on a contract alone is unlikely to resolve pending issues. Personal relationships and mutual trust are essential in order to build a solid foundation for repeat business in a highly competitive global environment. Both parties should keep in mind the long-term benefits of a business relationship when renegotiating existing agreements.

Experienced negotiators keep negotiating even after reaching agreement. In the end, satisfying and retaining current customers—by working together in solving problems through renegotiations—is less expensive and less time-consuming than seeking new partners or entering into costly litigation procedures. Skilled executives know that it is not the agreement alone that keeps a business going, but the strength of the relationship.

NOTES

1. See Jeswald W. Salacuse, *Making Global Deals: Negotiating in the International Marketplace* (Boston: Houghton Mifflin, 1991).
2. *Ibid*, p. 149.
3. James R. Pinnells, "Renegotiation Issues in International Sales Contracts," in *Readings in International Business Negotiations* (Geneva, Switzerland: International Trade Center—UNCTAD/WTO, 1997), pp. 125–131.
4. This section draws heavily from Jeswald W. Salacuse, *op. cit.*

9

Communication Skills for Effective Negotiations

Judge a man by his questions rather than by his answers.
—Voltaire

With a growing number of countries becoming actively engaged in world trade, resulting in intensified contacts between exporters and importers from different cultures, and with increased competition in both domestic and international markets, business executives are faced with a demanding environment for their commercial negotiations. In particular, those in small- and medium-size firms entering the global market for the first time need to master negotiating skills in a multicultural setting. Communication techniques are an important part of these skills. Negotiating is first and foremost about communications. It is a dialogue in which each person explains his or her position and listens to what the other person is saying. During this exchange of views, proposals are made and concessions are explored. The end result is intended to create added value for both parties.

In negotiations, communication occurs at two levels: the logical level (for example, a specific price offer) and the pragmatic level (for example, semantics, syntax, and style). The meaning of the communication received by the other party is a combination of logical and pragmatic messages. What matters is not simply what is said and how it is said, but also the inferred information intended, conveyed, or perceived. Thus, extreme care must be taken to control pragmatic messages. Many times negotiators are not aware of the potential of pragmatic miscommunication; therefore, they end up sending a wrong message—even with the best of intentions.

Communication between two negotiators tends to be more difficult and complex when it involves people from diverse cultural environments than when it involves people with similar backgrounds. For example, negotiators from a traditional culture often attach more importance to the way in which a proposal is made than to what is being said. In such discussions, what is not said may be just as important as what is said. In the opening minutes of the discussions, a negotiator has the opportunity to set the climate of the talks by making a short, clear statement of what is expected. Establishing credibility from the outset is essential if the negotiation is to progress smoothly. The first impression tends to influence the rest of the talks.

Negotiators discussing in a language other than their mother tongue should rely to a great extent on visual aids, printed materials, samples, and references to facts and figures. The old saying "A picture is worth a thousand words" is appropriate in this context. Furthermore, these negotiators should use simple, clear language with frequent questioning to ensure that the other person is following the discussions. Idioms, colloquialisms, and words with multiple meanings should be avoided. Similarly, certain words or phrases that can irritate the other party should be omitted. For example, phrases such as "To tell the truth," "I'll be honest with you," "I'll do my best," and "It's none of my business but . . ." convey a sense of distrust and make the other person more apprehensive and possibly less cooperative. Likewise, a negotiator should avoid stating or accepting from the other party the reply "No problem" when discussing a specific point. The negotiator should explain what he or she means or seek clarification about what the other party means.

In addition, one cannot assume that a message has been received and understood in the same way as the person speaking meant it to be. A typical example is when someone answers with a yes or no. In some cultures, *yes* means "Yes, I understood the question" or "Yes, I will consider it" or "Yes, I heard you." In certain cultural environments, the word *no* is uncommon and is replaced by a number of expressions to convey the message in an ambiguous or neutral manner.

In cultures in which conflict avoidance is predominant, the negotiator is unlikely to receive straightforward refusals to proposals, but will get vague responses instead. An inexperienced or unprepared negotiator may interpret these messages as relatively positive or may be led to believe that the other party is not ready to negotiate or is not in a position to make decisions. Vague replies should be followed by more discussion until it becomes clear what the problem is.

CROSS-CULTURAL COMMUNICATION-RELATED PROBLEMS

Communication with someone from a different culture can lead to two problems: perceptual bias and errors in processing information.[1]

Perceptual Bias

Perception is the process of attaching meaning to a message by the person who receives the communication. The receiver's own needs, desires, motivations, and personal experience create certain predispositions about the other party, which lead to perceptual bias, such as stereotyping, halo effects, selective perception, and projection.

Stereotyping: Stereotyping refers to assigning attributes to another party based on his or her membership in a particular society or group. Generally, the individual is assigned to a group based on very little perceptual information; then other characteristics of the person are derived or assumed. For example, at the first meeting, you see the negotiator, who happens to be in her fifties; you immediately think of her as "old" and perceive her to be conservative, risk-averse, and not likely to accept new ways of doing things. Cultural differences between negotiators significantly enhance stereotyping.

Halo Effect: The halo effect is the generalization made about numerous attributes of a person based on the knowledge of one attribute. For example, due to the halo effect, a negotiator may be judged as friendly, knowledgeable, and honest simply because he greets you with a smile in your language, following your custom. In reality, there may be no relationship between smiling and honesty, knowledge, and friendliness. Halo effects can be positive or negative. A good attribute leads to a positive halo effect and vice versa.

Halo effects are common in negotiations because people tend to form quick impressions of one another based on limited information such as appearance, group membership, and initial statements. Thus, matters such as clothing, a greeting, posture, tone of voice, eye contact, and so on, assume great significance.

Selective Perception: In terms of negotiations, selective perception means choosing certain information that supports one's earlier beliefs and leaving out other information from consideration. For example, based on initial impression, you judge another person as friendly and sensitive to your culture. Later in the day the person relates a joke that is not in good taste in your culture. According to selective perception, you tend to ignore the joke and remember only the information that reinforces your prior belief that the person has due regard for your cultural values.

Projection: Projection means using one's own attributes to describe the characteristics of another person. Projection occurs because people have a need to project their own self-concept. One person believes that honestly sharing the facts will enhance the process of negotiation. And that person assumes the other person has the same tendencies.

Errors in Processing Information

Negotiations involve sharing information. A person must correctly process the information received from the other party. Often, however, negotiators make systematic errors in processing the information. Such errors or cognitive biases can impede performance. Examples of such errors include the following:

- An irrational escalation of commitment (maintaining commitment to a chosen course of action even if it appears irrational)
- The mythical belief that issues under negotiation are a fixed pie (assuming the negotiation to be a zero-sum game of a win-lose exchange)
- The process of anchoring and adjusting in decision making (the effect of a faulty anchor or standard against which subsequent adjustments are made)
- Issue and problem framing (negotiators' perceptions of risk and behavior are determined by the manner in which a negotiation issue is framed)
- Availability of information (the information made available may be presented badly, leading to bias)
- Winner's curse (the feeling of discomfort generated by a quick settlement of the issue)
- Negotiator's overconfidence (leading him or her to accept less or give up more)
- The law of small numbers (drawing conclusions based on limited experience)
- Self-serving biases (justifying one's errors to unavoidable circumstances)
- The tendency to ignore others' cognitions (ignoring the perceptions and thoughts of the other party)
- The process of reactive devaluation (attaching little value to the concessions made by the other party)

IMPROVING COMMUNICATION IN NEGOTIATION

Communication is the core of negotiation. If communication is disrupted or distorted, negotiation fails. Parties have difficulty coming to an agreement if the communication process breaks down. This is true even when the goals of both parties are compatible. There are, however, techniques for improving the communication in negotiation. These include listening, asking questions, reversing roles, and ensuring clear understanding.

Listening

A major weakness of inexperienced negotiators in any cultural context is their inability to listen carefully to what the other person is saying. Their main concern is usually to present their case and then to counter objections made by the other party. This approach can only lead to a monologue, rather than a real discussion.

The perception that good negotiators talk a lot and dominate the discussions to achieve optimum results is false. In reality, skilled negotiators spend more time listening and asking questions to ensure that they fully understand the other side than they do talking. The ability to listen effectively is fundamental to the success of any business negotiation.

Good listeners do more than listen; they think, analyze, and assess what the other party is saying. They hear everything that is being said, not only what is important to them. By listening attentively, a negotiator can obtain valuable information about the other party and eventually gain more negotiating power. Effective listening contributes to identifying alternatives and options not considered during the preparatory phase. For example, by taking care to listen to an importer's needs and concerns, an exporter can adapt his or her offer and make counterproposals to meet the exporter's requirements.

In the context of listening, a major mistake is concentrating on what to say next instead of listening to what the other person is saying. Much useful information can be lost this way. Negotiators are thus prevented from exploring new options and identifying possible concessions, thereby slowing down the momentum of the discussions. Furthermore, reading between the lines is necessary to understand what the other person is saying, particularly among negotiators from different cultures. A negotiator should encourage the other party by indicating his or her willingness to listen longer by saying "Yes" or "Please go on" or by asking questions for clarification.

Good listening habits include observing body language. Studies on the effectiveness of communication reveal that words account for only 7 percent of the message being received versus the voice accounting for 38 percent and body language for 55 percent. For example, movements such as nodding one's head, inspecting a sample, taking notes, and moving the chair forward indicate interest in what is being said.

An experienced negotiator spends more than 50 percent of the time listening; the remaining time is used for talking and asking questions. By developing good listening skills and asking relevant questions, both parties can move closer to a negotiated agreement.

Three forms of listening can be distinguished:[2] passive listening, acknowledgment, and active listening.

- *Passive listening* amounts to receiving a message without providing any feedback. It tends to show one's complete lack of interest in what the other person is saying.
- *Acknowledgment* involves some interest in the information delivered. The acknowledgment occurs through nodding one's head, maintaining eye contact, or interjecting responses (such as "I see," "interesting," "sure," "go on," and "please continue.") Such acknowledgment encourages the other party to continue sending messages.
- *Active listening* means being thoroughly involved in the messages received and carefully analyzing and attaching meaning to the information contained in the messages. Active listening is characterized by placing greater emphasis on listening than on speaking, responding to personal rather than abstract points (i.e., feelings, beliefs, and positions rather than abstract ideas), following the other party rather than leading him or her into areas to explore, clarifying what the other party says without diverting attention away from what one thinks or feels, and responding to the feelings the other party expresses.

A good negotiator should engage in active listening. Using the skill encourages the other party to speak more fully about his or her feelings, views, and priorities. In this process, the other party is likely to state his or her position, which often leads to successful negotiation.

Asking Questions

In international business negotiations, one of the most important skills is the ability to ask good questions. By asking relevant questions, negotiators can obtain valuable information from the other party as well as test various assumptions they made when preparing for the discussions. During the preparatory phase, negotiators collect information, but not all data and facts may be available; negotiators need to supplement this information during the talks. A negotiator should not ask questions to show his or her knowledge of the subject or to impress the other party. Such an attitude can easily lead to a monologue. Instead, questions should be used to obtain information from the other party, to exchange concessions, and to move toward agreement. Therefore, they should be used selectively and they should be timely.

Good questions must be prepared in advance. For example, in the initial phase of the business discussions, exporters present their offers. The importers are most likely to want more details about the product specifications, after-sales service, payment conditions, delivery schedules, quantity requirements, price discounts, and so on. Information about such details is best obtained by asking relevant questions.

Broadly, questions can be classified as open-ended questions and probing or conditional questions. *Open questions* allow respondents to talk freely about their needs. In such situations, listening to the answers is extremely important as the essential elements must be sorted out, notes need to be taken of the key points, and critical information must be used to phrase succeeding questions. Open-ended questions are useful for clarifying specific points, for seeking details, for obtaining missing information, as well as for validating assumptions. For example, if a buyer refers to a product as being of inferior quality, the seller should ask what standards the buyer is applying, insisting on specifics.

A typical question an exporter is likely to hear after stating price is, "Can you do better than that?" This type of question should be answered with another question instead of a concession. For example, the exporter should reply by asking for clarification, such as, "What is meant by *better?*" or "Better than what?" At that stage, the importer may say that a competitor is offering better terms. Again, the exporter should ask for more details about the conditions and terms. These questions should continue until the exporter has a clear understanding of what the importer is looking for. At one point, the exporter must state his or her offer and stress that the offer is not only different from that of the competition, it is also better. Generally, the importer seeks the best product from the most reputable supplier at a price that is lower than that of other products being considered. In such cases, it is important for the exporter to clarify the offers from the competition and to ensure that both parties are comparing similar products and referring to identical quality, packaging requirements, performance guarantee, and so on.

Before asking a question, particularly in the early phase of the discussions, a negotiator should ask permission to do so. If the other party agrees, he or she is most likely to be more cooperative in replying to the question. Another benefit when the answer is yes is that the discussions begin with a positive answer, which is conducive to a productive atmosphere.

After a series of questions that give both the parties a good idea of what each other wants, the discussions enter into an exchange of proposals and counterproposals. This requires shifting from open questions to *conditional questions*. These are probing questions that seek specific information for repackaging of the proposal. Some of the most useful questions are, "What ... if" and "if ... then." For example, the exporter can say, "What if we agree to a two-year contract? Would you give us exclusive distribution rights in your territory?" This question permits one party to make a proposal subject to the acceptance of one or more conditions. The other party can accept the offer, make a counterproposal, or reject the offer. No harm is done in case of rejection. The other negotiator can continue making further conditional offers until common ground is reached.

An example of such conditional questions from the viewpoint of exporters and importers is provided in Figure 9-1. These questions illustrate how one party can make conditional offers while asking reciprocity through concessions. The other party can counter the offers with his or her own conditions. The conditional offer allows the negotiating process to move forward until common ground is identified and agreement is in sight.

Another advantage of using conditional questions is that they do not bind either party to a specific offer and do not require unilateral concessions by one party. Moreover, by countering a conditional proposal, the other party is indirectly supplying timely and valuable information that can be put to good use in succeeding phases of the discussions. For example, the exporter may counter the proposal with his or her own offer: "We would be ready to give you exclusivity provided you agree to a three-year contract." The two parties are exchanging information as well as their principal interests and priorities.

FIGURE 9-1
Example of Useful Questions When Negotiating

For the exporter or supplier:
- What do you think of our proposal?
- Why don't you give us a trial order to see for yourself our capacity to produce to your specifications?
- If you waive the penalty clause, would you be ready to accept ... ?
- If we maintain last year's prices, would you place an order by ... ?
- From where are you getting your supplies?
- If we guarantee weekly shipping, would you agree to ... ?
- Yes, I understand what you are saying. However, would you be ready to consider ... ?
- Yes, we could meet your additional requirements. But would you be willing to meet the extra costs?

For the importer or buyer:
- Can you provide us with the necessary additional information so we can reconsider your offer?
- Can you tell me more about your company's manufacturing process?
- If we give you assistance in this technical aspect, would you agree to ... ?
- If we modify our specifications, will you consider ... ?
- What is your exact production capacity?
- What are your quality assurance procedures?
- If we agree to a long-term contract, would you be ready to ... ?
- Your product is fine, but your prices are not competitive. Would you be willing to review your pricing structure?
- What is your price for a larger order?

Source: Claude Cellich, "Communication Skills for Negotiation," *International Trade FORUM*, 3/1997, p. 25.

This example also illustrates the conditional offer; both sides do not need to say no or cause embarrassment or loss of face, but can continue to negotiate cooperatively.

The use of "what if" is most appropriate when objecting to an offer. By responding with a conditional counterproposal, instead of rejecting it outright with a "no," a negotiator gives the other party the opportunity to provide more details about his or her offer. This exchange of offers and counterproposals eventually leads to the areas important to each side.

A negotiator should prepare a list of key questions in advance since this enhances the effectiveness of the negotiation. The questions should be well thought-out. They should generally be asked to obtain additional information currently unavailable and to test assumptions made when the negotiator was developing negotiating strategies and tactics. These questions should include finding out what is and is not negotiable, what is important to the other party, how badly the other party needs the transaction, and what the other party's minimum and maximum limits are. To gain this information, a negotiator should complete a thorough analysis of his or her strengths and weaknesses along with those of the competition.

Reversing Roles. The role reversal technique implies the negotiator putting himself or herself in the shoes of the other party and, then, contemplating various aspects of the negotiation. This will give the negotiator the opportunity to more completely understand the position of the other party. For example, another party may insist on certain terms you find unreasonable. But self-reversal role-playing allows you to appreciate the other party's position of asking for the terms. Subsequently, you can come up with a solution acceptable to both of you; i.e., modifying your position while responding to the needs of the other party. This way your respective positions become compatible, leading to the agreement.

Ensuring Clear Understanding

Techniques that can help provide clear understanding in negotiations include restating, rephrasing, reframing, and summarizing. Restatement of the other person's comments encourages clear communication between the parties. Repeating the main issues in different ways by rephrasing them is helpful during the discussions. For example, a negotiator can rephrase what he or she just heard by saying, "If I understand you correctly, what you are really saying is ..." The negotiator expresses in his or her own words the understanding of the point just made. This technique acknowledges the other person's point of view as well as indicates what was heard.

Reframing is also a useful tool for getting discussions back to the main issues. By reframing, a negotiator recasts what the other party said in a way that redirects attention of the discussions to the core theme that needs to be addressed.

Summarizing is considered a useful tool for bringing negotiations to a close. It consists of one person presenting in his or her own words the points agreed to and asking the other side to approve them. Precise note taking throughout the discussion can serve as the basis for summarizing. If the summaries are accurate, both parties can concentrate on the remaining issues or proceed toward finalizing the agreement. The person presenting the summaries must be careful to be factual.

NONVERBAL COMMUNICATION

Nonverbal communication refers to meaning given to behavior beyond words. It includes body language, facial expressions, physical appearance, space, time, and touch. In the context of cross-cultural negotiations, even when people do not speak a word, through nonverbal communication such as appearance, facial expression, and use of time, they send certain messages to another party. The other party receives the messages and attaches meanings to them. Unfortunately, the meanings a person attaches to nonverbal communication vary from culture to culture. Thus, without intending to do so, a negotiator nonverbal communication can send a wrong message to the other party, inadvertently harming the negotiations. Therefore, a negotiator must be aware of his or her nonverbal cues to avoid transmitting false or unilateral messages to the other party. After all, 60 percent to 70 percent of meaning in social interactions is interpreted from nonverbal cues.[3]

Figure 9-2 lists the different types of nonverbal behavior. All of these behaviors have an impact on negotiations, as illustrated below.

Body Language

Body movements vary from culture to culture. Consider the following conversation in a hotel lobby with a Japanese businessperson asking the North American about the hotel.

The American responds with a well-known "A-OK" ring gesture. To the Japanese, this means "money," and he concludes that the hotel is expensive. The Tunisian onlooker thinks that the American is telling the Japanese that he is a worthless rogue and is going to kill him. But the Frenchman, overhearing the question, thinks the hotel is cheap because the ring gesture in France means "zero."[4]

FIGURE 9-2
Different Types of Nonverbal Behavior

---

1. Body Language: gestures, body movement, facial movement, and eye contact
2. Vocalics (also called paralanguage): tone, volume, and sounds that are not words
3. Touching
4. Use of Space
5. Use of Time
6. Physical Appearance: body shape and size, clothing, jewelry
7. Artifacts: objects associated with a person, such as office size, office furniture, a personal library, and books.

Aspects of body language vary depending on where people are negotiating. Consider the case of eye contact. In the United States, maintaining eye contact is important because this shows a person is interested in what is being said. In Japan, however, anything more than brief eye contact is considered rude, amounting to invasion of privacy of the other party.

Vocalics

In the United States, people often raise their voice when they get upset. In China, on the other hand, people maintain prolonged silence when they are unhappy, rather than speaking in a loud tone. A wise negotiator should try to behave normally without using this aspect of vocalics to his or her advantage. For example, if a negotiator is not accustomed to pounding on the table to emphasize a point, the negotiator should not do so simply because he or she heard this would strengthen his or her argument in the context of the other party's culture. The best advice to follow is to be yourself.

Touching

In some cultures, people rarely touch each other. In other cultures, touching is common. For example, physical closeness between men is not commonplace in the United States. But men holding hands and hugging each other are gestures of friendship in some societies. In Latin America, a warm embrace, called *abrazo*, is common among well-acquainted businessmen, but is not found in other parts of the world.

What should a negotiator do when touching practices vary worldwide? The best thing to do is to avoid touching at all. This way he or she avoids doing the wrong thing. Just shaking hands is the safest way to avoid the touching dilemma.

Use of Space

In negotiations, space refers to the distance at which people feel comfortable when interacting with another person. In some parts of the world, such as Latin America, Italy, France, and the Middle East, people maintain short distances. The Americans, Germans, Chinese, and Japanese feel comfortable with more space. In addition, such factors as age, status, and gender of the opposite party affect the comfort distance.[5]

When a person with a preference for more space interacts with a person who likes less space, the latter ofter keeps coming closer to the first person to reduce the distance. The first person then begins to move back to maintain his or her comfort distance. Such a situation becomes very embarrassing for the parties involved.

What should be done when two negotiators have different perspectives on distance? The rule of thumb is to let the host set the distance limit, with the guest adapting to the cultural traits of the host.

Time

Different cultures have varying attitudes about time. In the United States, time is a precious commodity; the importance of the issue. The U.S. attitude toward time is common among Anglo-Saxons. In many societies, time is a boundless resource. It need not be distributed into time slots. People in such societies are relaxed about schedules and deadlines. If something cannot be accomplished today, it can always be accomplished tomorrow.

In negotiations, the time attitude becomes relevant with regard to three areas: keeping appointments, pursuing the meeting agenda, and devoting time to unrelated items. People who attach more importance to time like to start the meeting on time, like to discuss each item one at a time rather than moving from one issue to the other without any order, and prefer to avoid "wasting" time on unrelated matters. One type of attitude toward time is no better than the other. Both parties should adapt to the needs of the other through mutual respect and understanding.

Physical Appearance

There is a suitable business attire in each society. A person appears properly dressed following the professional perspectives of his or her society. A negotiator can expect the other party to dress according to his or her culture. No adaptation is necessary. A negotiator respects the way the other party appears and the other party respects the way the negotiator presents himself or herself. Not all people are alike. They dress differently and have different customs with regard to physical appearance.

Artifacts

In the United States, a large corner office on the top floor communicates status. Status symbols are common in other cultures too. A guest should abstain from criticizing the host about his or her artifacts. An executive may make positive comments about something with which he or she is familiar, but should otherwise ignore bothersome artifacts. For example, if an executive finds a picture on an office wall to be in bad taste, he or she should just ignore it instead of characterizing the other party based on the picture.

USE OF INTERPRETERS

Interpreters are the people who translate words from one language to another and who communicate them in the cultural context of one party to the other. Professional interpreters are highly qualified; they not only know both languages well, but also are knowledgeable about the two cultures. As a general rule, a negotiator should not communicate in the language of the other party unless he or she knows it extremely well. With a limited knowledge of the other party's language, the negotiator will be focusing his or her attention more on the language than on the substance of the negotiation.

Thus, when two parties speak different languages, they must hire the services of interpreters. The interpreter hired must be well versed in the language as well as the culture of the other party. In addition, when interpreters are present, both parties are obliged to speak slowly and to carefully repeat the important points. This means more time must be allocated to the negotiations. When negotiating through an interpreter, the parties should avoid the use of jargon, slang, or idioms common to their language; speak in small sentences; and not interrupt. Lastly, when a person speaks, he or she should address the other party, not the interpreters.

The following suggestions can be used for making effective use of an interpreter:[6]

1. A negotiation team should hire its own interpreter. Except in cases where special reasons for trust exist, do not rely on the other side's interpreter, unless someone on your team understands the language and can check the translation. Before hiring an interpreter, try to determine his or her skill and experience from independent, reliable sources.
2. Before negotiations actually begin, hold a briefing meeting with the interpreter to explain the nature of the deal, what you want in the way of translation, and why you want it. For example, if you want a word-for-word translation rather than a summary, make your requirements clear.

3. Guard against interpreters who, because of personal interest or ego, try to take control of the negotiations or slant them in a particular way. This risk may be present if the interpreter also works as a middleman, agent, or business consultant.

4. When negotiating, speak in short, bite-size statements and pause after each one to give the interpreter a chance to translate your words.

5. Plan each statement carefully so that it is clear; devoid of abbreviations, slang, and business jargon; and delivered slowly. Constantly ask yourself: How can my statements be misunderstood? One inexperienced American executive forgot this rule when he proudly told his Saudi counterparts that he represented a "blue chip company." This drew quizzical looks from both the interpreter and the Saudi executives. The American then launched into a long discussion of the expression "blue chip," only to be told that Saudi Arabia did not allow gambling.

6. Interpretation is difficult and extremely tiring work, so give your interpreter ample opportunity to take periodic breaks.

7. Treat the interpreters, both yours and the other side's, with the respect due professionals. Because the other side's interpreter speaks your language and presumably has insights into your psyche and culture that his employers do not, they may seek his advice about you—whether you are trustworthy, telling the truth, seem honest. If you have slighted or offended the other side's interpreter in some way during the negotiation, he or she may not give the other side the kind of advice that you would like them to hear. Conversely, if you develop a friendly relationship with the interpreter, he or she may provide you with much useful information about the other side, as one Japanese interpreter did when he let it slip that the head of his delegation believed he would lose face if he returned to Tokyo without a contract.

SUMMARY

To negotiate, a person must communicate. In negotiations, communication occurs at a logical level (for example, a specific price offer) and a pragmatic level (for example, semantics, syntax, and style). Communication between negotiators is more complex when the negotiators belong to different cultures even if the discussion takes place in the same language.

Cross-cultural communication leads to two problems: perceptual bias (i.e., attaching meaning to a message received by a person) and errors in processing information (e.g., maintaining an irrational escalation of commitment, considering negotiation to be a zero-sum game, using faulty standards, among others). These problems can be overcome by using the following techniques: listening, questioning, reversing roles, and incurring clear understanding. Three types of listening are passive listening, acknowledgment, and active listening. A good negotiator should engage in active listening. By asking relevant questions, negotiators can obtain valuable information. Two types of questions are open-ended questions and probing or conditional questions. In the context of negotiations, both types of questions make sense depending on the type of information sought. Reversing roles means putting oneself in the position of the other party and examining various aspects of the negotiations. This helps the negotiator understand the position of his or her counterpart. To seek clear understanding in communications, the parties should employ restating, rephrasing, reframing, and summarizing.

Nonverbal communication is equally important in cross-cultural negotiations. Even when a person does not speak a word, his or her appearance; facial expressions; and use of time, space, and touch send certain messages to the other party. Nonverbal communication takes place through body language, vocalics, touching, use of space and time, physical appearance, and artifacts. A person should control his or her behavior related to these matters in order to send the right message to the other party. Finally, if the two parties speak different languages, it is desirable to hire the services of interpreters.

NOTES

1. Discussion in this chapter draws heavily from Roy J. Lewicki, David M. Saunders, and John W. Minton, *Essentials of Negotiation*, 2nd Edition (New York: McGraw-Hill, 1997), pp. 114–122.
2. *Ibid*, pp. 124–127.
3. Donald W. Hendon, Rebecca A. Hendon, and Paul Herbig, *Cross-Cultural Business Negotiations* (Westport, CT: Quorum Books, 1996), pp. 63–64.
4. Michael Kublin, *International Negotiating* (Binghamton, NY: The Haworth Press, Inc., 1995), pp. 119–125.
5. Donald W. Klopf, *Intercultural Encounters: The Fundamentals of Intercultural Communications* (Englewood, CO: Morton, 1991), p. 197.
6. Jeswald W. Salacuse, *Making Global Deals: Negotiating in the International Marketplace* (Boston: Houghton Mifflin, 1991), pp. 31–33.

10

Demystifying the Secrets of Power Negotiations

Let us never negotiate out of fear. But let us never fear to negotiate.—John F. Kennedy

---

Chapter 2 passingly mentioned various forms of power and how power impacts negotiations. This chapter further explores the subject of power. The chapter is divided into four sections. The first section discusses the sources of personal negotiating power. The second section focuses on estimating negotiating power. The third section is devoted to using power effectively. In the final section, suggestions are made for increasing power.

SOURCES OF POWER

Negotiation power has a lot to do with perception. Although power can be real or perceived, what is important is how others see the negotiator. If the other party thinks the negotiator has power, he or she can negotiate from a position of strength. It is commonly believed that executives having personal charisma or representing larger firms have negotiation power. This view is based on the assumption that, due to their status or because they come from bigger companies, only executives have the power to achieve their goals, often at the expense of the other party. This, however, may not be true. Generally, the party who comes to the negotiation thoroughly prepared is the one likely to optimize the outcome. Successful negotiators develop their power based on superior preparation and excellent communication skills instead of a reliance on positional or visible power.

Although skilled negotiators rely on both positional and personal power, they tend to give more attention to personal power when preparing for discussions, interacting with the other party, and reaching agreement.[1] Personal negotiating power comes from a variety of sources, discussed below. The core of power is:

- Information and expertise—presenting information to prove one's viewpoint or pushing one's viewpoint based on special skills, knowledge, or experience.
- Control over resources—influencing the other party through the control of factors of production.
- Location in the organization—leveraging one's position in the organization to require concurrence from the other party.

Knowing Various Aspects of the Business Is Power

Knowing the company business and industry well and showing expertise about the issues being discussed projects an image of power. Because doing business on a global scale is becoming more complex, mastering all of the various aspects provides negotiating power. If there are areas about which an executive does not have much knowledge, he or she can call on staff members to join in the discussions or have them provide a briefing in advance about key issues. The Internet and mobile phones allow executives to reach company experts without incurring the costs of traveling. In case an executive does not have in-house expertise in a specific area, he or she can hire a consultant for the duration of the negotiations. What is important is to have this expertise readily available during the discussions. Displaying expertise at the right time enhances an executive's reputation and gains the executive respect in the eyes of the other party while advancing his or her own goals. The more expertise you demonstrate tactfully, the more power the other party is likely to give you.[2] However, overdoing it can become counterproductive.

Knowing the Other Party Is Power

Knowing the other party well increases one's negotiating power. The more an executive knows about the other party's interests, motivation, and negotiating style and what is important to him or her, the greater the negotiating power.

Effective negotiators put themselves in the other person's shoes when preparing their own strategies. If an executive has been dealing with the same party for some time, he or she probably has a fairly good idea of what to expect. Even in such cases, however, it is wise to consider the changes that have taken place since the last negotiations. For example, if a new competitor has entered the market and is making headway in the market or if new safety standards are being introduced that could affect product demand, the negotiator should revise his or her strategy.

When negotiating with a new party for the first time, the task is more demanding, time-consuming, and risky. In view of the difficulties of getting reliable information, a negotiator may need to make certain assumptions during the preparatory phase. However, these assumptions should be checked out during the initial discussions. The best way to test assumptions is to turn them into questions to be raised when meeting the other party. If a negotiator's early assumptions were incorrect, he or she should ask for a recess to readjust the negotiating plan.

Knowing the other party assumes the negotiator has a clear understanding of his or her negotiating style, whether it is task- or relationship-oriented. On the basis of preparation, the negotiator should be able to predict to some extent the negotiating style likely to be used by the other party. For example, if the other party is relationship-oriented, a negotiator can look forward to accommodating strategies and nonthreatening moves. Of course, the likelihood is that the other party relies on a combination of both approaches. If a negotiator's style differs significantly from that of the other party, the negotiator needs to find out how to best meet his or her own objectives by adapting the strategy and developing appropriate tactics. This advance groundwork provides greater negotiation power.

Knowing the Competition Is Power

Knowing the competition is key to making preparations. Unless a negotiator has an in-depth understanding of how he or she compares to competitors, including relative strengths and weaknesses, he or she does not have much bargaining power. Having such knowledge allows a negotiator to plan a strategy that will protect his or her interests as well as contribute to optimizing his or her goals.

If a negotiator has only limited knowledge about what the competition is doing, all the other party needs to say is, "We can get a better deal from the competition" to put the negotiator on the defensive. When the negotiator is prepared, he or she can neutralize this threat by justifying his or her position with valid arguments. Otherwise, the negotiator may be forced to make concessions to meet competitive pressures, without finding out what the competition is really offering. Even worse is the fact that the negotiator may begin making unnecessary concessions without receiving reciprocity.

As part of the preparation, a negotiator must find out whether the other party plans to negotiate with him or her only or with competitors too. If the other party plans to negotiate with several parties simultaneously, the negotiator must decide whether to get involved. If a negotiator is confident about the talks, he or she should devote all resources to preparing thoroughly. Otherwise, the negotiator should withdraw from the discussions. To avoid being compared to competitors, the negotiator must develop first-rate proposals to differentiate his or her company from them. In fact, negotiators can dominate the negotiations when they know more about competitors than the other party does—and when they know more about competitors than the competitors know about them.

Obtaining information about competition can be difficult, particularly when entering new markets. In international business, these difficulties can be a real handicap due to the lack of readily available data and its validity. Language and customs further complicate the gathering of relevant information. Experienced negotiators maintain a network of contacts and increasingly rely on the Internet to obtain up-to-date information about the competition and about latest market developments.

Knowing the competition in the market is crucial to achieving optimum results. Although being well informed is power, knowing how one compares to the competition provides "extra" bargaining power.

Developing Options and Alternatives Extends Power

Going into negotiations with a set of alternatives gives a negotiator bargaining power. Having several firms interested in doing business with his or her company puts the negotiator in a strong negotiating position. Even if you have weak alternatives, it may be sufficient to give you power as long as the other party is not aware of how strong or weak your alternatives are.[3]

Options provide leverage and increase a negotiator's chances of meeting the other party's interests as well as his or her own. When developing options, the negotiator can consider a wide range of possibilities, such as design modifications, packaging alterations, payment terms, faster delivery dates, quality improvements, increase of length of warranty, and proposed performances clauses. The more options and alternatives a negotiator develops, the greater the chances of reaching mutually beneficial outcomes.

Setting the Agenda Is Power

The party setting the agenda automatically gains power. For this reason, experienced negotiators propose to prepare it. By doing so, negotiators make sure their interests are well served. A critical review of the proposed agenda is crucial because it provides useful information: meeting time, place of the meeting, people expected to be in attendance, and the issues to be discussed. Sequence of the issues indicates the relative importance given to them by the initiating party. If a negotiator receives a proposed agenda from the other party for approval or information, he or she should request changes even if the draft is acceptable. By insisting on amendments, the negotiator becomes a real partner in the negotiation, thus gaining valuable bargaining power. Extra care is called for when reviewing the other party's agenda because what is not mentioned is often more important than what is written.

Negotiating in One's Own Environment Is Power

Power means the ability to influence others, and the best place to do so is in one's own environment. That is why successful negotiators propose to have the discussions at their site. Negotiating in a familiar place offers several advantages, particularly when doing business on a global scale. The main benefits are the ability to control the logistics (such as selecting the room, making seating arrangements, and overseeing planned interruptions) and access to staff, experts, and files. In addition, a negotiator does not suffer from jet lag and other discomforts from working in unfamiliar surroundings. It also provides the opportunity to showcase the company facilities.

Unfortunately, negotiating from one's power base is not fully utilized by executives from small and medium enterprises. Because they have limited travel budgets and staff, they should invite their foreign parties to visit them and offer to arrange the negotiations at their own site. Providing services such as booking hotels, facilitating visas, and arranging for cultural and social activities would place them in a dominant position to lead the discussions and control the environment.

When the negotiating parties decide to hold the discussions in a neutral location, the selected site should really be neutral. For example, if the other party has a subsidiary there, the location is not neutral.

Having Time to Negotiate and Setting Deadlines Is Power

Executives who have time to plan and interact with the other party gain valuable negotiation power. This power can be even greater if one party is under time constraints but the other is not. Negotiations do require substantial time for preparation and for the interface discussions. When a party enters a negotiation under time constraints, he or she may try to skip the early steps of discussions and rush into concessions in order to expedite the process. By doing so, he or she fails to identify the real needs of the other party, including priorities, and fails to build any rapport. On the other hand, the party without time constraints is patient, is comfortable with silence, listens to proposals, accepts concessions, and lets time run out. Consequently, the party with time on hand gains initial information, makes fewer concessions, and eventually takes control of the discussions.

When dealing in different cultures where the notion and value of time differs from that of the negotiator, it becomes crucial to set aside appropriate time to conclude the agreement. Likewise, a complex negotiation or an important business deal calls for the allocation of more time than a routine deal.

A golden rule among effective negotiators is that if you do not have time to negotiate, you should not enter into discussions; otherwise, you will be negotiating against yourself by giving up power to the other party. However, a negotiator can increase negotiating power by setting deadlines according to his or her own time requirements and having them approved by the other party. If, on the other hand, a negotiator does not believe the deadline suggested by the other party meets his or her timing, the negotiator should ask for an extension. If the other party refuses to do so, the negotiator should ask for clarification. If the explanations given are unsatisfactory, the negotiator should insist on rescheduling the negotiations to a date and for a duration that are acceptable to him or her. If the other party refuses to change the timing or is not providing satisfactory answers, the negotiator should reassess his or her strategy or find another party with whom to conduct business. By agreeing to work under tight deadlines to satisfy the other party's time schedule, a negotiator is, in effect, giving away negotiating power to the other side.

Listening Is Power

As negotiation is essentially an exchange of information between two or more parties, the party with superior communication skills gains power. Experience shows that most negotiations fail due to poor communications, particularly due to lack of active and sustainable listening. This is where negotiators can acquire considerable power.[4] Nothing is more important in negotiation than a negotiator letting the other party know he or she is listening. Once the other party realizes that fact, he or she will begin paying attention to what the negotiator has to say. In fact, good listeners send signals to the other party that they are interested in what is being said by asking clarifying questions, paraphrasing, reframing, acknowledging, observing body language, and paying attention to the feeling behind the words. Successful negotiators avoid using negative expressions, as these are likely to lead to breakdowns in the discussions. Only by encouraging understanding and exchanging information can both parties reach the final stage of negotiation.

A good listener also knows the power of silence. At times, the less a person says, the more power he or she receives from others. When asking questions, a negotiator must allow the other party sufficient time to think through the response before replying. Too often, due to impatience, the asking party provides the answer or moves on to another question. This is bad manners and may lead to misunderstanding on the part of the other party.

By improving your listening skills, you are putting yourself in an advantageous position to fully explore how best you can reach mutually beneficial outcomes.[5] It is worth remembering that listening brings parties together while arguing pulls them apart. That is why effective negotiators spend most of their time listening attentively to the other party and taking notes while less successful negotiators talk most of the time. When a negotiator can smile when listening and make the other person feel good, his or her communication power is that much more effective.

Knowing the Bottom Line Is Power

One negotiation power that is often underrated and frequently misunderstood is that of walking away. This is based on one's resistance point or bottom line. In other words, there is a limit beyond which it is no longer worthwhile to continue the negotiations. The bottom line must be based on a thorough calculation of real cost as well as opportunity cost. Knowing his or her bottom line coupled with alternative options to fall back on gives a negotiator greater bargaining power. Unfortunately, this type of power is not fully used by executives from smaller firms because of their inability to take the time to develop their bottom line and alternatives. Not knowing his or her bottom line only places a negotiator in a weak position, which may result in accepting outcomes that prove to be unprofitable in the long run. When a negotiator does not know his or her resistance limit, he or she may end up making unacceptable concessions. Knowing his or her bottom line and having the ability to walk away due to better alternatives influences a negotiator's overall approach and places him or her in a powerful position to lead the discussions.

Decision Making/Commitment Power

A type of power that is often neglected is the power to commit. This is a definite advantage when negotiating with larger organizations. With increasing global competition, greater reliance on suppliers, and just-in-time management, negotiators having the power to commit in the closing moments may well walk away with the deal. In contrast, negotiators from larger firms, besides being overconfident when dealing with smaller companies, may have limited authority, needing to seek prior approval from senior management. Not being outguessed by superiors or by committees gives negotiators from smaller firms an advantage because as more people get involved in decision making (whether directly or indirectly), the more delays can be expected. These delays not only slow down the process, but also lead to reopening of the negotiations with the introduction of new proposals, requests for more concessions, or involvement of new players. Moreover, dissension and disagreement among members is likely in larger teams, which can derail the negotiations over time.

Having the power to commit in the closing phase of a negotiation is critical. The party that is able to decide and commit on the spot gains power. Executives negotiating in cultures where quick decisions are associated with successful management performance are likely to find themselves in a dominant position when they have the power to commit.

ESTIMATING NEGOTIATING POWER

The previous section explored the role of power in negotiation. Before entering into negotiations, it is useful to estimate your own power as well as the power of the other party. This can be achieved by completing Figure 10-1, using the following ratings:

1. Do not have power
2. Have limited power
3. Do not know the power
4. Have some power
5. Have a great deal of negotiating power

When rating yourself, try to avoid the rating of 3, as it will fail to indicate a relative strength or weakness. Even when you do not have much information about the other party, try to estimate the extent of his or her power to the best of your knowledge.

If your score is 40 or better, you have negotiating power. If your score is between 35 and 39, you are in a relatively strong position with some weaknesses. If your score is below 34, your negotiating power is limited; you are likely to find yourself in a weak position, unless the other party is even weaker.

If you find that the other party has all the power and you have none, you should seriously reconsider entering into the

FIGURE 10-1

POWER ESTIMATE GRID		
Sources of Power	**Yours**	**Theirs**
Understanding the other party		
Knowing the competition		
Having expertise		
Having options and alternatives		
Setting the agenda		
Using home court advantage		
Having time		
Using listening and questioning skills		
Walking away/bottom line		
Being able to commit		
Totals		

negotiation. In such a case, it is better to postpone meeting with the other party until you can equalize your power or to find another party where you have a better chance to achieve your goals. For this reason, it is to your advantage to have more than one party interested in doing business with you.

By comparing your scores with those of the other party, you can gain a better understanding of what power you have and where you need to improve. If your overall score is less than that of the other party, look for those individual types of power where you have a lower score and find out how you can improve it.

BEING AN EFFECTIVE NEGOTIATOR

Effective negotiators do well because they are able to control the discussions, can offer the other party plenty of alternatives that will satisfy their needs, and are committed to reaching mutually beneficial outcomes.[6] A negotiator's personal power comes in handy in this endeavor. Listed below are a wide range of personal attributes that are found in most successful negotiators. You should review these attributes to determine whether you are an effective negotiator. If you possess most of these attributes, you have what it takes to be a successful negotiator. If you wish to further improve your negotiation skills, begin developing your personal power by reviewing your past experiences.

- Shows patience
- Prepares an agenda
- Has an opening range
- Tests assumptions
- Maintains flexibility
- Listens and asks relevant questions
- Prepares negotiation strategies and tactics
- Knows which concessions to make and to obtain in return
- Can withstand pressure
- Has developed arguments against possible objections
- Has power to make decisions
- Knows the firm's bottom line
- Has a good idea of the other party's BATNA
- Has developed multiple options and alternatives
- Displays creativity in finding mutually beneficial solutions
- Observes body language
- Is sensitive to cultural diversity
- Takes notes and summaries frequently

- Is willing to walk away
- Knows how and when to negotiate

SUMMARY

Generally, preparing well, acquiring negotiation know-how, improving communication skills, and learning from past mistakes increase negotiating power. However, effective negotiators never stop learning from their past experiences. After each negotiation, they review their performance by asking themselves the following questions:

- Am I satisfied with the outcome? Why or why not?
- Was my preparation thorough?
- Did I understand clearly the underlying needs of the other party?
- Who talked the most?
- Who asked the most questions?
- Was I able to explore new options by expanding the range of issues?
- Did I make too many concessions?
- Did I let the other party control and direct the discussions?
- How well did I manage time?
- Was I too emotional?
- What would I do differently next time?

Most types of power are within the range of any negotiator. Entering the negotiation with confidence because of preparation enables a negotiator to achieve superior outcomes. Moreover, when a negotiator is well prepared, the other party is respectful and gives the negotiator additional negotiation leverage. As successful negotiating is, to a large extent, the result of excellent preparations, it is desirable to be overprepared rather than underprepared and overconfident.

Skilled negotiators know when and how to apply various negotiating strategies and tactics while being people-sensitive and making decisions. In other words, successful negotiators possess the following traits:

- Negotiating skills
- People skills
- Decision-making skills

Effectively combining these three skills leads to superior and lasting outcomes. For this reason, negotiation is considered an art and not a science.

NOTES

1. W. M. Habeeb, *Power and Tactics in International Negotiation* (Baltimore: Johns Hopkins University Press, 1988).
2. John C. Banks, "Negotiating International Mining Agreements: Win-win Versus Win-lose Bargaining," *Columbia Journal of World Business*, Winter 1987, pp. 67–75.
3. P. Berten, H. Kimura, and I. W. Zartman, eds., *International Negotiations: Actors, Structure, Process* (New York: St. Martin's Press, 1999).
4. J. G. Cross, "Negotiation as Adaptive Learning," *International Negotiation*, No. 1, 1996, pp. 153–178.
5. D. Druckman, "Social Psychology and International Negotiations: Processes and Influences," in R. F. Kidd and M. J. Saks, eds., *Advances in Applied Social Psychology*, Vol. 2, 1983.
6. H. Raiffa, *The Art and Science of Negotiation* (Boston: Harvard University Press, 1982).

11

Negotiating on the Internet

*E-launch business activities often have to be carried out in an order that may seem totally illogical.—**Bill Gates***

In today's new economy, the Internet is changing the way business is carried out and is fast becoming an important channel of communication. It offers a wide range of business opportunities and challenges for enterprises, particularly those small- and medium-sized firms seeking new markets. Exporters, importers, suppliers, buyers, and agents are increasingly using the Internet to carry out their business transactions thanks to lower communication costs, reliability, and expediency.[1] As a result of its capabilities, many international executives have started to negotiate on the Internet.

Although the benefits from the Internet are numerous, inappropriate use can result in costly mistakes. In fact, most negotiations carried out over the Web fail due to a lack of clear communication resulting in a misunderstanding between the parties. As negotiation is about communication, negotiators must take the time to craft clear e-messages. By avoiding a few common pitfalls, negotiators doing business on the Internet can greatly improve their performance and optimize their outcomes.

MERITS OF NEGOTIATIONS OVER THE INTERNET

Because communicating on the Internet is relatively inexpensive, user-friendly, and timely, it is easy to maintain ongoing contact with the other party. The Internet also provides an effective means for a firm to promote its products or services anywhere in the world. By maintaining a web site, firms gain instant exposure and visibility worldwide, generating interest from potential customers.[2] Receiving inquiries on the Internet leads to dynamic interaction with quick exchanges of information. Communicating on the Web permits both parties to rapidly reach the concluding phase of negotiations. However, extra care is needed to determine the buyers' requirements, making offers competitive to improve one's chances of establishing a productive dialogue with the buyer. Similarly, the buyer needs to obtain vital information from the seller before considering concessions and counteroffers. Besides the Web being a neutral communication medium, it overcomes traditional barriers and allows greater interaction with potential partners on a global scale.

Eliminates Time Zones and Distances

Corresponding on the Internet reduces cultural, organizational, and gender barriers. Obtaining face-to-face appointments with key managers and getting involved in the bid process may be difficult for executives representing lesser-known firms. Thanks to the Internet, however, these same executives can communicate with their intended parties without any barriers.

In the e-economy, any business partner—regardless of location, availability, time zone, and position—can be easily contacted. This is a tremendous advantage considering how busy today's executives are. Even if the person an executive wishes to contact is not available, the message is getting through. Eventually the targeted person will look at his or her computer screen and respond. Being able to reach business partners on the Internet reduces the need to travel abroad, which is time-consuming and costly. Today buyers and importers seeking suppliers are less concerned with specific geographical locations as long as they believe a firm can be reached through the Internet. This option opens up new business opportunities for firms seeking an active role in global trade; more importantly, it projects an image of modern organizations relying on state-of-the-art technologies.

Reduces the Role of Status

Doing business on the Internet provides opportunities for junior or lower-ranked executives to interact with senior managers. In some countries and business organizations with a well-structured hierarchy, higher-ups may be reluctant to negotiate with junior personnel. In such cases, there will be undue delays, risk of changes in personnel, and/or breakdowns in communication. This problem is greatly reduced when the interaction takes place on the Internet. Generally, people are more inclined to respond to inquiries via e-mail regardless of age or status of the other person. The Net can be considered as an equalizer in situations where status, position, and age are considered essential in negotiating business deals.[3] This point is particularly significant in markets where culture and tradition play a major role in negotiations. In negotiation situations where one party is more relationship-oriented, the Internet should be used selectively with greater attention paid to crafting clear messages and addressing the other party properly. For example, in more traditional cultures, sending a junior executive to negotiate a contract where the other side is represented by a senior executive is a disaster in the making.

Erases Gender Biases

The Internet is an excellent medium that can be used to overcome gender biases in business negotiations where women executives are not expected to hold such key managerial positions. In specific geographic regions of the world as well as in certain organizations, women decision makers may face difficulties obtaining appointments with key managers or being invited to participate in negotiations. Doing business on the Internet neutralizes, to a large extent, this gender bias while allowing women executives to negotiate with their counterparts on an equal basis.[4] As the Internet reduces the need to travel, women managers are able to more effectively combine family obligations with their professional responsibilities.

Increases Personal Power

In addition, e-negotiations provide new sources of negotiating power to those executives who have difficulty interacting effectively in face-to-face discussions. E-negotiations also reduce the risk of discussions failing due to personality conflicts. By negotiating on the Internet, less-confident executives can gain greater personal power, thereby interacting with the other party on an equal, if not superior, basis.

Another benefit of e-negotiations is the home-court advantage enjoyed by both parties. Negotiating from one's own office offers a number of advantages. Besides being able to save on travel expenses and to avoid recuperating from jet lag, an executive has access to his or her files and staff and to any other expertise needed to carry out the discussions satisfactorily. Selecting the place for negotiations is no longer a sensitive issue when doing business on the Internet. For executives from small companies with limited travel budgets and limited office space, the Internet bypasses these impediments and puts the executives in a better position to negotiate with the other party.

Allows Simultaneous Multinegotiations

An important feature of e-negotiation is the ability to carry out several tasks simultaneously, including negotiating with other parties to maximize outcomes. For example, after sending out a message, an executive does not need to remain idle while waiting for an answer. Instead, he or she can undertake other priority tasks. Nothing stops the executive from checking out the competition to see whether his or her most recent offer is competitive. To improve his or her chances of success, the executive can negotiate simultaneously with other interested parties.

Expands One's Audience through New Technologies

With the introduction of new technologies, it is now possible to communicate on the Internet with video and interactive voice communication. Along with the exploding use of sophisticated mobile phones such as Wireless Application Protocol (WAP), digital communication generates greater virtual business opportunities. Using chat rooms and discussions groups, executives can negotiate with one or more parties. However, to ensure its effective use, a moderator is needed to manage the flow of communications. Due to technical and practical reasons, it is preferable to rely on the text channel only. Discussion groups are most useful for finding out what customers think of a product or service, for exchanging information, for finding new supply sources, and for testing the market.

PITFALLS OF INTERNET NEGOTIATIONS

Executives who rely on the Internet to keep in touch with existing customers and to seek access to new markets should be aware of a number of mistakes inexperienced e-negotiators tend to make. E-negotiations increase risk. Although the Internet provides worldwide opportunities, it also results in greater risks due to competitive forces dominating e-commerce. The ease with which companies can access global markets and do business using the Internet not only expands trading opportunities, but also gives more power to buyers. In other words, buyers and sellers must be extremely careful when corresponding via e-mail with business partners. All that is needed for an importer to switch to the competition for a better offer is to receive an unfavorable or unfriendly reply from an exporter.

Conflict Generation

A danger of Internet negotiations is that they may become antagonistic, as it is easier to become less agreeable when not dealing with another party face-to-face. Frequently, due to the absence of interface with the other party, e-negotiations can turn to "take it or leave it" offers, hardly the type of business strategies and tactics suitable for negotiating long-term agreements.[5]

Greater Emphasis on Price

E-negotiations allow an executive to carry out multinegotiations without the knowledge of the concerned parties. E-buyers also negotiate with several sellers to maximize their outcomes. As a result, e-negotiations often reflect a lack of cooperation coupled with more competitive moves centered on a single issue, namely, price.[6] Carrying out simultaneous negotiations with several parties may yield better outcomes, but mainly one-time deals. Multiparty negotiations are sometimes used to test the market and to determine whether one's offers are within an acceptable range. Generally, these initial contacts do not develop into full-scale negotiations.

STRATEGIES FOR NEGOTIATIONS ON THE INTERNET

Negotiating from one's office and exchanging information is an easy and comfortable way to carry out discussions. Reading e-messages on a computer screen and sending replies by e-mail is fast becoming an acceptable practice for business-to-consumer and business-to-business transactions. Unless negotiators take notice of the danger of negotiating on the Internet, they may develop "screen myopia" or "tunnel vision." In other words, negotiators enter an interpersonal game where messages are sent and received from one or more partners to obtain the best deal. After several rounds of exchanges, negotiators tend to become obsessed with winning at all costs and begin to take greater risks while relying on more conflictual tactics. By getting involved in this game, negotiators often fail to consider the context in which the transaction is taking place, do not consult others for advice, and forget the long-term consequences or benefits of their actions.[7] This explains the high failure rate of negotiations on the Internet.

SITUATIONS SUITABLE FOR E-NEGOTIATIONS

On a selective basis, initially, negotiating on the Internet should be limited to exchanging information, clarifying key issues, and finalizing specific clauses in an agreement. The Internet is also an excellent medium for preparing arrangements for a forthcoming face-to-face negotiation, such as making travel bookings, finalizing the agenda, selecting the location of the meeting, and agreeing to the number of people participating in the discussions. The Internet is also expedient when negotiating a repeat order or a small transaction that does not justify an investment in time, personnel, and financial resources.

To business executives, the Internet provides up-to-date information about the competition and buyers' technical requirements and offers a plethora of timely marketing intelligence. Companies must know who their competitors are and what buyers are looking for before their employees can reply to e-mail inquiries.

Because communication on the Internet is easy and fast, there is a tendency to respond immediately without taking time to prepare well. Negotiating on the Internet is no different than face-to-face negotiations; both require planning, preparing, displaying patience, understanding people, knowing the needs of the other party, and using persuasive skills and problem-solving capabilities (the four Ps of negotiations, i.e., preparation, patience, persuasion, and problem solving).

As e-enterprise involves receiving inquiries from parties operating in a borderless world, great care should be given to local business practices, legal aspects, and financial considerations. Payment and security concerns are sensitive issues requiring serious assessments, particularly when requests originate from unfamiliar markets or unknown parties.

PROPER PLANNING FOR E-NEGOTIATIONS

An executive should take time to think through the full implications of the negotiations on the Internet before communicating with the other party. Once a message is sent, particularly when it is printed, it can be viewed as a legal or binding document by the recipient. Furthermore, what is written tends to be taken more seriously by the other party and may come back to haunt the executive, especially when the message is of a negative or unpleasant nature. Frequently people use the Internet to send messages without planning and without assessing the long-term implications of their actions. Sending a message without preparing adequately is likely to be misunderstood, resulting in an exchange of unproductive communications. As a result, both parties may take positional stands, and instead of seeking common ground, they concentrate on exploiting their differences.

Too often a party's main concern is to reply as soon as possible. In fact, numerous e-commerce manuals recommend replying within 48 hours. For some business transactions, 48 hours may be too long; for others, 48 hours may not be long enough. Because many executives consider quickness in decision making a sign of superior management skills, they have a tendency to act rapidly. Acting quickly is easier on the Internet as a person is facing a screen instead of people. What is important is for a company representative to give each incoming and outgoing message full consideration, including assessing the risk over the long term and how the message will affect his or her position with their competition. To avoid being overwhelmed with incoming e-messages, the employee should thoroughly screen all incoming messages and set priorities allowing him or her to reply to genuine inquiries only. If the employee needs more time before replying, he or she can send an interim message.

Negotiators must use common sense and sound business practices to maintain open communication lines with potential clients while taking time to be well prepared for upcoming negotiations.

Combine E-negotiations with Face-to-Face Discussions

To reap the full benefits of e-commerce, negotiators may wish to combine off-line face-to-face meetings with online communication. Despite all the advantages of doing business on the Internet, when it comes to negotiations, face-to-face interaction is still preferred by most executives, particularly if the value of the deal justifies it. In more relationship-oriented cultures, online communication should be restricted to exchanging information, while the main issues are discussed off-line. One danger to be aware of is the impersonal nature of e-negotiations. Problems of trust and confidence are difficult to establish and maintain solely on the Net.[8] This is particularly true in situations where one party is only interested in pricing. Because of competitive pressures, buyers and sellers limit their exchanges to offers and counteroffers centered on the single issue of price. This scenario is at the heart of too many negotiations, whether they are held face to face or over the Internet. For example, sending ultimatums ("this is my last offer") or other forms of competitive moves tends to dominate e-negotiations. Although pricing is a key issue in any business negotiation, in the end, it is the firm's capacity to produce the required quality and quantity, timely delivery, and the firm's reputation that influence the decision. For this reason, each party should take the time to explore in detail what is required and take the time to develop sound proposals that can withstand competitive pressures and lead to repeat orders over the long run.

Cooperative versus Competitive Approach in E-negotiations

Basically, competitive behavior dominates e-negotiations. Given the fact that e-negotiations are impersonal, executives are inclined to pay less attention to personal relationships and cooperative strategies. This behavior is reflected by the wide use of irritants, negative expressions, and aggressive tones in e-communications. Moreover, as e-negotiators do not benefit from observing the other party's body movements, a great deal of information communicated through nonverbal cues is lost.

In e-negotiations, new technologies have an impact on the way negotiations are carried out, particularly on how fast they take place. Because e-negotiation is basically an exchange of information between two or more parties until each party's needs are satisfied, e-messages become the mainstay of communications. But sending ultimatums or responding with tit for tat is hardly the best approach for building a lasting business relationship. In any face-to-face negotiations, there is a mixture of competitive and cooperative strategies, with more collaborating prevailing in the concluding phase.

To ensure success, e-negotiators should avoid being too competitive in the early rounds, as such discussions can lead to a breakdown in communications. E-negotiators must encourage the sharing of information in the early rounds, allowing both parties to reach the closing phase through the exploration of joint solutions.

PROS AND CONS OF E-NEGOTIATIONS

The Internet has proven to be an excellent vehicle for business-to-business dealings. It is estimated that 80 percent of the growth in e-commerce will come from business-to-business transactions, mainly from global supply chains. Companies wishing to benefit from supply chains need to be connected with these global firms in order to be in contention for their procurements. The direct linkage between buyers and suppliers is likely to result in a restructuring of commercial distribution channels, with less reliance on intermediaries. As buyers' requirements will be accessible to anyone connected to the Internet, greater competition among suppliers can be expected, resulting in lower prices and reduced profit margins. E-negotiators will need to be well prepared to face the competition and must emphasize their technical capacities, delivery capacities, reputation, and long-term commitment. Finally, despite the benefits of negotiating on the Internet, negotiators should continue to travel to their markets to maintain personal contact with customers and to assess the local business environment.

SUMMARY

Until e-commerce is fully integrated into the global economy and management is committed to this new form of doing business by restructuring their processes, negotiators should continue face-to-face interaction supported by e-exchanges. But the Internet has changed the competitive landscape. It has given more power to buyers and has provided greater business opportunities to suppliers and exporters, regardless of time zones and distances. Thus, negotiations on the Internet are more competitive, impersonal, and adversarial, often resulting in negotiation failures. With e-commerce stimulating competition, firms engaged in business-to-business trade face greater price pressures, higher client turnover, and unpredictable markets conditions.

E-negotiation is no panacea to business-to-business deals, but if used effectively, it can lead to better agreements. Failing to do so, e-negotiators may find themselves without business deals, as other parties switch to the competition with a simple click of the mouse. By and large, e-negotiations are best for negotiating repeat business, taking and confirming orders, initiating trade leads, testing the market, clarifying specific points, providing additional information, providing after-sales service, giving details about shipping and deliveries, communicating with existing customers, checking the competition, and preparing face-to-face negotiations. But e-negotiation success requires sending well-crafted e-messages, considering long-term implications, consulting others before replying, carefully reviewing messages before sending them, being selective when replying, refraining from using negative/irritating expressions, adopting more cooperative strategies, avoiding discussing pricing issues from the outset, and avoiding developing "screen myopia."

NOTES

1. J. E. McGrath and A. B. Hollingshed, *Groups Interacting with Technology* (Thousand Oaks, CA: Sage Publications, 1999).
2. L. Sproull and S. Keisler, *Connections: New Ways of Working in the Networked Organization* (Cambridge, MA: MIT Press, 1991).
3. J. E. McGrath and A. B. Hollingshed, op. cit.
4. T. McGuire, S. Keisler, and J. Siegel, "Group and Computer-Mediated Discussion Effects in Risk Decision-Making," *Journal of Personality and Social Psychology*, Vol. 52, No. 5, pp. 917–930.
5. A. L. Dorlet and M. W. Morris, "Communication and Media and Interpersonal Trust in Conflicts: The Role of Rapport and Synchrony of Nonverbal Behavior," Unpublished manuscript, Stanford University, 1995.
6. R. Kramer, "Dubious Battle: Heightened Accountability, Dysphoric Cognition and Self-designing Bargaining Behavior," In R. Kramer and D. Mersick, eds., *In Negotiations as a Social Process* (Thousand Oaks, CA: Sage Publications, 1995), pp. 95–120.
7. Leigh Thompson, *The Mind and Heart of the Negotiator* (Upper Saddle River, NJ: Prentice-Hall, 1998), pp. 264–265.
8. V. Arunchalan and W. Dilla, "Judgment Accuracy and Outcomes in Negotiations," *Organizational Behavior and Human Decision Processes*, Vol. 61, No. 3, pp. 258–290.

12

Global Negotiations—Cases and Exercises*

*It is the interest of the commercial world that wealth should be found everywhere.—**Edmund Burke***

This chapter introduces five negotiation cases and exercises pertaining to different parts of the world: China, Europe, Latin America, the Middle East, and Asia. Each exercise begins with background information. Then a few discussion questions are raised. Finally, discussion on each question follows. These exercises are a learning tool for gaining insight into practical aspects of global negotiations. In addition, they pose managerial challenges and stimulate intellectual curiosity and thinking.[1]

CHINESE NEGOTIATIONS

EAST MEETS WEST IN SHOE MANUFACTURING NEGOTIATIONS

Background

Brown Casual Shoes, Inc., located in Houston, Texas, is a second-generation family-owned company that specializes in casual footwear for men, women, and children. The company has been in operation for 30 years and has manufacturing facilities in Houston, Texas, and Cincinnati, Ohio. Over the years, the company has expanded its operations throughout the United States and Canada. It sells directly to retail shoe stores such as Payless, to discount stores such as Wal-Mart and Kmart, and to wholesale outlets such as Costco. The company prides itself on manufacturing its shoes solely in the United States. Over the past five years, the company has felt the impact of cheap labor on the manufacturing of today's shoes. Local and international competition is

---

* Chapter 12 was prepared by Professor Gary Lefort, American International College, Springfield, MA. The authors gratefully acknowledge his help in this task.

making inroads on the company's niche markets. Sales have been down for the past two years. The president of the company, Robert Brown, Jr., is concerned that if the downward trend in sales continues, the company may be forced to close its doors. Labor costs in the United States have been a major concern. Mr. Brown is aware that the U.S. athletics footwear industry does most of its manufacturing in Asian countries such as China, South Korea, and Indonesia, where labor costs are appreciably lower.

The company must now find cheaper ways to manufacture its shoes, and it needs to expand its sales by entering the international marketplace. Mr. Brown called a board meeting to review his options. After much discussion, the board decided China was a good place to begin for a number of reasons: (1) The country has a cheap labor market, (2) the country already has footwear manufacturing contracts with U.S. companies, (3) China represents a potential new market with a population of over 1.3 billion people, and (4) China has been moving toward a free-market economy since the late 1970s. Mr. Brown decided he would visit China and bring with him Harry Livingstone, his senior vice president of operations, and Roberta Jackson, manager of the company's marketing department.

Mr. Livingstone was given the job of setting up the visit. He contacted business associates who had done business internationally to get some ideas of how to go about planning the visit. Mr. Livingstone also contacted several athletic footwear trade associations and was able to identify several Chinese companies interested in talking to his company about a business arrangement. One company, Chang Manufacturing, was located outside Beijing; the other company, Chung Sun Manufacturing, was located in Shanghai. After some discussion with Mr. Brown, the two of them decided to visit the Shanghai company because Shanghai was one of China's Special Economic Zones and would be supportive of Western ideas and business practices. The Beijing company was attractive, but Mr. Brown was somewhat concerned about the political and social risks of being so close to the country's capital and the seat of government.

Mr. Livingstone contacted Chung Sun Manufacturing and was eventually directed to Mr. Li Kim Son, who handled international business development for the company. Mr. Li spoke fluent English and had been involved in negotiating several footwear manufacturing contracts with U.S. companies. Mr. Livingstone explained Brown Casual Shoes' interest in wanting to manufacture its products in China. Mr. Li indicated that his company would be willing to discuss a business arrangement and invited Mr. Livingstone's company to visit the Chung Sun facility in Shanghai.

Mr. Livingstone was elated to hear this and immediately informed Mr. Brown. The meeting was scheduled for the following month, and the team went to work developing the business proposal. Some thought was given to hiring the services of a Chinese translator, but this was deemed unnecessary since Mr. Li spoke fluent English and had been involved in U.S. business negotiations.

The day of the departure finally arrived, and Mr. Brown and his team boarded their flight to Shanghai, China. They arrived in Shanghai at 9:30 in the morning. Upon their arrival, they were met by a company representative, who ushered them off to their hotel. A business meeting was scheduled for 3 P.M. The company representative would pick up Mr. Brown and his team at 2:30 P.M.

Upon arrival at the company's headquarters, Mr. Brown and his team were met by Mr. Li, who graciously greeted them with a bow and a handshake. They were immediately ushered off to a conference room to meet the company's president, Mr. Deng Kim Lee. Again, there was a cordial exchange of handshakes, bows, and business cards. After the introductions, Mr. Brown presented Mr. Deng with a small gift, beautifully wrapped in white paper and a ribbon, as a token of friendship. Mr. Deng seemed somewhat embarrassed to accept the gift. Mr. Brown insisted a second and third time before Mr. Deng accepted it. The team was introduced to Mrs. Wang Chu Jiang, who would be their Chinese translator throughout the visit. Almost immediately, Mr. Deng got into a discussion with Mr. Brown about his trip while Mr. Li engaged Mr. Livingstone and Mrs. Jackson in conversation. While talking to Mr. Deng, Mr. Brown would gently grasp the forearm of Mr. Deng in a gesture of friendship. At times, the U.S. team felt very uncomfortable because they knew very little Chinese. Refreshments were brought into the room, and everyone was invited to sit down. Before long, it was 5 P.M. and there had been no mention of why the U.S. team had visited the company. At this time, Mr. Li announced that an evening banquet in honor of the American guests had been arranged for 7 P.M. at the Great Wall of China Restaurant. Upon hearing this, Mr. Brown motioned with his finger for Mr. Livingstone to come see him. Mr. Brown had not expected such gracious hospitality and was unsure about how to reciprocate. The meeting came to a close, and Mr. Brown and his team returned to their hotel.

The banquet was very lavish and lasted for several hours. Mr. Brown, in appreciation for such hospitality, offered the first toast of the evening to his host. During the banquet, there was no mention of business. Conversation focused on China and its culture, the United States, family questions, and the team's flight to China. As the night came to a close, Mr. Brown wondered who should leave first.

The meeting began the next day at 9 A.M. Again, the meeting started with pleasantries. Thirty minutes into the meeting, Mr. Brown was asked to present his proposal to the company. With the assistance of his team (and some occasional help from Mrs. Wang), Mr. Brown explained how he would like to manufacture his shoes in China and that he was also interested in marketing his shoes in China. As Mr. Brown went through his presentation, Mr. Deng and his staff repeatedly asked questions; Mr. Brown thought he would never get through his presentation. By noon, it was time for a break. As Mr. Brown reflected back on the progress made at the morning meeting, he knew that more than one trip to China would be required to reach a business agreement with Chung Sun Manufacturing.

Questions

1. How would you assess the negotiations up to this point?
2. How culturally aware and sensitive do you think Mr. Brown and his team were? Give specific examples to support your position.

Discussion

You must research the Chinese culture to complete this exercise. This will give you an understanding of what to expect when conducting business in China and how the Chinese culture impacts negotiations. A good starting point is Hofstede's National Culture Model, which is defined in terms of four dimensions: (1) power distance, (2) uncertainty avoidance, (3) individualism versus collectivism, and (4) masculinity versus femininity.[2] The model provides valuable insight about what to expect when dealing with the Asian world. It is especially important that you understand the significance of "saving face" when dealing with Asians.

As part of your research, you should compile a summary chart of what you learn about the Chinese culture and how to do business with the Chinese. Discussion about the previous questions follows.

1. To a large extent, the success of negotiations depends on how thorough the prenegotiation activities are. In dealing with domestic negotiations, little time, if any, is spent on the

cultural dimension of the negotiations. The majority of time is spent on the technical and financial aspects of the negotiations. Even the formulation of negotiation strategies does not give serious consideration to cultural implications.

This all changes when a company gets involved in international negotiations. Certainly the technical and financial areas are important, but equally important (and maybe even more important) is the cultural dimension of the negotiations. For example, in negotiations with Asians, many contracts are lost because Western companies fail to understand the significance of not allowing either side to 'lose face' during business negotiations.

It is obvious that Brown Casual Shoes does not have a lot of international experience. Up to this point, the company's only exposure was in Canada. Mr. Livingstone had the right idea in asking his business associates and several athletics footwear trade associations for advice, but he should not have stopped there. Mr. Livingstone should have recognized the need for professional assistance from an international consulting firm that specializes in doing business with the Chinese, or at least the Asian region. This help is important because the company is in trouble and cannot afford to make mistakes in its international endeavors.

The company's failure to use professional help created problems when dealing with its Chinese counterpart. This was apparent in Mr. Livingstone's decision to rely on Mr. Li as an intermediary. An international consultant would have advised the company to get its own Chinese translator and to arrange to have a third party intermediary help with the negotiations. The use of an intermediary would help to minimize the chances of either party losing face during the negotiations. The international consultant also would have helped the company to better understand the Chinese way of doing business. For example, Mr. Brown was wise to go to China himself, but it is questionable whether he knew how important his visit was to the success of doing business with the Chinese company. If Mr. Livingstone had headed up the team, Chung Sun Manufacturing's president, Mr. Deng Kim Lee, would not have attended the meeting. The absence of Mr. Brown would have signaled that the visit was not of the utmost importance.

2. Brown Casual Shoes did a lot of work developing a comprehensive business proposal but spent little time learning

about Chinese culture and history or learning a little conversational Chinese. Again, the international consultant would have been helpful in this regard. This lack of cultural awareness and sensitivity jeopardized the success of the company's visit to China. The company had the time during the pre-negotiating stage to better prepare themselves culturally for the trip.

Cultural mistakes made by Mr. Brown and his team during their visit to Chung Sun Manufacturing include the following:

- Mr. Brown went to China with the idea that he would be able to negotiate a deal with his Chinese counterpart on the initial visit. He failed to realize that negotiations can be drawn out over an extended period of time. More than one visit is necessary; sometimes it can take a year or longer to complete a deal. The Chinese like to drag out negotiations with the intent of wearing a person down. Foreign companies must have patience and perseverance when dealing with the Chinese. The Chinese are looking for a long-term relationship that can only be developed over time. Mr. Brown began to realize this by the second day of the trip.

- It may not have been a good idea to bring a woman on the initial trip. Women still play a passive role in China. Even when women are in business, they do not hold senior management positions. The only Chinese woman present at the meeting was Mrs. Wang Chu Jiang; she was the Chinese translator.

- Not much information was provided about the introductions, but it is questionable whether Brown Casual Shoes' business cards were printed in English and Mandarin Chinese. It is also questionable whether Mr. Brown and his team appreciated the importance of bowing when greeting their Asian counterparts. Mr. Brown and his team also knew very little Chinese. Clearly, this showed a lack of cultural sensitivity on the part of the company.[3]

- The gift offered by Mr. Brown was appropriate providing Mr. Brown made a point of saying that the gift was offered to Mr. Deng by Mr. Brown's company to Mr. Deng's company. The color of the wrapping paper was not appropriate; in China, white is associated with funerals. It was also important that Mr. Brown offer the gift to Mr. Deng with both hands. Mr. Brown was wise to continue to offer the gift to Mr. Deng because it is customary for the Chinese to decline accepting a gift several times. This is an excellent example of a situation that could have led to both parties losing face.

- Mr. Brown was insensitive to Mr. Deng's personal space when, during their conversation, he grasped Mr. Deng's forearm in a gesture of friendship. The Chinese do not like being touched by people they do not know.

- Mr. Brown should not have been surprised that socializing and pleasantries are an integral part of doing business with the Chinese. Building long-term relationships is very important to the Chinese. Meetings begin with pleasantries such as tea, food, and small talk. Mr. Brown should not have been surprised to see that his Chinese counterparts had planned a banquet for their American guests. Mr. Brown will be expected to reciprocate at a later date. The first toast at the banquet is made by the host, not the guest. And the guest should leave the banquet before the host. North Americans have difficulty mixing business with pleasure. They want to get on with the business and socialize afterward if time permits.

- The messages conveyed by nonverbal communication must be considered when dealing with people from a different culture. Mr. Brown motioned with his finger for Mr. Livingstone to come see him. This way of using the finger to call someone is offensive in many Asian cultures. Instead, a person should turn his or her palm down and make a waving motion with the hand.

- The use of a third-party intermediary would have been a good idea at the first meeting. Many of the mistakes made by Mr. Brown and his team might have been avoided. Obviously, Mr. Brown was looking for someone to turn to for help. In all likelihood, an intermediary could also have served as a translator for Mr. Brown. During the business negotiations on the second day, Mr. Brown had to be uncomfortable relying on Mrs. Wang for translation assistance.

Mr. Brown did not understand the Chinese negotiating style. The Chinese like to drag out negotiations to wear down their counterparts. More than one visit is necessary to complete negotiations. The Chinese ask a lot of questions and revisit negotiated areas many times over. Renegotiations are a part of dealing with the Chinese because they see time as very dynamic. What is agreed to today can change tomorrow.

EUROPEAN NEGOTIATIONS

SOUTHERN CANDLE'S TOUR DE FRANCE

Background

Ronald Picard is the president of Southern Candles, Inc., located in Baltimore, Maryland. The company specializes in high-quality slow-burning scented and unscented candle products. The company also holds a patent on a special design process for making three-dimensional sculptured candles. The company's products are sold in retail stores, specialty shops, and franchised operations throughout the United States. In recent years, competition from other candle companies has intensified to the point that Southern Candles needs to seek out new markets. Past attendance at international trade shows has revealed a large candle market in Europe, especially in Western Europe. Mr. Picard is confident that the business experience gained in the U.S. market will carry over to the European market.

At this year's international trade show in Munich, Germany, Mr. Picard met Pierre Durand, a French retailer who owns a chain of specialty shops in France, Germany, and Belgium called Les Belles Choses. The specialty shops cater to an upper-class clientele. Its product line includes perfumes, beauty care products, clothing apparel, custom-made jewelry, and handcrafted home furnishings. Mr. Durand expressed an interest in selling Southern Candles products and wanted to hear more about the design process for making three-dimensional sculptured candles. Mr. Durand invited Mr. Picard to visit his company in Paris the following month to discuss a possible business arrangement. Mr. Picard cordially accepted the invitation.

Mr. Picard was very excited about the prospect of doing business in Europe. Southern Candles complemented the product line of Les Belles Choses. The opportunity also offered a way to gain product recognition, which could eventually lead to the company opening its own stores in Europe.

Mr. Picard pulled his staff together to strategize how to market its product line to Mr. Durand. Mr. Picard decided to take Marge Dubois, his marketing manager, and one technical staff member to discuss the design process for making the three-dimensional sculptured candles. After long hours of hard work, the team developed a comprehensive business proposal and was ready to make the trip to Paris. Mr. Picard was pleased to have Mrs. Dubois along because she had spent five years in Quebec, Canada, and spoke fluent French.

Mr. Picard and his team arrived in Paris at 9 A.M. and were met by Mr. Durand. Everyone exchanged handshakes and Mrs. Dubois extended a warm greeting in French. Mr. Durand acknowledged it with a smile. While traveling to the company, there was some light conversation with Mrs. Dubois occasionally speaking in French. Mr. Durand complimented her on her French and asked where she had learned to speak the language. Mrs. Dubois told him about the time she had spent in Canada. Again, Mr. Durand smiled.

At the company, Mr. Durand introduced Mr. Picard and his team to members of his staff. Business cards were exchanged. Mr. Picard examined the cards and was impressed to see that the cards were in English on one side and French on the other side. Mr. Durand escorted Mr. Picard and his team to the conference room. Twenty minutes into the meeting, Mrs. Dubois began feeling a little uncomfortable because she noticed several members of Mr. Durand's team repeatedly staring at her and smiling. She became somewhat intimated by this behavior. She decided to say something to Mr. Picard when they went to lunch. The group broke for lunch at 1 P.M., and much to Mr. Picard's surprise, it lasted over two hours. When they returned to the conference room, Mr. Picard, a little uncomfortable from a heavy lunch, decided to take off his coat, but no one else did.

The afternoon session went very well even though it got somewhat argumentative at times. Mr. Picard's presentation was well received, and it appeared that Mr. Durand would buy Southern Candles products. Pleased with himself, Mr. Picard gave a quick "okay" sign to his team members. Mr. Durand thanked Mr. Picard for his presentation and told Mr. Picard he would review the proposal with his staff. Following that review, he would let Mr. Picard know of his decision.

After the meeting, Mr. Durand invited Mr. Picard and his team to a small dinner party at his home at 8 P.M. Mr. Picard was picked up at his hotel at 7:30 P.M. and arrived at Mr. Durand's home at precisely 8 P.M. Several executives from Mr. Durand's company were already there.

Mr. Picard was introduced to Mrs. Durand. He graciously accepted her hand and gave her a beautiful bouquet of roses. Mrs. Dubois was also introduced to Mrs. Durand. Mrs. Dubois greeted her in French. Mr. Picard was then introduced to the other invited guests. The dinner was superb, leisurely served over several hours with light conversation. Several times Mr. Picard mentioned the business meeting earlier in the day, but conversation always drifted back to social amenities.

It was a lovely evening to what appeared to be a successful business day.

Mr. Picard arrived back at his hotel around midnight, totally exhausted from a very long day. He was glad that he had scheduled a late morning flight back to the United States.

Much to Mr. Picard's surprise, he received a cordial letter from Mr. Durand two weeks later stating that Mr. Durand had decided not to expand the Les Belles Choses' product line at this time.

Questions

1. Why did Mr. Durand decide not to carry the Southern Candles product line?
2. How culturally aware and sensitive do you think Mr. Picard was?

Discussion

You must research the French culture to complete this exercise. This will give you an understanding of what to expect when conducting business in France and how the French culture impacts negotiations. A good starting point is the Hofstede's National Culture Model, which is defined in terms of four dimensions: (1) power distance, (2) uncertainty avoidance, (3) individualism versus collectivism, and (4) masculinity versus femininity. The model provides valuable insight about what to expect not only in France, but also in other European countries. It is especially important that you understand how "nationalistic" and "social class conscious" the French can be when dealing with foreigners. Discussion about the previous questions follows.

1. Mr. Picard believed he had a good understanding of the European culture based on his past trips to Europe to attend international trade shows. He was confident that his business experience in the U.S. market would carry over to the European market. Many American businesses make this same mistake. A classic example of this is when Disney decided to open a park in Europe in 1992. Disney learned some valuable lessons the hard way about doing business in France. These lessons would have been helpful to Mr. Picard in preparing for negotiations with Mr. Durand.

   One can argue whether Mr. Picard needed to hire the services of an international business consultant. Mr. Picard certainly had acquired international experience over the years. He thought he knew the European market. A consultant may have made him more aware of the cultural differences between European countries.

Mr. Picard did not do any research about conducting business in France. Had he done so, he certainly would have realized how nationalistic the French are.[4] This fact alone would have told him that Mrs. Dubois's Canadian French was not an asset but a liability. When in France, one speaks Parisian French. Mr. Picard's lack of cultural awareness and sensitivity led to Mr. Durand's decision not to carry the Southern Candles products. Mr. Picard came across as bourgeois (middle class), which did not impress Mr. Durand, who was very social class conscious. (Remember, Les Belles Choses catered to an elite upper-class clientele.) Initially Mr. Durand saw Southern Candles as complementing his already exclusive line of products. He also seemed intrigued by the uniqueness of the three-dimensional sculptured candles. However, his one-day experience with Mr. Picard and his team (professionally and socially) made Mr. Durand realize that Mr. Picard was too uncouth to do business with.

2. Mr. Picard did not do any research about the French culture. He relied on the international experience he had gained while attending trade shows in Europe. He saw Europe as a single market with every country having the same culture. Cultural mistakes made by Mr. Picard include the following:

• Mr. Picard's first mistake was inviting Mrs. Dubois. He saw her ability to speak French an asset, which is normally true, except in France. There one should speak Parisian French, not Canadian French. Mrs. Dubois's French proved to be a liability throughout the trip. Even though Mr. Durand was polite, he obviously did not enjoy his conversations with her. The air of tolerance shown by Mr. Durand carried over to his French staff and to Mrs. Durand, who met Mrs. Dubois at dinner. With this gaffe, Mr. Durand probably began to sense that Mr. Picard and his company were "bourgeois."

• Mr. Picard was impressed to see the French business cards printed in English and French, which may mean that his business card was printed only in English. In today's global business environment, business travelers should have business cards printed in their own language on one side and printed in the language of the country with whom they want to do business on the other side. Besides bilingual business cards, some countries, such as Japan, go through a ritual of exchanging business cards; business cards should be handled with care.

- Mrs. Dubois should not have been shocked to see the Frenchmen staring at her. Frenchmen enjoy making eye contact with women; the behavior is not meant to be disrespectful or rude. An interesting comparison is the habit of Americans using the first names of people they just met. Most cultures consider this rude on the part of Americans, but Americans think nothing of it.

- Unlike Americans, many cultures take long lunch breaks, but work later in the day. This is true in France as well as most other European countries. The French also like to discuss business during lunch.

- The French are very social conscious and tend to be formal and reserved. If Mr. Picard had been culturally sensitive to this, he would not have taken off his coat after lunch. Doing so is considered too casual by French standards.

- Mr. Picard did not understand the French negotiating style. The French can be quite argumentative. They like a good debate. They tend not to accept information at face value. They are more analytical and critical, which leads to their argumentative negotiating style.

- The messages conveyed by nonverbal communication must be considered when dealing with people from a different culture. Mr. Picard used the "okay" sign to convey to his team that he thought things were going well. His hand gesture was inappropriate because in France, the "okay" sign means zero. The "okay" sign also has different meanings in other countries. For example, in Japan, the sign is associated with money; and in some European countries, it is considered an obscene gesture.[5]

- Mr. Picard's blunders did not end at the business meeting. They carried over to the dinner party at Mr. Durand's home. Mr. Picard should have checked with the hotel concierge before giving roses to Mrs. Durand. Roses are given at funerals. Mrs. Dubois's greeting to Mrs. Durand in her Canadian French probably did not help the situation. Likewise in bad taste was for Mr. Picard to mention business during the evening, regardless of how casual the comment may have been.

LATIN AMERICAN NEGOTIATIONS

BUSINESS AND SOCIALIZING GO HAND IN HAND IN MEXICAN NEGOTIATIONS

Background

Anita Rodriquez was a native Mexican who moved with her family to the United States in 1990 when she was 13 years old. Her family settled in Boston, Massachusetts. Over the years, she returned to Mexico twice to visit family and friends. She attended Boston University and earned her master's degree in Business Administration in 2001. While at the university, she met John Fitzgerald, who was studying economics. After graduation, Anita and John married and settled down in Boston. Anita had an entrepreneurial spirit and wanted to do business in Mexico. She spoke fluent Spanish and understood the Mexican culture. Even though John had never traveled internationally, he was very supportive of Anita's goal and helped her with the marketing research that led them to several U.S. manufacturing companies who were interested in doing business in Mexico. The companies had little international experience and were more than willing to let Anita do the initial work in identifying customers in Mexico. They were impressed with Anita's professionalism, aggressiveness, and Mexican background.

Anita and John were excited, and they set out to identify Mexican companies that would be interested in doing business with the U.S. companies. They began their search by contacting the U.S. Embassy in Mexico City to identify potential leads. They also contacted the regional office of the U.S. Department of Commerce and several trade associations. Their efforts paid off, acquiring the names of two Mexican companies—one located in Mexico City, the other in Monterrey.

Anita was excited and was anxious to contact them. She made telephone calls to set up meeting dates with each company. She and John planned a five-day trip to Mexico where they would spend two days with each company and use one day to tour Mexico City.

Anita made plans to arrive in Mexico City in the morning and to spend some time with the first company that afternoon. She was sure she could lay the foundation for a full-day discussion the next day. If everything went well, she and John would tour Mexico City on the third day and depart that evening for Monterrey.

Upon arriving at the airport, Anita was surprised that no one was there to greet her and John. She was sure she had given the company the right arrival time. The company representative arrived 45 minutes late with a warm, friendly welcome.

Tired from the trip, Anita and John expected to go immediately to their hotel, but much to their surprise, the company representative ushered them to a nearby restaurant to meet Mr. Raul Martinez, the company's business development manager. The lunch was cordial and dealt mainly with pleasantry and small talk. There was little mention of the reason for the business trip. At the end of lunch, Mr. Martinez invited the couple to dinner that night. Several senior executives from the company would be there.

Tired and somewhat frustrated, Anita and John arrived at the hotel. Both were hoping the evening dinner would provide an opportunity to discuss some business.

Dinner was at a fancy, but busy Mexican restaurant. The couple arrived on time and was surprised to find only Mr. Martinez there. Mr. Martinez welcomed them and explained that Mr. Jose Gonzalez, Vice President of Marketing, and Mr. Roberto Ortiz, General Plant Manager, would arrive shortly.

About 30 minutes later, both executives arrived and extended a warm welcome to their guests. The evening conversation centered on everything but business. It appeared that Anita and John's Mexican counterparts were out to have a good time. The evening ended with an invitation for Anita and John to meet at the company headquarters at 9 A.M. the next day.

They returned to their hotel somewhat frustrated that the day had flown by with no mention of the reason for their trip. Anita contemplated how she would handle the business meeting the next day.

Anita and John arrived at the company at 9 A.M. They were greeted by Mr. Martinez and Mr. Gonzalez and were taken to a large conference room. Shortly thereafter, Mr. Ortiz arrived with several department heads. Anita was the only woman present at the meeting.

Anita seized the initiative and began to talk about the purpose of her visit. She presented her business proposal to the company. Mr. Gonzalez was very interested and directed several questions to John. John deferred the questions to Anita. Forty-five minutes into the meeting, an assistant came into the conference room and spoke to Mr. Ortiz. Mr. Ortiz apologized, saying he had to leave the meeting but promising he would return later. Anita continued her presentation, disappointed Mr. Ortiz had to leave. At 2:30 P.M. Mr. Martinez suggested that everyone break for lunch at a nearby restaurant. Several hours later the meeting resumed. Mr. Ortiz had returned to the meeting, and he directed several questions to John. Anita, somewhat agitated by this time, responded. By 4 P.M., it was apparent that another day would be needed to conclude the discussions. Anita and John were invited to dinner that evening.

Back at the hotel, Anita and John reviewed the day's events. They were already behind schedule, with little hope of meeting with the second company as planned. Both of them had been on the go since their arrival and were exhausted. Yet they expected another long evening of socializing with little likelihood of discussing any business. Frustrated, they mapped out what they hoped to accomplish at the next day's meeting and discussed whether they should cancel the meeting with the second company and arrange to come at another time.

Questions

1. Does Anita really understand the Mexican culture and the Mexican way of doing business? Explain.
2. What went wrong on the visit to the first company?
3. Should Anita cancel the visit to the second Mexican company? Why or why not?

Discussion

You must research the Mexican culture to complete this exercise. This will give you an understanding of what to expect when conducting business in Mexico and how the Mexican culture impacts negotiations. A good starting point is the Hofstede's National Culture Model, which is defined in terms of four dimensions: (1) power distance, (2) uncertainty avoidance, (3) individualism versus collectivism, and (4) masculinity versus femininity. The model provides valuable insight about what to expect not only in Mexico, but also in other Latin American countries. It is especially important that you understand that Latin Americans like to socialize before they get into business. They like to know with whom they will be doing business. It is also important to recognize that women play a passive role in Latin American cultures, especially in the business world. Discussion about the previous questions follows:

1. Anita certainly understands her Mexican heritage, but it is questionable how well she understands the Mexican culture of today. She only visited Mexico twice during her adolescent

years. A lot of changes have taken place in Mexico over the past decade, especially with the advent of the North American Free Trade Agreement (NAFTA) in 1994. Anita had no experience doing business in Mexico. In fact, she had no real business experience to speak of considering she graduated from Boston University in 2001. It is not unusual that Anita would want to do business in her native country. That desire probably stems from her wanting to reconnect with her native country.

Anita had a lot of things going for her. She had her MBA. She had a Mexican background and spoke fluent Spanish. Her husband was supportive and had his own degree in economics. She was aggressive and had an entrepreneurial spirit. It was unfortunate that Anita did not recognize that her understanding of the Mexican culture may have been flawed.[6] There was also the question of how much she knew about international business in the first place. In light of these shortcomings, it would have been prudent for Anita to seek out the services of an international business consultant to make sure she was on the right track. One of the first things she would have learned was that women do not play a major role in business in Mexico.

If she did not want to hire an international business consultant, she should have at least done some research about how to do business in Mexico. This research also would have helped John, who had no international experience and knew little about Mexico and its culture.

2. Anita started out on the right track by using private and public sources to find potential Mexican companies. Her success in setting up the two business appointments made her believe she could negotiate a deal for her U.S. clients. It never occurred to her that the Mexican contacts might have seen her as the secretary making appointments for her manager.

Anita, to some extent, experienced reverse cultural shock in going to Mexico City. After many years in the United States, she had become too Americanized in many ways. For example, Mexicans are polychronic, so Anita should not expect them to be punctual or driven by a schedule like monochronic Americans. It should not have surprised Anita that the driver was late picking up her and John at the airport or that Mr. Gonzalez and Mr. Ortiz arrived late for dinner. Another example is Mr. Ortiz leaving the meeting to take care of other matters. Polychronic cultures tend to do more than one thing at a time. In Latin American cultures, the family is very important, and taking care of family matters takes priority over a business meeting. Another example is the amount of socializing done in the course of doing business with Mexicans. Mexicans want to know with whom who they are going to do business. They want to know business contacts personally. Anita should not have been surprised that little to no business was conducted on the first visit. Scheduling the second company on the first trip showed that Anita did not understand how business was conducted in Mexico.

The biggest problem Anita faced dealing with the first company was the executives' unwillingness to deal with her as the person in charge. This is the "male machismo" ingrained in Mexican men from birth. Women do not play an active role in business. Anita was not seen as the lead negotiator. This explained why Mr. Gonzalez and Mr. Ortiz directed their questions to John, not to Anita. Anita failed to recognize that this was the Mexican way of doing business.

3. Anita and John should cancel the visit to Monterrey. They are exhausted and somewhat frustrated. Her five-day trip to meet with the two companies was too ambitious, especially since she wanted to spend one day touring Mexico City with John. They need time to regroup and assess what they have learned. One major area that Anita needs to address is her willingness to let John take a more active role in future negotiations. Maybe now is the time for them to do more cultural research or to hire an international business consultant to help.

MIDDLE EASTERN NEGOTIATIONS

PRENEGOTIATION ACTIVITIES IMPORTANT TO SUCCESSFUL NEGOTIATIONS

Background

Frank Rogers heads up the international division of a U.S.-based fast-food company that wants to open up franchising operations in the Middle East. The company specializes in family and individual meals and specialty sandwiches. The company's menu offers fish and meat entrees, including roasted chicken, beef, and baked ham. The company opened franchising operations in Europe five years ago and now operates in seven Western

European countries and two Eastern European countries. Two years ago the company entered the Latin American market, initially in Mexico; it expanded its franchising operations to South America, Brazil being the first market. The company would like to enter the Middle Eastern market, beginning with Saudi Arabia.

Mr. Rogers believes the success of the company's international expansion program has been due to the two-step negotiation approach used by the company. The first step focuses on pre-negotiation activities; the second step is the negotiation itself. Experience in Europe and Latin America have shown that the first step is critical to successful negotiations. The pre-negotiations step is the work done by the company in preparation for the negotiations. This preparation is more complex than preparing for negotiations in the United States because of the different cultural, political, legal, and economic environments found in other countries.

The prenegotiation steps followed by Mr. Rogers's company consist of the following activities:

- *Selecting the right team members.* The negotiating team either makes or breaks the negotiations. When selecting members, one must consider their past negotiating experience and in what countries they have negotiated; the technical, personal, and social skills required; and the role each team member must play during the negotiations. Is a third-party intermediary needed? If so, what role does he or she play?
- *Providing appropriate training.* It is important to understand the cultural environment of the new market. Cultural awareness and sensitivity can help make the negotiations a 'win-win' situation. Training needs to focus on more than the cultural traits of the country. Negotiating styles and work ethics also vary between countries.
- *Identifying negotiations objectives.* The company, going into the negotiations, needs a clear understanding of what it wants to achieve during the negotiations. The other party's objectives may be different from what the company hopes to accomplish. For example, American objectives tend to be more pragmatic than Asian objectives, which are aimed more toward building long-term relationships.
- *Establishing a negotiations agenda.* A company must have a clear plan of how it wants the negotiations to go. The time factor becomes important because long stays away from

home can weaken the bargaining power of the negotiator. If a negotiator understands the negotiating style of the other party, he or she will know when to take a firm stance.

- *Developing concession strategies.* To make negotiations a 'win-win' situation, a company must have considered fall-back positions prior to negotiations. This helps to bracket what is or is not acceptable to the company. Many times a reasonable counterproposal is rejected (which can lead to a breakdown in negotiations) because the other party did not consider fallback positions earlier. Successful negotiations do not follow a "take it or leave it" approach. Of course, once the bottom line has been reached, the company may need to regroup to determine whether it has more room to negotiate.

Question

Prepare a prenegotiations strategy for Saudi Arabia based on what you know about Mr. Rogers' company.

Discussion

A number of factors must be considered up front when doing business in Saudi Arabia. First is the influence of the Islam religion on every aspect of a Muslim's life. Second is the role of women in the society. Foreign women are tolerated providing they follow the local practices with regard to proper behavior and attire. These factors vary in intensity based on the country one is in. Some countries, such as Jordan, Egypt, and Lebanon, are more liberal; other countries, such as Saudi Arabia and other Gulf States, are more restrictive.[7]

Selecting the Right Team Members

Mr. Rogers' company needs to decide whether to include a woman on the negotiating team. The company must exercise care when selecting a woman for assignment in Saudi Arabia.

The company must recognize the need to have a local sponsor to arrange appointments. The sponsor is not part of the team but is essential in conducting any kind of business in Saudi Arabia. The company should select a sponsor who is well connected in Saudi Arabia. Contacts should be established through the Federation of Saudi Chambers of Commerce and Industry or through any of the various chambers of the Kingdom.

Providing Appropriate Training

The company must have a clear understanding of the Saudi culture and the influence of the Islam religion on the culture. Important cultural traits include the following:

- Gentle, limp handshakes are common. Business cards should have one side printed in English and the other side printed in Arabic.
- The Middle East is a collective, polychronic, touch-oriented, and high-context culture.
- Nothing happens quickly; patience is necessary; trust and mutual respect are important and can be cultivated only over time.
- To a Saudi, business is an honorable career; connections/networking is important.
- Saudis like to conduct business in person; there should not be an overreliance on telecommunications.
- It is important to show harmony/agreement in business dealings; businessmen want to get to know people before getting down to business.
- Interruptions are common throughout the day.
- Socializing is part of doing business.
- Saudis like to stand close to people they are talking to. This can make Americans uncomfortable.

Identifying Negotiations Objectives

Mr. Rogers's company clearly wants to expand its market into the Middle East. The company should be receptive to using local nationals, including those who can provide managerial training. This will reinforce the company's commitment to the country. Remember, the Saudis are more concerned with relationships, trust, and mutual respect in their business dealings.

Establishing a Negotiations Agenda

This can be the most challenging part of the prenegotiations activities. Americans like to finish negotiations quickly, which does not happen in Saudi Arabia. The selection of a sponsor with the right connections can expedite the negotiation process. When building a timetable, one should recognize the Middle

Eastern culture as collective, polychronic, and influenced by Islamic values. Delays are common.

Developing Concession Strategies

Concession strategies will be needed in areas such as menu items, store locations, store hours (to accommodate daily prayer and holidays such as Ramadan), exclusive versus nonexclusive franchising arrangements, use of local nationals versus expatriates, personnel training, financial commitment, settlement of disputes, revenue repatriation, and social/community responsibilities. A good negotiator knows when to trade off one concession for another. The bottom line is to make the negotiations a win-win situation for both sides.

ASIAN NEGOTIATIONS

NEGOTIATING IN VIETNAM—A RISING ASIAN ECONOMIC TIGER

Background

Since the United States normalized diplomatic ties with Vietnam in 1994, there has been a surge of economic activities in the country. A steady stream of U.S. foreign investments has poured into Vietnam. The country's current economic growth has the potential to challenge that of the Pacific Rim countries. If such growth continues, Vietnam could become a major economic force in Asia in the twenty-first century.

Even though Vietnam offers many business opportunities, the wise foreign investor needs to be aware of the economic, political, and social risks associated with doing business in Vietnam. Despite the unification of North and South Vietnam economic progress in the northern part of the country has significantly lagged behind that of the southern part. There is also a dire need for improvement of the country's infrastructure, especially in the areas of transportation and telecommunications. Even though Vietnam's government has created a political and legal environment more conducive to a free market system, the government is still overtly involved in business activities, especially when they involve foreign companies. Violations of basic human rights and social freedoms are major concerns as well.

C&A Electronics, Inc., is a U.S.-based company that specializes in the manufacturing of electronic communication switches for telecommunications systems. The company's main focus has been marketing to developing countries where improvements in telecommunications systems are a top priority. During the past ten years, the company has expanded its operations into Eastern Europe, Latin America, and Asia. The main market in Asia has been China. In 2001, C&A Electronics decided to expand its operations into Southeast Asia. A preliminary marketing research identified Vietnam as the entry point. Dick Bernard, the company's business development manager, made initial contact with the Vietnamese government in May 2001 and was linked up with a privately owned telecommunications company, Vietnam Telecommunications Services, Inc. (VTS), located in Ho Chi Minh City. VTS was under contract to the Vietnamese government to upgrade the telecommunications system throughout Vietnam. VTS had been negotiating with large foreign telecommunications companies such as AT&T, Siemens, NEC, and Ericsson.

Mr. Bernard's first meeting with VTS went very well. VTS was impressed with C&A Electronics' experience in other developing countries and felt more comfortable dealing with a small company. It was clear from the outset that the Vietnamese government would be a party to any future negotiation. The first meeting ended on a positive note with an agreement to meet in 90 days, at which time C&A Electronics would submit a formal proposal to VTS.

In September 2001, Mr. Bernard met with VTS and provided a detailed proposal of how his company's communication switch could be integrated into VTS's telecommunications infrastructure. C&A Electronics was willing to enter into a licensing arrangement under which it would retain control over the switching technology. C&A Electronics would provide the switches to VTS based on an agreed-upon schedule. VTS was pleased with the proposal and requested a formal meeting for its senior management to review the proposal in more detail. Both companies agreed to meet in Hanoi, Vietnam, in October 2001.

On October 14, 2001, Mr. Bernard arrived in Hanoi prepared to discuss his company's proposal in more detail. Upon arriving at the VTS facilities, he was ushered into a conference room where, much to his surprise, he found several high-ranking government officials in attendance. The meeting began with introductions, and then the senior government official, Mr. Nguyen Van Quoc, took over the meeting. Mr. Nguyen stated that the development of an up-to-date telecommunications system was critical to Vietnam's future economic success. There were, however, several governmental requirements in the area of technology transfer, foreign currencies, and operational staffing.

The Vietnamese government considered the telecommunications system an essential industry to the country. The government's intention was to have the capability to produce the complete system in Vietnam, which meant that the switching technology was essential. The Vietnamese government recognized C&A Electronics' concern over safeguarding its intellectual property rights (IPRs). The government was also concerned with the payment mechanism. In fact, the Vietnamese government wanted to use a countertrade buyback arrangement. Under this arrangement, C&A Electronics would provide VTS with the required technology, machinery, and equipment needed for in-country production. Once operations were up and running, C&A Electronics would buy back from VTS an agreed-upon portion of the switching production. This approach would help Vietnam better manage its foreign trade account. The Vietnamese government was also concerned with development of a cadre of technicians and managers who could oversee the implementation of the system throughout Vietnam. C&A Electronics' experience in markets of other developing countries would prove to be invaluable.

To show Vietnam's commitment to doing business with C&A Electronics, Mr. Nguyen closed by saying that his government would be willing to help C&A Electronics market its products to other Southeast Asian countries. Mr. Nguyen thanked Mr. Bernard for providing a comprehensive proposal and turned the meeting over to VTS.

Questions

1. Do you think C&A Electronics should be negotiating with VTS? Explain your position.
2. What should be the negotiating position of C&A Electronics toward governmental requirements raised by Mr. Nguyen?

Discussion

Discussion about the previous questions follows.

1. This case shows the difficulty encountered in doing business with a centrally planned Communist country. A high degree of political, economic, and social risks is associated with doing business in such a country. However, the degree of risk varies from country to country. For example, China is a

Communist country that has moved somewhat toward a free market economy since the 1970s. China has experienced high annual economic growth over the past decade that is expected to continue well into the twenty-first century. This growth has been due in part to China's willingness to liberalize its international trade laws and its recent admission to the World Trade Organization. Since normalizing its trade relations with the United States in 1994, Vietnam has likewise shown economic growth. If this growth continues, Vietnam can become a major economic driving force in Southeast Asia in the twenty-first century.

There are, however, concerns in doing business with Vietnam. Even though the Vietnamese government has created a political and legal environment more conducive to a free market system, the government is still overtly involved in business activities, especially when they involve foreign companies. This exercise illustrates that type of involvement. The Vietnamese government has a history of not safeguarding intellectual property rights, which should be a major concern to C&A Electronics. There is also the opportunity cost of not seeking out and evaluating new business opportunities or fully exploiting existing business activities, such as in China. (Remember, China represents a very large market with 1.3 billion people.) Lastly, there is the danger that due to a high level of government involvement, the venture could fail, which would damage C&A Electronics' reputation not only in Southeast Asia but internationally as well.

From the foregoing discussion, one can make an argument *for* or *against* doing business with Vietnam.

2. The three requirements raised by Mr. Nguyen are in the areas of technology transfer, payment mechanism, and operational staffing.

Technology Transfer

It is not surprising that the Vietnamese government would want access to the technology. As Mr. Nguyen stated, the development of an up-to-date telecommunications system is critical to Vietnam's economic success in the future. Since this is an essential industry in Vietnam, the government wants the capability to produce the complete system in-country.

With regard to intellectual property rights, C&A Electronics will have a difficult time negotiating this issue. Vietnam has a history of not safeguarding intellectual property rights. Compromise of the technology could have far-reaching consequences for C&A Electronics. It really comes down to a question of trust: How comfortable is C&A Electronics in doing business with Vietnam? The company realizes that the Vietnamese government is a party to any business arrangement with VTS. Assuming the trust is there, C&A Electronics should agree to the release of the technology—with two caveats. The first caveat is that VTS cannot sell the technology outside Vietnam. The second caveat is a guarantee by the Vietnamese government not to violate the company's intellectual property rights. If a violation occurs, the government will be prosecuted to the full extent of international law.

Payment Mechanism

It is questionable whether C&A Electronics has encountered any form of countertrade in the past. The Vietnamese government's request is not unreasonable. The government is trying to manage its trade balance account. But C&A Electronics may have several concerns. First, what impact will foreign manufacturing have on its domestic manufacturing operations? Will the company be operating at full capacity? Will the shift in manufacturing impact its labor force? The second concern is product quality. Will the switches produced in Vietnam meet C&A Electronics' quality standards? The answer to this question depends on how successful VTS is in incorporating the technology into the system. If C&A Electronics concedes on this issue, VTS must agree to use C&A Electronics' technical support and assistance until quality standards are met.

Operational Staffing

C&A Electronics should have no problem with this requirement, especially if the company agrees to release the technology to VTS. The hiring of local nationals is a good way for a foreign company to improve its relations with the host government. It likewise shows a commitment to the local community. In addition, it will cut down on C&A Electronics' operating expenses since maintaining a large expatriate cadre in Vietnam can be costly.

SUMMARY

The chapter illustrates five different kinds of negotiation situations in different parts of the world. The exercises highlight a variety of issues related to global negotiations, such as (a) role of culture in cross-boarder negotiations, (b) importance of prenegotiation planning, (c) government's involvement in negotiations, (d) international protection of intellectual properties, (e) payment through buyback deals, and (f) barriers to women serving as overseas negotiators.

NOTES

1. See Dean Allen Foster, *Bargaining Across Borders* (New York: McGraw-Hill, 1992).
2. Geert Hofstede, *Cultures and Organizations* (London: McGraw-Hill Europe, 1992).
3. George A. Bolden, Wayne A. Conaway, and Terri Morrison, *Kiss, Bow, or Shake Hands* (Holbrook, MA: Adams Media Corporation, 1994).
4. Philip R. Harris and Robert T. Moran, *Managing Cultural Differences*, 5th Edition (New York: Gulf Publishing Co., 2000).
5. Richard E. Porter and Larry A. Samovar, *Communications Between Cultures*, 4th Edition (New York: Thomson Learning, 2001).
6. John L. Graham and R. A. Herberger, "Negotiations Abroad: Don't Shoot From the Hip," *Harvard Business Review*, July–August 1983, pp. 160–168.
7. Jeswald W. Salacuse, *Making Global Deals: Negotiating in the International Marketplace* (Boston: Houghton Mifflin, 1991).

Note: The exercises in this chapter are based on stereotypes for illustration purposes only. They may not reflect the actual behavior of experienced global negotiators from the countries referenced therein.

SELECTED BIBLIOGRAPHY

Achebe, Chinua. (1959). *Things Fall Apart*. New York: Ballantine.

Acuff, Frank. (1993). *How to Negotiate Anything with Anyone Anywhere*. Chicago: AMACOM.

Adler, Nancy J., Theodore Swartz Gehrke, and John L. Graham. (1987). "Business Negotiations in Canada, Mexico and the United States." *Journal of Business Research* 15 (October), 411–430.

Allas, Tera, and Nikos Georgiades. (2001). "New Tools for Negotiators." *The McKinsey Quarterly*, no. 2, 8–97.

Allison, Graham. (1971). *Essence of Decision: Explaining the Cuban Missile Crisis*. Boston: Little Brown.

Altany, David. (1998). "Wise Men from the East Bearing Fights." *International Management* (UK) 37(5) (May), 67–68.

Arrow, Kenneth, Robert Mnookin, Lee Ross, Amos Tversky, and Robert Wilson. (1995). *Barriers to Conflict Resolution*. New York: Norton.

Axtell, Roger, ed. (1985). *Do's and Taboos Around the World* 3rd edition. New York: John Wiley & Sons.

Axtell, Roger. (1998). *The Do's and Taboos of Body Language Around the World*. New York: John Wiley & Sons.

Baker, James A. (1995). The *Politics of Diplomacy: Revolution, War and Peace: 1989–1992*. New York: G. P. Putnam & Sons.

Banks, John C. (1987). "Negotiating International Mining Agreements: Win-Win versus Win-Lose Bargaining." *Columbia Journal of World Business* (winter), 67–75.

Banthin, Joanna. (1991). "Negotiating with the Japanese." *Mid-Atlantic Journal of Business* 27 (April), 79–81.

Barnum, Cynthia, and Natasha Wolniansky. (1989). "Why Americans Fail at Overseas Negotiations." *Management Review* 78(10) (October), 55–57.

Bennett, Douglas C., and Kenneth E. Sharpe. (1979). "Agenda Setting and Bargaining Power: The Mexican State versus Transnational Corporations." *World Politics* 32(1) (October), 57–89.

Berton, Peter, Hiroshi Kimura, and I. William Zartman, eds. (1999). *International Negotiation: Actors, Structure, Process, Values*. New York: Bedford/St. Martin's.

Big World Inc. (1992). "Negotiating in Today's World" (videotape). Boulder, CO.

Bilder, Richard B. (1981). *Managing the Risks of International Agreement*. Madison: University of Wisconsin Press.

Binnendijk, Hans, ed. (1987). *National Negotiating Styles.* Washington, DC: Foreign Service Institute, U.S. Department of State.

Bird, Arthur. (2001). "Using video clips in the classroom." AIB *Insights,* Third Quarter, 20–22.

Black, J. Stewart, and Mark Mendenhall. (1989). "A practical but theory-based framework for selecting cross-cultural training methods." *Human Resource Management* 28(4), 511–539.

Black, J. Stewart, and Mark Mendenhall. (1993). "Resolving Conflicts with the Japanese: Mission Impossible." *Sloan Management Review* (spring), 49–53.

Boyer, Benjamin, B. Starkey, and John Wilkenfeid. (1999). *Negotiating a Complex World.* New York: Rowman and Littlefield.

Boyer, Brook, and Laurent Cremieux. (1999). "The Anatomy of Association: NGOs and the Evolution of Swiss Climate and Biodiversities Policies." *International Negotiation* 4(2), 255–282.

Breslin, J. William, and Jeffrey Z. Rubin. (1991). *Negotiation Theory and Practice.* Cambridge, MA: Program on Negotiation at Harvard Law School.

Brett, Jeanne, et al. (1998). "Culture and Joint Gains in Negotiation." *Negotiation Journal* 14, 61–86.

Brett, Jeanne M. (2001). *Negotiating Globally.* San Francisco: Jossey-Bass.

Brunner, James A., and Wang You. (1988). "Chinese Negotiating and the Concept of Face." *Journal of International Consumer Marketing* 1(1), 27–43.

Bryan, Robert M., and Peter C. Buck. (1989). "The Cultural Pitfalls In Cross-Border Negotiations." *Mergers and Acquisition* 24(2) (September–October), 61–63.

Burt, David N. (1984). "The Nuances of Negotiating Overseas." *Journal of Purchasing and Materials Management* (winter), 2–8.

Burt, David N. (1989). "The Nuances of Negotiating Overseas." *Journal of Purchasing and Materials Management* 25, 56–64.

Cai, Doi A., and Lendel E. Drake. (1998). "The Business of Business Negotiation: Intercultural Perspectives." In M. E. Roloff, ed. *Communication Yearbook 21,* Newbury Park, CA: Sage, 153–189.

Campbell, Nigel C. G. (1987). "Negotiating with the Chinese—A Commercial Long March." *Journal of Marketing Management* 2(3), 219–223.

Campbell, Nigel C. G., John L. Granham, Alain Jilbert, and Hans Gunther Meissner. (1988). "Marketing Negotiations in France, Germany, the United Kingdom and the United States." *Journal of Marketing* 52(2) (April), 49–62.

Casse, Pierre. (1991). *Negotiating across Cultures.* Washington, DC: United States Institute of Peace Press.

Casse, Pierre, and Surinder Deol. (1985). *Managing Intercultural Negotiations.* Yarmouth, ME: Intercultural Press.

Cavusgil, S. Tamer, and Pervez N. Ghauri. (1990). *Doing Business in Developing Countries: Entry and Negotiation Strategies.* London: Routledge.

Christensen, Carl Roland, David Garvin, and A. Sweet, eds. (1991). *Education for Judgment: The Artistry of Discussion Leadership.* Cambridge, MA: Harvard Business School Press.

Cialdini, Robert B. (1984). *Influence: The Psychology of Persuasion.* New York: William Morrow.

Clavell, James. (1975). *Shogun.* New York: Atheneum.

Cohen, Herb. (1980). *You Can Negotiate Anything.* Secaucus, NJ: Lyle Stuart.

Cohen, Raymond. (1993). "An Advocate's View." In G. O. Faure and Jeffrey Z. Rubin eds. *Culture and Negotiation.* Thousand Oaks, CA: Sage.

Cohen, Raymond. (1997). *Negotiating Across Cultures: International Communication in an Interdependent World.* Rev. ed. Washington, DC: U.S. Institute of Peace.

Contractor, Farok J., and Peter Lorange. (1988). *Cooperative Strategies in International Business.* Lexington, MA: Lexington Books.

Copeland, Michael J., and Larry Griggs. (1985). *Going International.* New York: Random House.

Cormick, George (1989). "Strategic Issues in Structuring Multi-Party Public Policy Negotiations." *Negotiation Journal* 5:125–132.

Cova, Beverly, Frank Nazet, and Robert Salle. (1996). "Project Negotiations: An Episode in the Relationship." In Pervez N. Ghauri and Jean-Claude Usunier eds. *International Business Negotiation.* New York: Elsevier.

Covey, Stephen. (1989). *The 7 Habits of Highly Effective People.* New York: Simon & Schuster.

Crichton, Michael. (1992). *Rising Sun.* New York: Alfred A. Knopf.

Cross, James G. (1969). *The Economics of Bargaining.* New York: Basic Books.

Cross, James G. (1996). "Negotiation as Adaptive Learning." *International Negotiation* 1, 153–178.

Cutcher-Gershenfeld, J., and Watkins. (1997). "Toward a theory of representation in negotiation." Presented at the Academy of Management, Boston.

de Bourbon Busset, J. (1963). *La Grande Conference.* Paris: Gallimard.

De La Torre, J. (1981). "Foreign Investment and Economic Development: Conflict and Negotiation." *Journal of International Business Studies* (fall), 9–32.

Dennett, Raymond, and Joseph E. Johnson. (1989). *Negotiating with the Russians.* New York: World Peace Foundation.

Deverge, Michael. (1986). "Negotiating with the Chinese." *Euro-Asia Business Review* 5(1) (January), 34–36.

Drake, Laura E. (1995). "Negotiation Styles in Intercultural Communication." *The International Journal of Conflict Management* 6(1) (January), 72–90.

Druckman, Daniel. (1983). "Social Psychology and International Negotiations: Processes and Influences." In R. F. Kidd and M. J. Saks eds. *Advances in Applied Social Psychology,* vol. 2. Mahwah, NJ: Erlbaum.

Druckman, Daniel, A. A. Benton, F. Ali, and J. S. Bagur. (1976). "Cultural Differences in Bargaining Behavior: India, Argentina and the United States." *Journal of Conflict Resolution* 20, 413–448.

Dupont, Charles. (1994). *La Negociation: Conduite, Théorie, Applications.* 4th ed. Paris: Dalloz.

Dupont, Charles. (1996) "Negotiation as Coalition-Building." *International Negotiation* 1(1), 47–64.

Eibl-Eibesfeldt, I. (1972). "Similarities and Differences between Cultures in Expressive Movements." In Robert A. Hinde ed. *Non-Verbal Communication.* Cambridge, NY: Cambridge University Press.

Ekman, Paul. (1971). "Universals and Cultural Differences in Facial Expressions of Emotion." In J. Cole ed. *Nebraska Symposium on Motivation.* Lincoln, NE: University of Nebraska Press.

Elgstrom, Ohoman. (1994). "National Culture and International Negotiations." *Cooperation and Conflict* 29(3).

Engholm, Christopher. (1992). "Asian Bargaining Tactics: Counterstrategies for Survival." *East Asian Executive Reports* (July), 9–25.

England, George W. (1978). "Managers and Their Value Systems: A Five-Country Comparative Study," *Columbia Journal of World Business* (summer), 35–42.

Fang, Tony. (1999). *Chinese Business Negotiating Style.* Newbury Park, CA: Sage.

Faure, George O. (1991). "Negotiating in the Orient." *Negotiation Journal* 7, 279–290.

Faure, George O. (1998). "Negotiation: The Chinese Concept." *Negotiation Journal* 14(1).

Faure, George O. (1995). "Nonverbal Negotiation in China." *Negotiation Journal* 11(1), 11–18.

Faure, George O. and Jeffrey, Z. Rubin ed. (1993). *Culture and Negotiation.* Newbury Park, CA: Sage.

Fayerweather, John, and Ashok Kapoor. (1976). *Strategy and Negotiation for the International Corporation.* New York: Ballinger Publications.

Fisher, Glen. (1980). *International Negotiations: A Cross-Cultural Perspective.* Chicago: Intercultural Press, Inc.

Fisher, Roger. (1991). "Negotiating Inside Out: What Are the Best Ways to Relate Internal Negotiations with External Ones?" In J. W. Breslin, and J. Rubin eds. *Negotiation Theory and Practice.* Cambridge, MA: Program on Negotiation Books.

Fisher, Roger, et al. (1994). *Beyond Machiavelli: Tools for Coping with Conflict.* Cambridge, MA: Harvard University Press.

Fisher, Roger, William Ury, and Bruce Patton. (1991). *Getting to YES: Negotiating Agreement without Giving In* 2nd ed. New York: Penguin Books.

Fisher, Roger, and Scott Brown. (1989). *Getting Together: Building Relationships As We Negotiate.* New York: Penguin Books.

Foster, Dean Allen. (1995). *Bargaining Across Borders: How to Negotiate Business Successfully Anywhere in the World.* New York: McGraw-Hill.

Frances, June N. P. (1991). "When in Rome? The Effects of Cultural Adaptation on Intercultural Business Negotiations." *Journal of International Business Studies* 22(3) (Third Quarter), 403–428.

Frank, Sergy. (1992). "Global Negotiating." *Sales & Marketing Management* (May), 64–70.

Frazier, Gary L., James D. Gill, and Sudhir H. Kale. (1989). "Dealer Dependence Levels and Reciprocal Actions in a Channel of Distribution in a Developing Country." *Journal of Marketing* 53 (January), 50–69.

Galante, Steven. (1984). "U.S. Firms Aim to Avert Cultural Clashes." *The Wall Street Journal* (July 30).

Gannon, Martin J. (1994). *Understanding Global Cultures: Metaphorical Journeys Through 17 Countries.* Thousand Oaks, CA: Sage.

Gardner, Howard. (1999). *The Disciplined Mind.* New York: Simon & Schuster.

Ghauri, Pervez N. (1986). "Guidelines for International Business Negotiations." *International Marketing Review* (autumn), 72–82.

Ghauri, Pervez N. (1988). "Negotiating with Firms in Developing Countries: Two Case Studies." *Industrial Marketing Management* 17(1) (February), 49–53.

Ghauri, Pervez N., and Jean-Claude Usunier, eds. (1996). *International Business Negotiation.* New York: Elsevier.

Gilbert, Nick. (1985). "The China Guanxi." *Forbes* (July), 104.

Gleick, James. (1987). *Chaos: Making a New Science.* New York: Viking Press.

Golden, Arthur. (1997). *Memoirs of a Geisha.* Toronto: Vintage Canada.

Gosling, Lester Arthur Peter. (1990). "Your Face Is Your Fortune: Fortune Telling and Business in Southeast Asia." *Journal of Southeast Asia Business* 6(4), 41–52.

Graham, John L. (1986). "Across the Negotiating Table from the Japanese." *International Marketing Review* (autumn), 58–70.

Graham, John L. (1983). "Brazilian, Japanese, and American Business Negotiations." *Journal of International Business Studies* 14(1) (spring–summer), 44–66.

Graham, John L. (1993). "Business Negotiations: Generalizations about Latin America and East Asia Are Dangerous." UCINSIGHT University of California Irvine GSM (summer), 6–23.

Graham, John L. (1983). "Business Negotiations in Japan, Brazil, and the United States." *Journal of International Business Studies* 14 (spring–summer), 47–62.

Graham, John L. (1984). "A Comparison of Japanese and American Business Negotiations." *International Journal of Research in Marketing* 1, 51–68.

Graham, John L. (1985). "Cross Cultural Marketing Negotiations: A Laboratory Experiment." *Marketing Science* (spring), 130–146.

Graham, John L. (1987). "Difference Given the Buyer: Variation Across Twelve Cultures." *Cooperative Strategies in International Business,* Peter Lorange and Farok Contractor, eds. Lexington, MA: Lexington Books, 473–484.

Graham, John L. (1985). "The Influence of Culture on the Process of Business Negotiations: An Exploratory Study." *Journal of International Business Studies* 16(1) (spring), 81–96. (Study of the United States, Japan, and Brazil.)

Graham, John L., Arthur T. Mintu, and Wayne Rodgers. (1994). "Explorations of Negotiation Behaviors in Ten Foreign Cultures Using a Model Developed in the United States." *Management Science* 40(1), January, 72–95.

Graham, John L., and Chi-Yuan Y. Lin. (1986). "A Comparison of Marketing and Negotiations in the Republic of China (Taiwan) and the United States," *Advances in International Marketing,* S. Tamer Cavusgil, ed. Greenwich, CT: JAI Press.

Graham, John L., and Chi-Yuan Y. Lin. (1987). "A Comparison of Marketing Negotiations in the Republic of China (Taiwan) and the United States." *Advances in International Marketing* 2, Greenwich, CT: JAI Press, 23–46.

Graham, John L., Dong Kim, Chi-Yuan Lin, and Michael Robinson. (1988). "Buyer-Seller Negotiations around the Pacific Rim: Differences in Fundamental Exchange Processes." *Journal of Consumer Research* 15 (June), 48–54.

Graham, John L., and Harry G. Meissner. (1986). "Content Analysis of Business Negotiations in Five Countries." Working Paper, University of Southern California.

Graham, John L., and J. Douglas Andrews. (1987). "A Holistic Analysis of Cross-Cultural Business Negotiation." *Journal of Business Communication* 23, 63–77.

Graham, John L., Leonid I. Evenko, and Mahesh N. Rajan. (1992). "An Empirical Comparison of Soviet and American Business Negotiations." *Journal of International Business Studies* (Third Quarter), 387–418.

Graham, John L., and Richard A. Herberger. (1983). "Negotiators Abroad: Don't Shoot from the Hip." *Harvard Business Review* (July–August), 160–168.

Graham, John L., and Yoshihiro Sano. (1984). *Smart Bargaining: Doing Business with the Japanese.* Cambridge, MA: Ballinger.

Graham, John L., and Yoshihiro Sano. (1989). *Smart Bargaining: Doing Business with the Japanese.* New York: Harper Business.

Graham, John L., and Yoshihiro Sano. (1990). *Smart Bargaining: Doing Business with the Japanese* 2nd ed. Cambridge, MA: Ballinger.

Graham, Robert J. (1981). "The Role of Perception of Time in Consumer Research." *Journal of Consumer Research* 7 (March), 335–342.

Griffin, Trenholme J., and W. Russell Daggatt. (1990). *The Global Negotiator: Building Strong Business Relationships Anywhere in the World.* New York: Harper Business.

Grindsted, Annette. (1994). "The Impact of Cultural Styles on Negotiations: A Case Study of Spaniards and Danes." *IEEE Transactions on Professional Communication* 37(1) (March), 34–38.

Gross, Stein H. (1988). "International Negotiation: A Multidisciplinary Perspective." *Negotiation Journal* 4(3), 221–232.

Guittard, Stephen W. (1974). "Negotiating and Administering an International Sales Contract with the Japanese." *International Lawyer* 8, 823–831.

Guittard, Stephen W., and Sano Yoshihiro. (1989). *Smart Bargaining: Dealing with the Japanese.* New York: Harper & Row.

Gulbro, Robert, and Paul Herbig. (1995). "Differences in Cross-Cultural Negotiating Behavior between Industrial Product and Consumer Firms." *Journal of Business and Industrial Marketing* 10(3), 18–28.

Gulbro, Robert, and Paul Herbig. (1996). "Negotiating Successfully in Cross-Cultural Situations." *Industrial Marketing Management* 24 (March), 1–12.

Habeeb, William Mark. (1988). *Power and Tactics in International Negotiation.* Baltimore: Johns Hopkins University Press.

Hall, Edward T. (1959). *The Silent Language.* Greenwich, CT: Fawcett.

Hall, Edward T., and Mildred Hall. (1987). *Hidden Differences: Doing Business with the Japanese.* Garden City, NY: Anchor Books, Doubleday.

Hall, Edward T., and Hall Mildred. (1990). *Understanding Cultural Differences: Germans, French and Americans.* Yarmouth, ME: Intercultural Press.

Hampden-Turner, C., and F. Trompenaars. (2000). *Building Cross Cultural Confidence.* New York: John Wiley & Sons.

Hampson, Fred O. (1994). *Multilateral Negotiation.* Baltimore: Johns Hopkins University Press.

Harris, Philip R., and Robert T. Moran. (1991). *Managing Cultural Differences.* Houston: Gulf Publishing Company.

Harrison, George W., and Ben H. Saffer. (1980). "Negotiating at 30 Paces." *Management Review* (April), 51–54.

Haskel, Barbara G. (1974). "Disputes, Strategies and Opportunities and Opportunity Costs: The Example of Scandinavian Economic Market Negotiations." *International Studies Quarterly* 18(2), 3–30.

Hawrysh, Brian Mark, and Judith Lynne Zaichkowsky. (1990). "Cultural Approaches to Negotiations: Understanding the Japanese." *International Marketing Review* 7(2), 28–42.

Hay, M., and J. C. Usunier. (1993). "Time and Strategic Action: A Cross-Cultural View." *Time and Society* 2(3) (September).

Heiba, Farouk I. (1984). "International Business Negotiations: A Strategic Planning Model." *International Marketing Review* 1/(4) (autumn), 5–16.

Hendon, Donald W., and Rebecca Angeles Hendon. (1990). *World-Class Negotiating: Dealmaking in the Global Marketplace.* New York: John Wiley & Sons.

Hendon, Donald W., Rebecca A. Hendon, and Paul Herbig. (1996). *Cross Cultural Business Negotiations.* Quorum Books.

Herbig, Paul A., and Hugh E. Kramer. (1991). "Cross-Cultural Negotiations: Success Through Understanding." *Management Decision* 29(1), 19–31.

Herbig, Paul A., and Hugh E. Kramer. (1992). "The Dos and Don'ts of Cross-Cultural Negotiations." *Industrial Marketing Management* 20(2), 1–12.

Herbig, Paul A., and Hugh E. Kramer. (1992). "The Role of Cross-Cultural Negotiations in International Marketing." *Marketing Intelligence and Planning* 10(2), 10–13.

Hobson, Charles. (1999). "E-Negotiations." *Negotiation Journal* 15, 201–209.

Hofstede, Geert. (1989). "Cultural Predictors of National Negotiation Styles." In Frances Mautner-Markhof, *Process of International Negotiations.* Boulder, CO: Westview Press.

Hofstede, Geert. (1992). *Cultures and Organizations.* London: McGraw-Hill Europe.

Hofstede, Geert. (1994). *Culture's Consequences.* London: Sage.

Hofstede, Geert, and Jean-Claude Usunier. (1996). "Hofstede's Dimensions of Culture and Their Influence on International Business Negotiations." In Pervez Ghauri and Jean-Claude Usunier, *International Business Negotiations.* Oxford: Pergamon.

Holbrooke, Richard. (1998). *To End a War.* New York: Random House.

Hopmann, P. Terrence. (1996). *The Negotiation Process and the Resolution of International Conflicts.* Columbia, SC: University of South Carolina Press.

Husted, Bryan W. (1994). "Bargaining with the Gringos: An Exploratory Study of Negotiations between Mexican and U.S. Firms." *The International Executive* 36(5), 625–644.

Ikle, Fred Charles. (1964). *How Nations Negotiate.* Millwood, NY: Kraus Reprint Co.

Ikle, Fred Charles. (1982). *How Nations Negotiate.* New York: Harper and Row.

International Negotiation Institute. (1982). "Effective Preparation for Negotiation." *Monographs on International Business Negotiation* No. 1. Princeton, NJ: International Negotiation Institute.

Janosik, Robert. (1987). "Rethinking the Culture-Negotiation Link." *Negotiation Journal* 3, 385–395.

Jayachandran, Chandra. (1991). "International Technology Collaborations: Issues in Negotiations." *Management Decision: Quarterly Review of Management Technology* 29(6) (November), 80–85.

Jensen, Kevin and Ike Unt. (2002). *Negotiating Partnerships.* New York: Prentice-Hall.

Johnson, Robert. (1993). *Negotiation Basics.* Newbury Park, CA: Sage.

Jonsson, Claude. (1989). "Communication Processes in International Negotiation: Some Common Mistakes." In F. F. Mautner-Markhof ed. *Processes of International Negotiations.* Boulder, CO: Westview Press.

Jonsson, Claude et al. (1998). "Negotiations in Networks in the European Union." *International Negotiation* 3, 319–344.

Kale, Sudhir H., and John W. Barnes. (1992). "Understanding the Domain of Cross-National Buyer-Seller Interactions." *Journal of International Business Studies* (First Quarter), 101–132.

Kapoor, Ashok. (1970). *International Business Negotiations: A Study in India.* New York: New York University Press.

Kapoor, Ashok. (1974). "MNC Negotiations: Characteristics and Planning Implications." *Columbia Journal of World Business* (winter), 121–132.

Kapoor, Ashok. (1975). *Planning for International Business Negotiations.* Cambridge, MA: Ballinger.

Kazuo, Ogura. (1979). "How the 'Inscrutables' Negotiate with the 'Inscrutables': Chinese Negotiating Tactics Vis-à-vis the Japanese." *The China Quarterly* 79, 529–552.

Kellerman, Barbara, and Jeffrey Z. Rubin, eds. (1988). *Leadership and Negotiation in the Middle East.* New York: Praeger.

Kemper, Robert, and David Kemper. (1999). *Negotiation.* N.J.: Literature Scarecrow Press.

Kennedy, George. (1985). *Doing Business Abroad.* New York: Simon & Schuster.

Kennedy, George. (1987). *Negotiate Anywhere!* London: Arrow Books.

Kennedy, Robert, and Howard Raiffa. (1992). "Structuring and Analyzing Values for Multiple-Issue Negotiations." In P. Young ed. *Negotiation Analysis.* Ann Arbor: University of Michigan Press.

Kersten, George, and Sam Noronha. (1999). "Negotiation Via the World Wide Web: A Cross-Cultural Study of Decision Making." *Group Decision and Negotiation* 8(3).

Kim, Wen C. and Robert Mauborgne. "Fair Process: Managing in the Knowledge Economy." *Harvard Business Review* (July–August), 197.

Klein, Gary (1998). *Sources of Power: How People Make Decisions.* Cambridge, MA: MIT Press.

Kreisberg, Paul H. (1994). "China's Negotiating Behavior." In Thomas W. Robinson and David Shambaugh eds. *Chinese Foreign Policy: Theory and Practice.* Oxford: Clarendon Press.

Kremenyuk, Victor, ed. (1991). *International Negotiation.* San Francisco: Jossey-Bass.

Lakos, Amos. (1989). *International Negotiations: A Bibliography.* Boulder, CO: Westview Press.

Lall, Arthur. (1966). *Modern International Negotiation.* New York: Columbia University Press.

Lapeyre, Benedicte, and Pamela Sheppard, *Negotiate in French As Well As in English: Negocier en Anglais comme en Francais.* London: Nicholas Brealey Publishing.

Lavin, Franklin L. (1994). "Negotiating with the Chinese." *Foreign Affairs* 73.

Lax, David A., and James K. Sebenius. (1986). *The Manager as Negotiator.* New York: Free Press.

Lax, David, and James Sebenius. (1991). "The Power of Alternatives or the Limits to Negotiation." In J. W. Breslin and Jeffrey Rubin eds. *Negotiation Theory and Practice.* Cambridge, MA: Program on Negotiation Books.

Lax, David, and James Sebenius. (1991). "Thinking Coalitionally." In P. Young ed. *Negotiation Analysis.* Ann Arbor: University of Michigan Press.

Lee, Eve. (1980). "Saudis as We, Americans as They," *The Bridge* (fall), 3–5, 32–334.

Lee, Kam-hon, and Thamis Wing-Chun Lo. (1988). "An American Business People's Perceptions of Marketing and Negotiating in the People's Republic of China." *International Marketing Review* 5(2), 41–51.

Lewicki, Roy, D. Saunders, and J. Minton, (1993). *Negotiation* 3rd ed. Burr Ridge, IL: McGraw-Hill.

Lewis, Richard. (2003). *The Cultural Imperative.* London: Nicholas Brealy Publishing.

Lewis, Richard. (1996). *When Cultures Collide.* London: Nicholas Brealy Publishing.

Li, X. (1999). *Chinese-Dutch Business Negotiations.* Amsterdam: Rodopi.

Lundberg, Kim. (1996). "The Oslo Channel: Finding a Secret Path to Peace." Case C113–96-1333.0, John F. Kennedy School of Government, Harvard University.

March, Robert M. (1982). "Business Negotiation as Cross-Cultural Communication: The Japanese Western Case." *Cross Currents* 9(1) (spring).

March, Robert M. (1985). "East Meets West at the Negotiating Table." *Winds* (April), 55–57.

March, Robert M. (1991). *The Japanese Negotiatior.* Tokyo: Kodansha International.

March, Robert M. (1985). "No No's in Negotiating with the Japanese." *Across the Border* (April), 44–50.

Mautner-Markhof, F., ed. (1989). *Processes of International Negotiations.* Boulder, CO: Westview Press.

McCall, John B., and Mathew B. Warrington. (1990). *Marketing By Agreement: A Cross-Cultural Approach to Business Negotiation* 2nd ed. New York: John Wiley & Sons.

McCreary, Don R. (1986). *Japanese-U.S. Business Negotiations: A Cross-Cultural Study.* New York: Praeger.

McKersie, Rich B., and Norm Fonstad. (1997). "Teaching Negotiating Theory and Skills over the Internet." *Negotiation Journal* 13, 363–368.

Meridian Resources Associates. (1992). "Working with China" (videotape series). San Francisco.

Min, Harry, and Wes Galle. (1993). "International Negotiation Strategies of U.S. Purchasing Professionals." *International Journal of Purchasing and Materials Management* (summer).

Mintzberg, Henry. (1987). "Crafting Strategy." *Harvard Business Review* (July–August).

Mintzberg, Henry. (1990). "Strategy Formation: Schools of Thought." In J. Fredrickson ed. *Perspectives on Strategic Management.* New York: Harper Business.

Mistry, Rohinton. (1995). *A Fine Balance.* Toronto: McClelland & Stewart.

Mnookin, Robert, and Linda Susskins, eds. (1999). *Negotiating on Behalf of Others.* San Francisco, CA: Sage Publications.

Moncrief, William C. (1993). "A Comparison of Sales Activities in an International Setting." In Erdener Kaynak ed. *The Global Business: Four Key Marketing Strategies.* New York: Haworth Press.

Moran, Robert T. (1985). *Getting Your Yen's Worth: How to Negotiate with Japan, Inc.* Houston: Gulf Publishing Company.

Moran, Robert T., and William G. Stripp. (1991). *Successful International Business Negotiation.* Houston: Gulf Publishing Company.

Morrison, Terri, Wayne A. Conaway, and George A. Borden. (1994). *Kiss, Bow, or Shake Hands: How to Do Business in Sixty Countries.* Holbrook, MA: Bob Adams, Inc.

Nakane, Chie. (1970). *Japanese Society.* Berkeley: University of California Press.

National Film Board of Canada. (1985). "Final Offer." South Burlington, VT: California Newsreel.

Natlandsmyr, Jan Halvor, and Jorn Rognes. (1995). "Culture, Behavior, and Negotiation Outcomes: A Comparative and Cross-Cultural Study of Mexican and Norwegian Negotiators." *The International Journal of Conflict Management* 6(1), 5–29.

OctoberFilms. (2002). "The Siege of Bethlehem." London.

Odell, John S. (1980). "Latin American Trade Negotiations with the United States." *International Organization* 34 (spring), 207–228.

Oikawa, Naoko, and John Tanner, Jr. (1992). "Influence of Japanese Culture on Business Relations and Negotiations." *Journal of Services Marketing* 6(13) (summer), 1–12.

Oxnam, Robert B. (1989). *Cinnabar: A Novel of China.* New York: St. Martin's Press.

Parker, Victor. (1996). "Negotiating Licensing Agreements." In Pervez Ghauri and Jean-Claude Usunier eds. *International Business Negotiation.* New York: Elsevier.

Pendergast, William. "Managing the Negotiation Agenda." *Negotiation Journal* 6, 135–145.

Pfeiffer, John. (1988). "How Not to Lose the Trade Wars by Cultural Gaffes." *Smithsonian* 18, 145–156.

Posses, Frederick. (1978). *The Art of International Negotiation.* London: Business Books, Brookfield Publishing.

Puffer, Sheila M., ed. (1996). *Management Across Cultures: Insights from Fiction and Practice.* Cambridge, MA: Blackwell.

Putnam, Robert. (1988). "Diplomacy and Domestic Politics: The Logic of Two-Level Games." *International Organizations* 42(3): 427–460.

Pye, Lucian W. (1992). "The Chinese Approach to Negotiating." *The International Executive* 34(6) (November/December), 463–468.

Pye, Lucian W. (1982). *Chinese Commercial Negotiating Style.* Cambridge, MA: Oelgeschlager, Gunn & Hain.

Pye, Lucian W. (1992). *Chinese Negotiating Style: Commercial Approaches and Cultural Principles.* New York: Quorum Books.

Pye, Lucian W., and Stan R. Hendryx. (1986). "The China Trade: Making the Deal." *Harvard Business Review* 64(4) (July/August), 74–85.

Quinn, John. (1992). "Strategic Change: 'Logical Incrementalism.'" In Henry Mintzberg and J. Quinn eds. *The Strategy Process: Concepts, Contexts and Cases.* Englewood Cliffs, NJ: Prentice Hall.

Radway, Robert J. (1978). "Negotiating in the Caribbean Basin: Trade and Investment Contracts." *International Trade Law Journal* 4 (winter), 164–169.

Raiffa, Howard. (1982). *The Art and Science of Negotiation.* Cambridge, MA: The Belknap Press of Harvard University Press.

Raiffa, Howard. (1991). "Mock Pseudo-Negotiations with Surrogate Disputants." In J. William Breslin and Jeffrey Rubin eds. *Negotiation Theory and Practice.* Cambridge, MA: Program on Negotiation Books.

Raiffa, Howard. (1992). "Preparing for Negotiations." Li & Fung Lecture, Chinese University of Hong Kong.

Rangaswany, Arvind, Jehoshua Eliashberg, Raymond R. Burk, and Jerry Wind. (1989). "Developing Marketing Expert Systems: An Application to International Negotiations." *Journal of Marketing* 53(4) (October), 24–38.

Raval, Dinker, and Bina Raval. (1998). "Cultural Shift in Indian Managers' Perceptions: Implications for MNC's Negotiation Strategy." *Proceedings of the ASC Conference,* 337–345.

Reardon, Kathleen Kelley, and Robert E. Spekman. (1994). "Starting Out Right: Negotiation Lessons for Domestic and Cross-Cultural Business Alliances." *Business Horizons* (January–February), 71–79.

Riker, William. (1986). *The Art of Political Manipulation.* New Haven, CT: Yale University Press.

Robinson, Robert J. (1997). "Errors in Social Judgment: Implications for Negotiation and Conflict Resolution, Part 1: Biased Assimilation of Information." HBS no. 9-897-103. Boston: Harvard Business School Publishing.

Robinson, Robert J. (1997). "Errors in Social Judgment: Implications for Negotiation and Conflict Resolution, Part 2: Partisan Perceptions." HBS no. 9-897-104. Boston: Harvard Business School Publishing.

Roemer, Charles, P. Garb, John Neu, and John L. Graham. (1999). "A Comparison of American and Russian Patterns of Behavior in Buyer-Seller Negotiations Using Observational Measures." *International Negotiation* 4, 37–61.

Rosegrant, Susan, and Michael Watkins. (1995). "Carrots, Sticks and Question Marks: Negotiating the North Korean Nuclear Crisis" (A) and (B). Cambridge, MA: John F. Kennedy School of Government Case nos. 1297.0 and 1298.0.

Rosegrant, Susan, and Michael Watkins. (1996). "Getting to Dayton: Negotiating an End to the War in Bosnia." Cambridge, MA: John F. Kennedy School of Government Case no. c125-96-1356.0.

Rosegrant, Susan, and Michael Watkins. (1994). "The Gulf Crisis: Building a Coalition for War." Cambridge, MA: John F. Kennedy School of Government Case no. 1264.0.

Rosegrant, Susan, and Michael Watkins. (1996). "A 'Seamless' Transition: United States and United Nations Operation in Somalia—1992–1993" (A) and (B). Cambridge, MA: John F. Kennedy School of Government Case nos. 1324.0 and 1325.0.

Rosegrant, Susan, and Michael Watkins. (1996). "Sources of Power in Coalition Building." *Negotiation Journal* 12(1) 47–68.

Rosen, Stanley, and Mat Watkins. (1998). "Rethinking 'Preparation' in Negotiation." Harvard Business School Working paper no. 99–042.

Ross, Lawrence, and Art Ward. (1995). "Psychological Barriers to Dispute Resolution." *Advances in Experimental Social Psychology* 27: 255–304.

Roston, John. (1992). McGill Negotiation Simulator. Instructional Communications Centre, McGill University: Montreal.

Rubin, Jeffrey Z., Dean G. Pruitt, and Sung Hee Kim. (1994). *Social Conflict: Escalation, Stalemate and Settlement* 2nd ed. New York: McGraw-Hill.

Rubin, Jeffrey Z., and George O. Faure. (1993). *Culture and Negotiation.* San Francisco, CA: Sage.

Rubin, Jeffrey, and Frank Sander. "When Should We Use Agents? Direct v. Representative Negotiation." In J. William Breslin and Jeffrey Rubin eds. *Negotiation Theory and Practice.* Cambridge, MA: Program on Negotiation Books, 1991.

Salacuse, Jeswald W. (1999). "Intercultural Negotiation in International Business." *Group Decision and Negotiation* 9(3).

Salacuse, Jeswald W. (1991). *Making Global Deals: Negotiating in the International Marketplace.* Boston: Houghton Mifflin.

Saunders, Henry. "We Need a Larger Theory of Negotiation: The Importance of Pre-Negotiating Phases." *Negotiation Journal* 1, 249–262.

Sawyer, John, and Harry Guetzkow. (1965). "Bargaining and Negotiation in International Relations." In H. Kelman ed. *International Behavior.* New York: Holt, Rinehart and Winston.

Schneider, Susan C., and Jean-Louis Barsoux. (1997). *Managing Across Cultures.* London: Prentice-Hall.

Schecter, John. (1998). *Russian Negotiating Behavior.* Washington DC: U.S. Institute of Peace Press.

Schon, Donald (1983). *The Reflective Practitioner: How Professionals Think in Action.* New York: Basic Books.

Schuster, Camille P., and Michael J. Copeland. (1996). *Global Business: Planning for Sales and Negotiations.* Fort Worth: Dryden Press.

Schuster, Paul. (1993). "Sensitivity to Differences in Cultures Can Smooth Dealings." *The Business Record* (November 29–December), 15.

Sebenius, James. (1996). "Introduction to Negotiation Analysis: Structure, People, and Context." HBS Note no. 896-034.

Sebenius, James. (1998). "Negotiating Cross-Border Acquisitions." *Sloan Management Review* 39, 27–41.

Sebenius, James. (1984). *Negotiating the Law of the Sea.* Cambridge, MA: Harvard University Press.

Sebenius, James. (1992). "Negotiation Analysis: A Characterization and Review." *Management Science* 38, 1, 18–38.

Sebenius, James. (1996). "Sequencing to Build Coalitions: With Whom Should I Talk First?" In R. Zekhauser, R. Keeney, and James Sebenius eds. *Wise Choices: Decisions, Games, and Negotiations.* Boston: Harvard Business School Press.

Sen, Sondra. (1981). "The Art of International Negotiating: Doing Business in the Middle East." *Art of Negotiating Newsletter* 11(3) (December).

Shell, George. (1999). *Bargaining for Advantage.* New York: Viking.

Shenkar, Oded, and Simcha Ronen. (1987). "The Cultural Context of Negotiations: The Implications of Chinese Interpersonal Norms." *The Journal of Applied Behavioral Science* 23(2), 263–275.

Sheth, Jag. (1983). "Cross-Cultural Influences on the Buyer-Seller Interaction/ Negotiation Process." *Asia Pacific Journal of Management* 1(1), 46–55.

Silkenat, John, and James Anesty, eds. (1999). *The ABA Guide to International Business Negotiations.* Chicago: ABA.

Solomon, Richard H. (1999). *Chinese Negotiating Behavior.* Washington, DC: U.S. Institute of Peace Press.

Stein, Janice Gross, ed. (1989). *Getting to the Table: The Process of International Prenegotiation.* Baltimore: Johns Hopkins University Press.

Stein, Janice Gross. (1989). "Getting to the Table: The Triggers, Stages, Functions, and Consequences of Prenegotiation." In J. Stein ed. *Getting to the Table: The Process of International Prenegotiation.* Baltimore: Johns Hopkins University Press, 239–268.

Stein, Janice Gross. (1988). "International Negotiation: A Multidisciplinary Perspective." *Negotiation Journal* 4, 221–231.

Stewart, Edward C., and Milton J. Bennett. (1991). *American Cultural Patterns: A Cross-Cultural Perspective*. Rev. ed. Yarmouth, ME: Intercultural Press.

Stewart, Sally, and Charles F. Keown. (1989). "Talking with the Dragon: Negotiating in the People's Republic of China." *Columbia Journal of World Business* 24(3) (fall), 68–72.

Stoever, William A. (1979). "Renegotiation: The Cutting Edge of Relations Between MNCs and LDCs." *Columbia Journal of World Business* (spring), 5–13.

Stoever, William A. (1981). *Renegotiations in International Business Transactions: The Process of Dispute Resolution Between Multinational Investors and Host Societies*. Lexington, MA: Lexington Books.

Stone, Ray. (1989). "Negotiating in Asia." *The Practicing Manager* 9(2) (autumn), 36–39.

Sullivan, Sam E., and Hien Tu. (1995). "Developing Globally Competent Students: A Review and Recommendations." *Journal of Management Education* 19(4), 473–493.

Swierczek, Fredric William. (1990). "Culture and Negotiation in the Asian Context." *Journal Managerial Psychology* 5(5), 17–25.

Thiederman, Sondra. (1991). *Profiting in America's Multicultural Marketplace: How to Do Business Across Cultural Lines*. New York: Lexington Books.

Ting-Toomey, Stella. (1988). "Intercultural Conflict Styles: A Face-Negotiation Theory." In Young Yun Kim and William B. Gudykunst eds. *Theories in Intercultural Communication*. Beverly Hills: CA: Sage.

Tomlin, Brian W. (1989). "The Stages of Prenegotiation: The Decision to Negotiate North American Free Trade." In Janice Gross Stein ed. *Getting to the Table*. Baltimore: Johns Hopkins University Press.

Trompenaars, Fons, and Charles Hampden-Turner. (1998). *Riding the Waves of Culture* 2nd ed. London: Nicholas Brealey Publishing.

Tse, David K., James Francis, and John Walls. (1994). "Cultural Differences in Conducting Intra- and Inter-Cultural Negotiations: A Sino-Canadian Perspective." *Journal of International Business Studies* 25(3), 537–555.

Tucker, John B. (1996). Interagency Bargaining and International Negotiation: Lessons from the Open Skies Treaty Talks. *Negotiation Journal* 12, 275–288.

Tung, Rosalie L. (1984). *Business Negotiations with the Japanese*. Lexington, MA: Lexington Books.

Tung, Rosalie L. (1984). "Handshakes across the Sea: Cross-Cultural Negotiating for Business Success." *Organizational Dynamics* 23(3), 30–40.

Tung, Rosalie L. (1984). "How to Negotiate with the Japanese." *California Management Review*, vol. XXVI, no. 4, 62–77.

Tung, Rosalie L. (1989). "A Longitudinal Study of United States-China Business Negotiation." *China Economic Review* 1(1), 57–71.

Tung, Rosalie L. (1982). "U.S.-China Trade Negotiations: Practices, Procedures, and Outcomes." *Journal of International Business Studies* 10(3) (fall), 25–37.

Underdal, Arild. (1991). "The Outcomes of Negotiation." In Victor A. Kremenyuk ed. *International Negotiation.* San Francisco: Jossey-Bass.

Ury, William. (1991). *Getting Past No: Negotiating Your Way from Confrontation to Cooperation.* New York: Bantam Books.

Usunier, Jean-Claude. (1996). "Cultural Aspects of International Business Negotiations." In Pervez Ghauri and Jean-Claude Usunier eds. *International Business Negotiation.* New York: Elsevier.

Van Zandt, Howard F. (1970). "How to Negotiate in Japan." *Harvard Business Review* 48, 45–56.

Walmsley, Adam. (1995). "The Deal That Almost Got Away." *Report on Business Magazine* (August), 26–36.

Walton, Richard, and Robert McKersie. (1965). *A Behavioral Theory of Labor Negotiations.* Ithaca, NY: ILR Press.

Walton, Richard, Robert McKersie, and Joel Cutcher-Gershenfeld. (1994). *Strategic Negotiations: A Theory of Change in Labor-Management Relations.* Boston: Harvard Business School Press.

Watkins, Michael. (1998). "Building Momentum in Negotiations: Time-Related Costs and Action-Forcing Events." *Negotiation Journal* 14(3), 241–256.

Watkins, Michael. "Dynamic Negotiation: Seven Propositions About Complex Negotiations." Harvard Business School Note #9-801-267.

Watkins, Michael. (1998). "Shaping the Structure of Negotiations." Program on Negotiation Monograph no. 98-1, Program on Negotiation, Harvard Law School.

Watkins, Michael, and Kim Winters. (1997). "Intervenors with Interests and Power." *Negotiation Journal* 13(2): 119–142.

Watkins, Michael, and Sam Passow. (1996). "Analyzing Linked Systems of Negotiations." *Negotiation Journal* 12(4): 325–339.

Watkins, Michael, and Sydney Rosen. "Rethinking Preparation in Negotiation." Harvard Business School Note #9-801-286.

Weiss, Stephen E. (1993). "Analysis of Complex Negotiations in International Business: The RBC Perspective." *Organization Science* 4(2) (May), 269–282.

Weiss, Stephen E. (1987). "Creating the GM-Toyota Joint Venture: A Case in Complex Negotiation." *Columbia Journal of World Business* (summer), 23–37.

Weiss, Stephen E. (1995). "International Business Negotiations Research: Bricks, Mortar, and Prospects." In B. J. Punnett and O. Shenkar eds. *Handbook on International Management Research.* Cambridge, MA: Blackwell.

Weiss, Stephen E. (forthcoming). (International Business Negotiations Research: Revising "bricks, mortar, and prospects.") In B. J. Punnett and O. Shenkar, *Handbook of International Management Research* (forthcoming), 2nd ed. Ann Arbor: University of Michigan Press.

Weiss, Stephen E. (1994). "Negotiating with the Romans—Part 1." *Sloan Management Review* 35(2) (winter), 51–62.

Weiss, Stephen E. (1994). "Negotiating with the Romans—Part 2." *Sloan Management Review* 35(3) (spring), 85–97.

Weiss, Stephen E. (1985). Negotiating with Foreign Business Persons: An Introduction for Americans with Propositions on Six Cultures. New York: New York University Faculty of Business Administration, Working Paper, no. 1, February 12.

Weiss, Stephen E. (forthcoming). Teaching the cultural aspects of negotiation: A range of experiential techniques. *Journal of Management Education.*

Weiss, Stephen E., and C. H. Tinsley. (1999). "International Business Negotiation." *International Negotiation* 4(1).

Winham, George R. (1980). "International Negotiation in an Age of Transition." *International Journal* 35, 1–20.

Winham, Gilbert. (1979). "Practitioners' Views of International Negotiation." *World Politics* 32, 111–135.

Wolf-Laudon, G. (1989). "How to Negotiate for Joint Ventures." In F. Mautner-Markhof ed. *Processes of International Negotiations.* Boulder, CO: Westview Press.

Yamada, Haru. (1997). *Different Games, Different Rules: Why Americans and Japanese Misunderstand Each Other.* New York: Oxford University Press.

Zartman, I. William. (1994). *International Multilateral Negotiation.* San Francisco: Jossey-Bass.

Zartman, I. William. (1989). "Prenegotiation: Phases and functions." In Janice Gross Stein ed. *Getting to the Table: The Processes of International Prenegotiation.* Baltimore: John Hopkins.

Zartman, I. William, and Maureen Berman. (1982). *Practical Negotiator.* New Haven, CT: Yale University Press.

Zhang, Danian, and Kenji Kuroda. (1989). "Beware of Japanese Negotiation Style: How to Negotiate with Japanese Companies." *Northwestern Journal of Law and Business* 10 (fall), 195–212.

Zimbardo, Philip, and Michael Lieppe. (1991). *The Psychology of Attitude Change and Social Influence.* New York: McGraw-Hill.

INDEX

Note: **Boldface** numbers indicate illustrations.